THE VALUE OF THINKING

THE VALUE OF THINKING

FOR A COGNITION THAT SATISFIES THE HUMAN BEING
THE RELATIONSHIP BETWEEN SPIRITUAL SCIENCE
AND NATURAL SCIENCE

Eleven lectures given in Dornach on 20 August and between
17 September and 9 October 1915

TRANSLATED AND INTRODUCED BY
CHRISTIAN VON ARNIM

RUDOLF STEINER

RUDOLF STEINER PRESS

CW 164

Rudolf Steiner Press
Hillside House, The Square
Forest Row, RH18 5ES

www.rudolfsteinerpress.com

Published by Rudolf Steiner Press 2023

Originally published in German under the title *Der Wert des Denkens für eine den Menschen befriedigende Erkenntnis. Das Verhältnis der Geisteswissenschaft zu Naturwissenschaft* (volume 164 in the *Rudolf Steiner Gesamtausgabe* or Collected Works) by Rudolf Steiner Verlag, Dornach. Based on shorthand notes that were not reviewed or revised by the speaker. This authorized translation is based on the second German edition (2006), edited by Hella Wiesberger with the assistance of Hans Huber for Part I, and Gian A Baiaster and Maurice Martin for Part II

Published by permission of the Rudolf Steiner Nachlassverwaltung, Dornach

© Rudolf Steiner Nachlassverwaltung, Dornach, Rudolf Steiner Verlag 2006

This translation © Rudolf Steiner Press 2023

All rights reserved. No part of this publication may be reproduced, stored in a retrieval system, or transmitted, in any form or by any means, electronic, mechanical, photocopying or otherwise, without the prior permission of the publishers

A catalogue record for this book is available from the British Library

ISBN 978 1 85584 609 8

Cover by Morgan Creative
Typeset by Symbiosys Technologies, Vishakapatnam, India
Printed and bound by 4Edge Ltd., Essex

Contents

Publisher's Note ix
Introduction, by Christian von Arnim x

I

THE VALUE OF THINKING FOR A COGNITION THAT
SATISFIES THE HUMAN BEING

First Lecture
Dornach, 17 September 1915

The difficulty of entering a relationship with the spiritual world. The question of the value of thinking. The human path of cognition in the sense of the Aristotelian words: There is nothing in the intelligence which did not first pass through the senses. Leibniz's addition. Thinking, an activity of the etheric body. Question about the reality of thoughts. Intellectual activity: dead images. Forgotten ideas as life-promoting and life-inhibiting forces. World of possible memories: imaginations. World of the unconscious life of ideas: inspirations.

Pages 3-18

Second Lecture
18 September 1915

The submergence of ideas into the unconscious; a threshold process. Memory. Difference between the review exercise and ordinary memory. The mobile thoughts in the etheric body using the example of Goethe's thoughts about metamorphosis. The development from unconscious imaginative cognition via physical to conscious imaginative cognition: a descent and a renewed ascent. The world of coming into being and passing away and the world of wrath and punishment.

Pages 19-35

Third Lecture
19 September 1915

Atavistic, visionary clairvoyance: a regression to the Old Moon intelligence. (Example: the figure of Theodora in the Mystery Dramas.) Imaginative cognition in Jakob Böhme and Saint-Martin. Living one's way into the inspired world: an experience of the Old Sun facts. The Old Moon existence continues to work in embryology, the sun existence in artistic inspiration. Intuitive cognition, a return to the Old Saturn existence. The progress from moon existence to earth evolution. The creative concepts of the angels on the Old Moon and their connection with the forms of the present animal kingdom. The progression of the earth human being to emotionless, objective concepts.

Pages 36-50

FOURTH LECTURE
20 SEPTEMBER 1915

Summary of the aforesaid: dead physical cognition, living imaginative cognition, inspired cognition and its connection with the Old Moon and Sun existence. The objective laws of the experiences of inspiration. Feeling the facts of nature as matters of a person's own heart. The distinction between deeds and personality in judging people. Wrong tendencies in modern jurisprudence. The task of the spiritual scientist: not to judge a person's deed but to understand it. Necessary effort of the soul to reach higher knowledge. Humour as a counterweight. The linkage of the human organization with the Old Sun development through air and warmth. The relationship between breathing and inspiration.

Pages 51-66

II

THE RELATIONSHIP BETWEEN SPIRITUAL
SCIENCE AND NATURAL SCIENCE

Discussion of the pamphlet *Science and Theosophy* by F. von Wrangell as an example of how texts can be discussed in branches

FIRST LECTURE
DORNACH, 26 SEPTEMBER 1915

Wrangell's characterization of the materialistic-mechanistic worldview. The spiritual-scientific method of characterization by letting facts or personalities speak. Discussion of the first chapters of Wrangell's pamphlet: 'The basic assumptions of a materialistic-mechanistic worldview—Examination of these basic assumptions—Freedom and morality—The riddle of the universe—Origin of the idea of conformity with laws—Freedom of the will cannot be proven experientially—Epistemological review.'

Pages 69-91

SECOND LECTURE
27 SEPTEMBER 1915

Poems, life and personality of Marie Eugenie delle Grazie as a testimony of the materialistic-mechanistic worldview being taken really seriously. Discussion of more of Wrangell's chapters: 'Formation of concepts—Ideas of space and time—The principle of causality—Application of the idea of arbitrariness to the environment—Observation of uniformly proceeding phenomena—Essence of all science—Astronomy, the oldest science—Uniform motion—Measuring—The principle underlying clocks.'

Pages 92-115

THIRD LECTURE
2 OCTOBER 1915

Recapitulation of what has been said so far. Discussion of more of Wrangell's chapters: 'Limit of error in measuring—Absolute validity of logical and mathematical truths—All laws of nature are taken from experience, therefore have only conditional validity—Chemical laws—Physical laws—Knowledge progresses from the simple to the intricate—Extension of the mechanistic conception to the organic—Difference between inanimate and animate bodies—Consciousness—Spiritual phenomena—The occult faculties of the human being—Essence of the teaching of Jesus.'

Pages 116-143

FOURTH LECTURE
3 OCTOBER 1915

Continuation of the discussion of Wrangell's chapters: 'Essence of the teaching of Jesus—Essence of the theosophical teachings—Secret teachings—Difference between sensory science and spiritual science—Theosophy, a religion.'

Pages 144-160

FIFTH LECTURE
4 OCTOBER 1915

The meaning of materialistic culture on the basis of Wrangell's last chapters: 'Materialism—Doubts about the materialistic worldview—Agnosticism—The sources of the error of occult perceptions lie in the subject as well as in the object—Continued existence of the soul after death—Reincarnation and karma—Lessing's view of the teaching of rebirth—Brief summary of the line of reasoning.' The atomistic model of the world. The need for a School of Spiritual Science. The engagement with contemporary science in Rudolf Steiner's public lectures.

Pages 161-185

SIXTH LECTURE
9 OCTOBER 1915

The examinations of criminal brains by the criminal anthropologist Moriz Benedikt. The too short occipital lobe in criminals and its corrective through appropriate education. The psychological research results of the school of Avenarius: it is not the truth of a worldview that determines the acceptance of the same but the emotional predestination.

Pages 186-201

III

EPISODIC OBSERVATIONS ABOUT SPACE, TIME, MOVEMENT

DORNACH
20 AUGUST 1915

Episodic observations about the mechanical concepts of space, time and speed. Differentiation of two types of division and discussion of the kinematic formula: Velocity = Distance/Time. The concepts of distance and time are abstractions; velocity is the fundamental mechanical concept that belongs to mechanical things as life belongs to living bodies. Thus motion faster than the speed of light or the thought of a human life shortened to a few seconds or extended to millennia are unreal concepts. Since every body is related to the light ether and this is what moves light, no body can move faster than the speed of light. On the basis of experimental results, important present-day physicists (e.g. Max Planck) are impelled towards the idea: there is actually no matter but only holes in an ether, to which no material but only spiritual properties may be ascribed.

Pages 205-218

Notes 219

Rudolf Steiner's Collected Works 231

Significant Events in the Life of Rudolf Steiner 245

Index 261

Publisher's Note

The lectures collected in this volume were given during the First World War to a group of co-workers and members at the Goetheanum in Dornach, whose number had been greatly reduced by the circumstances of war. At the time, some confusion had been created by a pathological personality within the community. This incident lies behind occasional hints in these lectures—comments that were probably intended to clarify this confusion. For this reason, it was likely already being considered to publish them at the time, for there are some textual corrections in Rudolf Steiner's hand and three drawings inserted by him in the typewritten transcripts of lectures 1 to 5.

Introduction

Mention Rudolf Steiner to someone and, if they recognize the name and happen not be an anthroposophist, they will probably most likely associate it with the practical fields of activity inspired by anthroposophy: Waldorf education, the Camphill communities for people with special needs or biodynamic agriculture. Probe a bit further and they might also have heard of anthroposophy—spiritual science—itself, as something to do with the acceptance of a spiritual reality and the paths by which knowledge of the spiritual world that surrounds us and all its beings might be achieved.

But while the value of the practical achievements are often recognized, the systematic underpinnings of anthroposophy, because it deals with the spiritual world and calls itself a science of the spirit, tend to be seen as something rather wishy-washy and not possessing the rigorous thinking of natural science. Much of the criticism of anthroposophical medicines, for example, and indeed of some of the methods of biodynamic farming, is based on the allegation that they are pseudoscientific and have no foundation in science—by which it means no foundation in natural science. (The fact that there are by now quite a number of academic studies showing the efficacy of anthroposophical medical therapies, for example, when assessed with the appropriate methods is not seen as relevant by such criticism.)

Yet all of the critique of Steiner's lack of scientific rigour and understanding of modern science ignores the fact that Steiner, through his studies in the sciences at the Vienna University of Technology and his subsequent career, was in fact well versed in the science and general culture of his time, and when he sought to extend natural science into the spiritual realm he was speaking from a position not of ignorance but of familiarity with materialistic science. If there is one thing that can be said about Rudolf Steiner it is that he always sought to engage with the thinking of his time.

In his early career he worked in a conventional academic and intellectual setting and once he started to develop anthroposophy and spiritual science he always wanted to connect it with the mainstream. He saw anthroposophical medicine, for example, as complementing and extending conventional medicine, not seeking to replace it. In education, too, he sought to intervene positively in the social conditions of his time with the foundation of the first Waldorf school in Stuttgart for the children of the workers at the Waldorf Astoria cigarette factory, and his thoughts about the threefold nature of the social organism formed the basis of extensive ideas as to how to reform society to create better social conditions.

As he emphasized repeatedly himself, in setting out the ideas of spiritual science he sought out the intellectual currents of his time with which he could connect. Spiritual science, Steiner says, seeks to immerse itself in the facts and to allow the facts to speak for themselves. Thus he states quite unambiguously in the present lectures that unless anthroposophists can engage in the debate about the validity of spiritual science on the basis of a thorough understanding of modern conventional science and intellectual currents in general, they will merely make themselves appear ridiculous.

So while in the first series of lectures in this volume Steiner discusses the nature of thinking and cognition itself in the context of human and planetary evolution, the second series of lectures is a detailed analysis of the pamphlet *Science and Theosophy* by an author with impeccable scientific credentials. As well as his intention of illustrating how contemporary ideas can be discussed in the anthroposophical branches—indeed that they should be discussed there rather than just 'internal' anthroposophical topics—this look at theosophy from the outside, setting it against a materialistic view of the world, was used by Steiner as something against which the ideas of anthroposophy could be measured and developed.

Steiner does not reject materialism and all that materialistic science has revealed about the world out of hand. It is fully justified in its place and necessary at a certain time in human development but needs to be extended and to reach beyond itself if we are to understand reality, including spiritual reality, to its full extent. That is where spiritual science comes in. Where he is critical of materialism is when it refuses to go further and acknowledge the reality of anything beyond itself. It should be a method of research and not a worldview, Steiner argues.

The final lecture in Part III of this volume, 'Episodic Observations about Space, Time, Movement', was actually given before all the others and might almost be seen as a kind of preparation for the discussion of sections of the pamphlet on *Science and Theosophy*. Both this lecture and parts of that discussion about the pamphlet often give the impression of being more in the nature of a science lesson for his listeners, tying in with his attempt to make them understand that that they must engage with the wider world and be scientifically literate rather than just cocooning themselves in anthroposophy. The spiritual scientific movement had to extend its threads out into the world in general—spiritual science was not something apart but had to be integrated into the fabric of the world.

And clearly he was not convinced that his listeners were always making the best use of their time in his lectures. At one point he urges them not just to painstakingly—in his own words—'scribble down' every word he says but that it would be much more productive for them if they rather concentrated on listening properly to what he was saying. Enough material has already been published to work with in the branches, he tells them, and it would be better if they made good use of that and in the meantime listened seriously to what he was saying.

In short, he wanted the members of the Anthroposophical Society to engage properly with the world around them because that was essential for any serious spiritual striving—not to dismiss it because in their view they were concerned with much more serious spiritual matters; and, to put it crudely, he wanted them to think for themselves a bit more. Lastly, and very importantly, he wanted them to do so with a sense of humour. As he put it in the last lecture of the first section in this volume, keeping the soul free and open to humour is a good way to take the serious matter really earnestly: 'Otherwise you debase yourself, the serious matter turns into a lie through sentimentality, and sentimentality is the worst enemy of real earnestness for the serious things of life.'

Christian von Arnim
March 2023

I

THE VALUE OF THINKING FOR A COGNITION THAT SATISFIES THE HUMAN BEING

First Lecture

DORNACH, 17 SEPTEMBER 1915

For research in and contemplation of the physical world it is above all what we may call a matter of the heart for human beings to find their bearings in the relationships between the physical world—in which they spend their existence between birth and death—and the higher worlds to which they actually belong. We are, after all, quite clear about the fact that in the human being, however vague their thinking, there nevertheless lives an eminently clear feeling, a clear sense, that they should know at least something about these relationships in some form. For no matter how vaguely the human being may think about the higher worlds, no matter how much they may, for various reasons, despair of being able to know anything about them, it is simply natural and appropriate to human feeling and sensibility to relate to a higher world.

Certainly, we might object that there are nevertheless numerous people, especially in our present materialistic age, who either deny in some form or other that there is a spiritual world at all, or at least deny that the human being can know anything about it. But we can also say that a person first has to learn to behave 'negatively' towards the spiritual world, so to speak; for it is not 'natural' for human beings to deny a spiritual, a supersensory world. They first have to get there through all kinds of theories; they must first be 'mistaught', we might say, in order to deny a spiritual world with any degree of seriousness. So that when we speak of the natural human being, we can nevertheless do so in such a way that it is appropriate to their feeling to turn the soul's gaze upwards in some way to the spiritual worlds.

However, if there is even just a possibility that there are people who want to know nothing at all about spiritual worlds there must be something in human nature that makes it difficult to determine the relationship with the spiritual world. And this relationship seems to be difficult, difficult to think about. For we see that in the course of history, which we can trace, a very great number of all kinds of philosophies and worldviews have appeared which seem to contradict each other. But I have often explained that it only seems to be so, for if it were easy for human beings to determine their relationship with the supersensory world, then seemingly contradictory worldviews would not fill the history of worldviews. So it is already clear from this that it is difficult in a sense to determine the relationship with the spiritual world. And therefore we can ask where this difficulty comes from, what is actually present in the soul of the human being, that they find it difficult to relate to the spiritual world.

Now, if we examine all the attempts that are made outside a spiritual-scientific worldview, that is, let us say, in plain philosophy or in external science, and ask ourselves what these attempts are actually aiming at, what underlies them, then we must say: If we study these attempts, if we look at what kind of soul power people mainly use to find out about the relationship between the physical and the spiritual world, then we find that people again and again—discounting isolated attempts, let me say—see above all in the thinking that soul ability, soul activity, which, properly applied, could lead to saying something, to determining something about the relationship of the human being to the supersensory worlds. It is therefore necessary to consider the thinking, the thinking work of the soul, and to ask ourselves: What is it about the thinking, about giving thought, regarding the relationship of the human being who lives in the physical world with the spiritual worlds? What is it about this relationship of the thinking with the spiritual worlds?

So the question: What is the value of thinking for a cognition that satisfies the human being? I would like to consider this question today in preparation for the discussion of other questions with you. I would like us to prepare ourselves, as it were, for a worthy discussion by considering the question of the value of thinking for cognition.

Well, we get behind the thinking, so to speak, if we go about it in the following way. After all, we have already indicated in the course of the last lectures[1] that certain peculiarities of the thinking, or better still, of the thoughts, need to be considered. I have pointed out how there are many people who see it as a downright mistake in all scientific thinking if this scientific thinking is not just a mere copy, a mental photograph of an external reality. For these people say: If thinking is to have any relationship at all with what is real, with reality, then it must not add anything of itself to this reality; for at the moment when thinking adds something to reality, we are not dealing with an image, with a photograph of reality, but with a fantasy, with a fantasy image. And so that we do not have to deal with such a fantasy image, we must strictly see to it that no one includes in their thoughts anything that is not a mere photograph of external reality.

Now, an easy line of thought will immediately lead you to say to yourself: Indeed, for the outer physical world, for what we call the physical plane, this seems to be quite correct and self-explanatory. It seems to correspond to a quite correct feeling that we must not add anything to reality through the thinking if we don't want to have fantasy images instead of an image of reality. For the physical plane we can indeed truly say that it is absolutely correct to abstain from adding anything through the thinking to that which we receive from the outside through perception.

Now I would like to draw your attention to two philosophers, Aristotle and Leibniz, in relation to the view that is found in what has just been said.

Aristotle—who to a certain extent summarizes the Greek worldview—is a philosopher who himself was no longer initiated in any way into the secrets of the spiritual world but who lived in the very first period after what I might call the 'age of initiation'. Whereas before, all philosophers were still somehow affected by their initiation when they expressed philosophically what they knew as initiates—Plato, for example, who was a kind of initiate of the highest degree but expressed himself philosophically—with Aristotle we have to say that he no longer had any trace of initiation but that there still existed all kinds of after-effects of initiation. So here we have a philosopher who speaks only philosophically, without initiation, without any impulse of initiation but who gives in his philosophy by way of reason what the initiates who went before him gave in a spiritual way. So here we have Aristotle.

Aristotle is the source of the words[2] we now intend to consider. [Writes on the blackboard:]

There is nothing in the intelligence which did not first pass through the senses.

So let us consider these words: There is nothing in—we can add—'human' intelligence that is not in the senses.

These words of Aristotle must not be interpreted in any kind of materialistic way, for Aristotle is far removed from any worldview that is even remotely materialistically tinged. In Aristotle, these words are not to be taken in terms of how we see the world but epistemologically. That is, Aristotle refuses to believe that we can obtain knowledge of any world from within but claims that we can have knowledge only by turning the senses towards the external world, by receiving sense impressions and then forming concepts from these sense impressions with our reason; but he does not of course deny that we receive spiritual things with the sense impressions. He thinks of nature as being permeated by the spirit; only, he says, we cannot arrive at the spiritual if we do not look out into nature.

Here you can notice the difference to the materialist. The materialist concludes: There are only material things outside, and we only create concepts of material things. Aristotle thinks of the whole of nature as being filled with spirit, but the way of the human soul to reach the spirit is such that we must start from the sense perception and process the sense impressions into concepts. If Aristotle himself had still been touched by an impulse of initiation, he would not have said this; for then he would have known that if a person frees themselves from sense perception in the way we have described, they will attain knowledge of the spiritual world from within. So he did not want to deny the spiritual world but only to show the path that human knowledge must take.

These words then played a major role in the Middle Ages and were reinterpreted materialistically in the materialistic age. We need only change one small thing in these words of Aristotle—there is nothing in the world for the intellect that is not in the senses—and we have immediately formed materialism from it. It is the case, after all, that we need only make that which, in the sense of Aristotle, is the human path of knowledge into the principle of a worldview and then we have materialism.

Leibniz came up with similar words, so let us look at them as well. Leibniz is not yet that far in the past; in the seventeenth century. Let us now also consider these words of Leibniz. So Leibniz now says: There is nothing in the, we can again say, 'human' intelligence—I only add 'human'—that is not in the senses, except the intelligence itself, except the intellect itself.

[Writes on the blackboard:]

There is nothing in the human intelligence that is not in the senses, except the intelligence itself, except the intellect itself.

So the intellect that the human being has working within themselves is not in the senses. In these two sentences in particular you see proper textbook examples of how we can be completely in agreement with the formulation of a sentence, and yet how the sentence can be incomplete.

Now I don't want to dwell on the extent to which this sentence of Leibniz is also philosophically incomplete. Let us first note that Leibniz was of the opinion that the intellect itself is not somehow already founded in the senses but that human beings must add the work of the intellect to what the senses give them. So that we can say: The intellect itself is an inner activity that has not yet passed through the senses.

If you have followed the last lectures, you know that this inner work is already free of the senses and takes place in the etheric body of the human being. In our language we can say: There is nothing in the intelligence working in the etheric body that is not in the senses, except the intelligence itself working in the etheric body; what is at work there does not enter from the senses.

But thinking as such is in reality, if we look at it in true self-knowledge, such work in the etheric body, and this is what the philosophers call the intellect. So this thinking is work, working we can say. And because for our spiritual-scientific insight Leibniz, even if he is not absolutely right, is nevertheless more right than Aristotle, we can say: This thinking—or rather, this thinking activity, this thinking work in the human being which is an activity of the etheric body—is not in the outer reality of the physical plane. For the physical plane reaches its limit in what it lets us recognize through the senses. So, by placing ourselves as human beings on the physical plane, we introduce the intellect into it which, however, is not itself in the physical world.

And here we arrive at the difficulty of those philosophers who want to get to the bottom of the riddle of the universe through the intellect. These people must say to themselves: Indeed, when I think about it, the intellect does not belong to the world of the senses; but I am now in a peculiar position. I know of no spiritual world other than only the intellect; it is a spiritual world behind the senses. So where does that leave the intellect as far as I am concerned? After all, it can get nothing, no content, if it does not inform himself about the outer physical world through the senses. It only stands for itself. But then the philosopher is confronted with a rather peculiar thing. He has to consider: I have in me an activity, the activity of the intellect. Through this activity of the intellect I want to get behind the secrets of the sensory world. But I can only consider what is out there in the sensory world with thoughts; but these arise from something that does not itself belong to the sensory world. So how are these thoughts connected with the sensory world? Even if I know that the intellect is something spiritual, I must still despair of being able to approach anything that is reality with the spiritual thing that I have there.

Now I want to try to address the matter by means of a comparison. After all, we expressed the same thing in a different way in the last lectures.[3] We expressed it by arriving at the recognition that we have mirror images of reality in what we produce through our thinking, that these mirror images are actually an addition to reality and are not realities themselves.

You see, this is the same truth, only expressed differently philosophically here. We had to say: The intellect forms mirror images. These mirror images as an image of the reality that is being reflected are of indifference to reality, because the reality that is being reflected does not need these mirror images. So that we could come to doubt the whole reality, the whole value of the reality of the thinking, of intelligence, to ask ourselves: Does the thinking have any real meaning? Doesn't it actually already add something to external reality through what it is? Does any single thought have any real value if it is actually nothing more than a mirror image in relation to reality?

But let us now endeavour to properly seek out the reality of the thought. In other words, we want to answer the question: Is a thought really something merely imaginary that has no real value? Or we can approach the question from another angle: Where then does thought have a reality? Well, as I said, I will try to illustrate this by a comparison. Here we have a clock; I pick up the clock, now have it in my hand. Everything that is the clock is external to the muscles and nerves of my hand. My hand and the clock are two different things. But let us assume that it is dark here, that I have never seen the clock and that I perceive the clock only by feeling, then I would perceive something of the clock by stretching out my hand and grasping it. If you direct your attention to the clock, you will say to yourself: I can experience something of the reality of the clock by having it in my hand, by grasping it. But let us hypothetically assume for a moment that I had only one hand and not two, I would not be able to grasp the first hand with the second as I can now grasp it in reality. I would probably be able to grasp the clock with one hand but I would not be able to touch the hand itself with my other hand—at most with my nose, but we'll not do that right now. Nevertheless, the hand is just as real as the clock. How do I convince myself of the reality of the clock? By taking it in my hand, touching it. How do I convince myself of the reality of the hand? I could not convince myself by touching it if I did not have a second hand; but I do know with inner certainty that I have a hand, that I possess the thing I have on me to grasp the clock with just as much reality as I can vouch for the clock being real by grasping it. Do you notice the difference between the real hand and the real clock? I have to experience the reality of the hand in a different way from the reality of the clock.

You can transfer this comparison wholly to human thinking, to the intellect. You can never grasp the intellect's comprehension so directly through the intellect itself; just as you cannot touch your own hand with the same hand. The intellect cannot perceive itself in the same way it perceives other things; but it is nevertheless convinced of its reality through inner certainty. It is an inner certainty whereby the intellect is convinced of its reality. But we must then understand this intellect, this work of the intellect, as an activity of the human subject; we have to be clear that the intellect is spiritually only a hand, as it were, that is stretched out to grasp something. We are speaking metaphorically here, but in very real images. And just as, on the one hand, my hand is able to convince me of the reality of the clock— namely by the fact that I am able, for example, to feel with my hand the heaviness of the clock, the smoothness of the clock; I am able, therefore, through the nature of my hand to learn everything that is real about the clock—so, on the other hand, I am able through the reality of the intellect to learn something about things other than what the senses learn. The intellect is therefore a grasping organ in the spiritual sense which we must perceive in ourselves not in the outside world.

And you see, here lies the difficulty for philosophers. They believe that when they have thoughts about the world, the thoughts must come to them from outside, and then they realize that they do not come in from outside at all but that the intellect makes these thoughts. And since they regard the intellect as alien to external reality, they must actually regard all thoughts as fantasy images. But we must ascribe a subjective reality to the intellect, a reality that is experienced internally. Then we have the realm of reality in which the intellect is perceived. Thus, by examining the actual nature of the intellect, we come to be able to say to ourselves: Yes, everything that the intellect brings about may or need only be a reflection of external reality, but this reflection has come into being through the work of the real intellect. It is a human activity. And its reality consists in that the human being is at work as they acquire knowledge of the reality of the intellect through the intellect. So that we can say that the intellectual activity of the human being works in the human being, but it works to begin with in such a way that it is quite justified to say: What this intellect works on has no meaning for the world in which it works—just as the hand has no meaning for the clock, because for the clock it is supremely irrelevant whether or not it is grasped by the hand—the intellect is something that is there for the human being and in the human being, so that they produce some kind of image of things for themselves through the intellect. With regard to the things of the physical plane, however, everything that this intellect works on is unreal, a mirror image, dead, nothing living. We can say that the images of the physical world worked on in the intellect are lifeless, dead images.

[Writes on the blackboard:]

Intellectual activity—dead images.

Thus the images that the human being produces for themselves of the physical world are also dead images. We fail to understand the actual nature of this content of the intellect if we ascribe to it something other than that it can be a copy of the physical world.

But the matter immediately becomes quite different when the human being reaches the point of living with the experiences of their existence over time. When we confront the things of the outside world and form images of them through the intellect, we get dead concepts; but if we allow these concepts to be present in our soul, then after some time, when the experience of which we have formed an image has long passed, we can, through memory, as we say, bring up the image of that experience from memory. We can say: Well, I know nothing about the experience now; but when I remember, it arises. It may not have been in my consciousness before I remembered, but it is there, somewhere down in my soul, that is unconsciously, I just have to raise it from the unconscious first.

So the image of an earlier experience that I saw in the past is down there in the unconscious. Fine, it's down there, I'll raise it. But down there is not so devoid of meaning. You have only to take the quite ordinary difference between a conception which we receive from an experience such that it gives us joy, elevates us, and a conception from some experience which has given us no joy. Now we can push down into the unconscious a conception that has given us pleasure, and we can push down into the unconscious a conception that has not given us pleasure. Very few people think about what might be said about the difference between such a joyful and such a sorrowful, painful conception. But there is a huge difference. And this difference occurs especially when we try to get behind the reality value of such conceptions that have actually already faded from normal memory.

So let us keep to a conception which has given a person pleasure but which they have had no reason to think back to in later life, or a conception which has caused them pain and which they have also had little reason to think back to. They do not rise into their consciousness but they play a role in the unconscious life of the soul. If only people were willing to understand out of spiritual science what conceptions stored in the soul mean, even if they are completely forgotten. We are actually always the result of our experiences. The countenance we bear, especially in the more intimate gestures, is indeed a reflection of what we have experienced in this incarnation of ours. You can tell from the faces of people whether they have experienced a lot of sadness in their childhood. So what is going on down there is, in other words, involved in the life processes of the human being. Whatever inhibiting, sad ideas are pushed down into oblivion, into the unconscious, that wears us out, it cuts off our vitality. The joyful and uplifting things we have experienced revive us. And if we study the fate of our mental life in the unconscious, then we find how tremendously dependent the present mood, the whole condition of a person is on what rests there in their subconscious below.

Now compare the conceptions in our memory, the conceptions that have then already entered the unconscious soul life, with the conceptions that we currently have in our consciousness. Then you will say to yourself: The conceptions that we currently have in our consciousness are dead. Dead conceptions are not involved in our life process. They do not begin to be involved in our life process until they delve down into the unconscious, when they become life-enhancing or life-inhibiting ideas. So that the conceptions do not properly begin to live until they are forced down into the deeper recesses of the soul. I have always drawn attention to this in the lectures I have given in various places on the hidden grounds of the soul life.[4] So the conceptions that are initially dead conceptions begin to live when they are implanted into our soul life; but the more unconscious they become for us, the more they begin to take on life.

If we now follow the process with spiritual-scientific cognition, then something very peculiar happens, which I can actually only describe in this way [begins to draw]:

Assume that this is the boundary between conscious and unconscious; this line is the boundary between 'conscious', which is above, and 'unconscious', which is below. And now we have formed all kinds of conceptions in our consciousness. Let me designate them schematically by various shapes. We have formed these conceptions; let's assume that these conceptions go down into the unconscious. They go down here [draws arrows].

So, you see, if we now follow these conceptions with spiritual-scientific cognition, then they are transformed. Outwardly we have seen that they become life-enhancing or life-inhibiting; inwardly it becomes apparent through spiritual-scientific cognition that, in sliding down below the surface, as it were, they become imaginations. There in the unconscious or subconscious, everything that goes down becomes imagination, everything becomes an image. You can have the most abstract conceptions in your ordinary day-consciousness: when you go down below the threshold of ordinary day-consciousness, everything becomes imagination. That is to say, there

is a process in the human being, a sum of events, which is always endeavouring—in that the dead conceptions of the earthly, ordinary, materialistic consciousness go into the subconscious—to transform in every human being, before they arrive at imaginative cognition, all the cognitions in their consciousness into images, into imaginations in the unconscious.

If, then, we wish to designate what we have of our conceptual life in the unconscious, if we wish to become acquainted with it, we must actually say: All of it consists of unconscious imaginations, and all the conceptions which we can in turn raise from the unconscious into consciousness we must raise by an activity which also remains unconscious to us. We must bring them back into consciousness but strip them of their image character, transform them back into abstract, non-pictorial conceptions. And when you are actively considering: Let me think, I experienced something; what was it?—and make an effort—you all know the process—to remember something, then that is the effort which you must make in order to strip the image that sits down there of its pictorial character and transform it back into the imaginative form of consciousness.

But from this you will see that when we push the conceptions down into the unconscious, they become more spiritual. So we have to say: If we take what the intellect offers us into the unconscious, then we have to characterize the conceptual world that is there in us and that we have pushed down as a higher, as a more spiritual world. So we have to say: The world of possible memories—please note that I say the world of possible memories; not all the conceptions that go down there need to be remembered again but they are all down there in the unconscious life of the soul—the world of possible memories actually consists in imaginations, in unconscious imaginations.

[Writes on the blackboard:]

World of possible memories—imaginations.

Now for the normal consciousness of a person there is sometimes the possibility—and perhaps we will be able to talk about other such possibilities in the next few days—of bringing up into consciousness these images that would otherwise never pass from a possible memory into a real memory. Take the experiences that drowning people sometimes have! And if you could compare with this the experiences of people who have passed through the gateway of death, you would find that even there some conceptions, where the effort in ordinary physical life is not sufficient to bring them up again, then rise up as if of their own accord. But episodes, parts also rise up in the ordinary dream world. The dream, too, as it confronts us, is a complicated reality because the things which are experienced actually lie behind it in many instances. But the conceptions we wrap around it are taken from the memory. So the dream, the experiences of those wrestling with death, such as drowning people and the like, and experiences had immediately after passing through the gateway of death—these reveal this world of imagination which is a more spiritual world than the world of ordinary human intelligence on the physical plane.

But if you take what I described earlier, that these conceptions which have passed into the region of possible memories work to enhance life or inhibit life, you will say to yourself: There is some life in there. Whereas the conceptions of the ordinary intellect are dead, some life enters in there, but it is not a very strong life. But even there, ordinary experience can offer something that can show you that what happens with these conceptions that descend into the subconscious region can nevertheless mean an even stronger life.

I have already pointed out the very common fact that people who have to learn something by heart in order to recite it, learn it and sleep on it, and that this sleeping on it is part of making the memory more capable. This, however, is only a faint hint at something which spiritual science shows much more clearly, indeed completely clearly, namely that our entire conceptual world, in that we shape it and push it down into the subconscious, becomes more and more alive and vivid in the subconscious, while it is dead in the consciousness.

But now the conceptions that rise up again are not even those that are most involved in enhancing or inhibiting life, but it is those conceptions that are even more intimately connected with us.

Conceptions that we often only see as accompanying life, to which we don't pay that much attention in life, they connect with our life-enhancing or life-inhibiting forces to a much greater extent. Let us assume for a minute that someone is engaged in spiritual science. They begin by taking it in, this spiritual science, as worked on by the physical intellect. That is what they have to start with. We have to build on what the physical intellect perceives through the senses. Otherwise I would not be able to speak about the spiritual world at all, because language is there for the physical world. But there is a difference in how we, I might say, take in such a conceptual world as it is clothed in life.

Suppose a person takes in the truths of spiritual science with seriousness and dignity such that they feel: seriousness, profound seriousness is involved. Another person takes in the ideas of spiritual science in such a way that they actually only listen to them theoretically and does not let them approach with any seriousness. The one receives them in an atmosphere of superficiality, as it were, the other in an atmosphere of seriousness. We do not need to be very aware of how we receive them; it is much more connected with how we go through life without always thinking about it. Those who are predisposed or accustomed to taking things seriously, and not frivolously or cynically, do not always think about how to take them; they behave seriously and naturally. Likewise the person who is only superficially inclined takes them superficially; they can't help it. In this way, we accompany our conceptual life with something that we do not bring to mind, which is really something that runs in parallel to our consciousness. But the thing that runs in parallel with our consciousness goes much deeper into the unconscious than what we think consciously. So the way we form our conceptions goes down much deeper into the unconscious than what we consciously think. And when a person is asleep and their astral body and I are out of the physical and etheric body, then this way of forming conceptions plays an infinitely great role in the astral body and I. We can thus say: A person who takes in any conceptions with the necessary seriousness has these conceptions in their astral body and in their I in such a way that they are contained in them like the enlivening power of the sun is contained in the plant. They are truly enlivening forces to the highest degree. And they take into these conceptions that which is enlivening, enlivening and transcending the present incarnation, and creating the preconditions for the next incarnation. Here we already see through the creative soul that you have something in the subconscious that is more spiritual than that which can be raised through a dream.

Here we have a world of the unconscious conceptual life connected with the entire essence of a person's being at its core. This way of taking life penetrates, as it were, into our spiritual life forces, and it is just like unconscious inspiration.

[Writes on the blackboard:]

World of the unconscious conceptual life—inspirations.

I will go on to explain to you—today we no longer have the time—how ordinary life already shows that these unconscious inspirations then unconsciously work in the human being even in the incarnation in which they are formed, but just unconsciously. Then I will further show you that there is still a higher world for human beings. But you can see from what has been set out today that the human soul life has an inner movement, that that which is experienced on the physical plane through the physical intelligence is experienced further down, that it then ascends into more spiritual regions, ultimately into even more spiritual regions, than we experience on the physical plane. [The arrows were drawn.] So the conceptual life is in inner movement, in an ascending movement. And now remember what I drew for you yesterday:[5] how certain processes of the human being were represented in a descending movement. So that you can say to yourself: When I have the human being before me, there is a descending current and an ascending current in the human being, and they work together. How they work together will then be discussed tomorrow.

[Diagram on the blackboard]:

World of the unconscious conceptual life : inspirations

World of possible memories : imaginations

Intellectual activity : dead images

Second Lecture

DORNACH, 18 SEPTEMBER 1915

I spoke yesterday about a kind of ascending movement that is rooted in human nature. And basically, through the contemplation of this ascending movement, we have found again everything that we already know; namely, on the lowest level, the knowledge that is only applicable to the facts of the physical plane, the physical knowledge which is called object knowledge in *Knowledge of the Higher Worlds. How is it Achieved?*[6] So physical knowledge is what I want to call it today. We then got to know the next higher level of knowledge, the so-called imaginative knowledge; but we considered it as unconscious imaginative knowledge; conscious imaginative knowledge can, after all, only be present in a person who tries to attain it in the way described in the book *Knowledge of the Higher Worlds. How is it Achieved?*. [The words 'physical knowledge', 'unconscious imaginative knowledge', 'conscious imaginative knowledge' were written on the blackboard, see diagram 4 page 33.]

But as a fact, the content of imaginative knowledge, that is imaginations, is in every human being. So that actually the development of the human soul in this respect is nothing other than an extension of consciousness into an area that is always within the human soul. So we can say: This imaginative knowledge is no different from the way it would be with objects that are in an initially dark room. For in the depths of the human soul all the imaginations that first come into consideration for the human being are just as present as the objects of a dark room. And just as these are not increased by a single one when light is brought into the room, but just as all remain as they are, only that they are illuminated, so, too, after the consciousness of imaginative knowledge has awakened, there is no content in the soul other than what was there before; it is only illuminated by the light of consciousness. So, to a certain extent, we experience nothing more through the ascent to the imaginative level of cognition than what has long been previously present in our soul as a sum of imaginations.

If we look back once more at what became clear to us yesterday, we know that when our ideas, which we gain about the objects around us through our physical perceptions, sink down into the realm of possible memories—that is, are lowered into the unconscious so that we find ourselves in the position of not knowing anything about them for some time, not having lost them but being able to bring them up again from the soul—then we must say that we lower down into the unconscious that which we have in ordinary physical consciousness. The world of conceptions we obtain through physical knowledge of the outer world is therefore constantly absorbed by our spiritual part, by the supersensory; it continually slips into the supersensory realm. At every moment it is the case that we obtain conceptions of the outer world through the physical perceptions, and these conceptions are handed over to our supersensory nature. It will not be difficult for you to reflect on this after all that has been said over the years, because this is precisely the most superficial supersensory process that is conceivable, a process that is continually taking place: the transition of ordinary conceptions into conceptions we can remember. So it is natural to think, which is also true according to spiritual research, that everything that takes place when we perceive the outer world is a process of the physical plane. Even when we form conceptions based on the physical external world, this is still a process of the physical plane. But the moment we let the conceptions sink down into the unconscious, we are already at the entrance to the supersensory world.

This is indeed a very important point which must be taken into consideration by anyone who wants to attain an understanding of the occult world not through all kinds of occultist twaddle but through serious human effort of the soul. For there is already a quite essential fact hidden in the words which I have just spoken: when we as human beings face the things of the outer world and form conceptions, then this is a process of the physical plane. At the moment when the conception sinks down into the unconscious and is kept there until it is brought up again by a memory, a supersensory process, a real supersensory process, takes place. So that you can say to yourself: If we are able to follow this process, which consists in the fact that a thought which is above in the consciousness sinks down into the subconscious and is there below as an image, if we can, in other words, follow an idea as it is down in the unconscious, then we actually already begin to slip into the realm of the supersensory. For just think: When you carry out the ordinary process of recollection, the conception must first come up into the consciousness, and you then see it up in the consciousness, never down in the unconscious. You must distinguish ordinary recollection from following the conceptions down into the unconscious. You can compare what takes place in remembering with a swimmer who sinks below the water and whom you continue to see until they are completely submerged. Now they are down and you don't see them anymore. When they come back up, you'll see them again! [Draws.] It is the same with human conceptions: you have them as long as they are on the physical plane; when they go down, you've forgotten them; if you remember them again, then they come up again like the swimmer. But this process that I'm talking about now, which already points to imaginative cognition, could be compared to you submerging yourself and thus being able to see the swimmer below in the water, so that they do not disappear from your sight when they submerge.

But nothing less follows from this than that the line I drew earlier, the base, as it were,—below which the imagination sinks into the unconscious, into possible memories—is the threshold of the spiritual world itself, the first threshold of the spiritual world. This follows with absolute necessity. It is the first threshold of the spiritual world! Just think how close the human being is to this threshold of the spiritual world. [The words 'threshold of the spiritual world' were written next to the diagram.]

22 ✳ The Value of Thinking

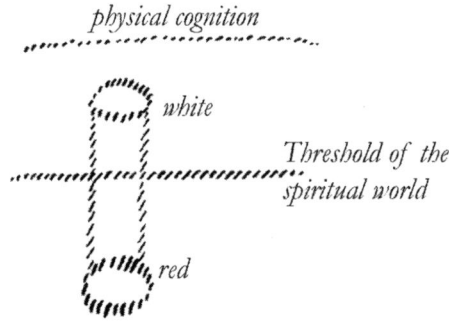

physical cognition

white

Threshold of the spiritual world

red

And now take a process by which we can try to get down there properly, to submerge. The process would be that you endeavour to pursue conceptions down into the unconscious. This can really only be done by trying. It can happen by doing something like the following. You have formed a conception of the outside world; you try to artificially evoke the process of memory independently of the outside world. Think of how this is recommended in *Knowledge of the Higher Worlds. How is it Achieved?*, in which the quite ordinary rule of looking back on the day's events is given. When you look back on the day's experiences, you practise entering, as it were, into the ways which the imagination itself takes by being submerged and rising again. So the whole process of recollection is designed to pursue the conceptions that have sunk below the threshold of consciousness.

It is further said there in *Knowledge of the Higher Worlds. How is it Achieved?* that we do well to trace back the conceptions we have formed in reverse, that is, from the end to the beginning; and if you want to review the day, to follow the stream of events backwards from evening to morning. As a result we have to make a different effort than is made by way of ordinary recall. And this different effort leads us to grasp below the threshold of consciousness, as it were, what we had as a conception of our experience. And in the course of trying, we come to feel, to experience inwardly how we pursue the conceptions, pursue them down below this threshold of consciousness. It is really a process of inner experiential trying that is under consideration here. But it is a matter of doing this review really seriously, not doing it in such a way that after a while we slacken in terms of the seriousness of the matter. But then, if we go through this process of looking back for a longer period, or in general go through the process of bringing up from memory an experience, a world of conceptions arising from our experience—so that we imagine the matter in reverse, that is, make more effort than we have to make when we remember in the ordinary sequence—then we now also have the experience that we are no longer in a position to grasp the conception from a certain point onwards in the way we have grasped it in ordinary life on the physical plane.

On the physical plane, memory lives itself out in such a way—and it is best for memory on the physical plane if it lives itself out in this way—that if we raise the conception that we want to remember or should remember faithfully according to the context in life, we raise it simply in the way that we have formed it on the physical plane. But if through trying as we spoke about we gradually get used to pursuing the conceptions to below the threshold of consciousness, as it were, then we don't discover them down there as they are in life. That is the mistake people always make when they think they will find in the spiritual world a copy of what is in the physical world. You have to anticipate that the conceptions down there will be different. In reality they look like this under the threshold of consciousness, that they have shed everything that is characteristic of them on the physical plane. Down there they completely become images; and they become wholly such that we sense life in them. We sense life in them. It is very important to keep these words in particular in mind: we sense life in them. You can only be convinced that you have really followed a conception down there below the threshold of consciousness when you have the feeling: the conception begins to live, to stir. When I compared the ascent to imaginative knowledge with sticking your head into an anthill, I explained it from a different point of view. I said everything begins to stir, everything becomes animated.

So suppose, for example, that during the day—I will take a very ordinary experience—you were sitting at a table and had a book in your hand. Now at some point in the evening, vividly imagine what that was like: the table, the book, you sitting there, as if you were outside yourself. And in this context it is always good to imagine the whole thing pictorially from the outset, not in abstract thoughts, because abstraction, the capacity for abstraction, has no meaning at all for the imaginative world. So you imagine this picture: yourself sitting at a table, with a book in your hand. With table and book I simply want to say, imagine as vividly as you can some slice of daily life. Then, if you really let your soul's gaze rest on this image, if you really intensely meditate on it, then from a certain moment on you will feel different from usual; indeed, let me say as a comparison, as if you were to take a living creature in your hand.

When you take a dead object in your hand, you have the feeling: the object is still, it does not tingle or prickle in your hand. Even if you have a moving dead object in your hand, you reassure yourself with the feeling that its life is such that it does not emanate from the object but is mechanically assigned to it. It is a different matter if you happen to have a living object, say a mouse, in your hand. For example, let's say you have reached into a cupboard thinking you have picked up some object and discover you have picked up a mouse. And then you feel the prickling and tingling of the mouse in your hand, don't you? There are people who start screeching when they suddenly feel a mouse in their hand. And the screeching is no less if they haven't yet seen what's prickling and tingling in their hand. There is therefore a difference between holding a dead object and holding a living object. You first have to get used to the living object to be able to bear it in a certain way. People are used to touching dogs and cats, aren't they?; but they first have to get used to it. But if you put a living creature into someone's hand in the night, in darkness, without them knowing about it, they are also shocked.

It is this difference that you feel between touching a dead object and a living object that you have to be clear about. When you touch a dead object, you have a different feeling than when you touch a living one. Now, if you have a conception on the physical plane, you have a feeling that you can compare with touching a dead object. But as soon as you really descend down below the threshold of consciousness, that changes; so that you get the feeling: the thought has life inside it, begins to stir. It is, if you like, the same as the discovery you make—as a comparison for the inner feeling—when you have grasped a mouse: the thought tingles and prickles.

It is very important that we pay attention to this feeling if we are to get an idea of imaginative cognition; because in the moment that the thoughts we bring up from the subconscious begin to tingle and prickle, begin to behave in such a way that we have the feeling: down there, below the threshold, everything is actually bubbling and teeming away, we are in the imaginative world. And while upstairs everything is quite calm and the thoughts can be controlled so nicely, just like machines can be controlled, down below one thought pursues the other, the thoughts tingle and prickle, bubble and teem; down there they suddenly turn into a very lively world. It is important to acquire this feeling, because in that moment when you begin to feel the life of the world of thoughts you are inside the imaginative or elemental world. That's where you are! And you can get in so easily if only you follow the very, very simple rules given in *Knowledge of the Higher Worlds. How is it Achieved?*; if only you don't try to get into it by way of all kinds of 'practices'[7] alluded to in the last few days. You really can get in so easily. Just think that one of the very first things clearly stated in the book *Knowledge of the Higher Worlds. How is it Achieved?* is that one should try, for example, to follow the life of a plant: how it gradually grows, how it gradually dies away. Indeed, if you really follow this, you must go through this life of the plant in your thoughts. First you have the thought of the very small seed, and if you do not make the thought mobile, you will not be able to keep up with the plant in its growth. You have to make the thought mobile. And then again, when you think of the plant defoliating, gradually dying, withering away, then again you have to think of it shrinking, wrinkling up. As soon as you start thinking about the living sphere, you have to make the thought itself mobile. The thought must begin to gain inner mobility through your own power.

There are two beautiful poems by Goethe. One is called 'The Metamorphosis of Plants', the other 'The Metamorphosis of Animals'. You can read these two poems, you can find them beautiful, but you can also do the following. You can try to really think the thought in these poems as Goethe thought it, from the first line to the last, and then you will find: if you do this, the thought can move inwardly from the beginning to the end. And anyone who does not follow the thought of these poems in this way has not understood metamorphosis. But the person who pursues the thought in this way and then lets it sink down into the unconscious, and again, after they have done this often, recalls this particular thought of metamorphosis—for this is no other thinking than the one you should pursue in *Knowledge of the Higher Worlds. How is it Achieved?*—the person, then, who does this, who makes this thought sink down and then endeavours to do this fifty, sixty, a hundred times, and it might take a hundred and one times, they will be able to raise it up at some point. But then this thought, which they have practised in this way, will be a mobile one. You will experience that it does not rise up like a small machine but—forgive the example once more—like a small mouse; you will experience how it itself is an inwardly mobile, living element.

I said that we can so easily dive down into this elemental world if we only tear ourselves away a little from the tendency of all people towards abstract thoughts. This tendency to have limited, abstract thoughts instead of inwardly mobile thoughts is so terribly great. You see, people are so eager to say with everything what this or that is and what is meant by it, and are so satisfied when they can say that this or that is meant by it, because that gives them a thought which, like a machine, does not stir. And people become so terribly impatient in ordinary life when you try by all possible means to convey to them fluid and not such abstract thoughts in a box. For all the outer life of the physical plane and all the life of outer science consists of such dead thoughts in a box, of nested thoughts. How often have I had to experience people asking me about this or that: Why is that, then? What is it? They wanted a completed, rounded thought that they could write down in order to be able to read it off again, to repeat it as often as they wanted, whereas the aspiration must be to have an inwardly mobile thought, a thought that lives on, really lives on.

But you see, the thing with the mouse also has its very serious side. Because why do some people screech when they discover they have reached into a cupboard and have a mouse in their hand? Because they're scared! And this feeling also really occurs at the moment when you realize, truly realize: the thought is alive! That's when you start to get scared too! And that is precisely what the good preparation for this event consists of, that you get rid of the fear of the living thought. The materialists do not want to come to such living thoughts, I have often emphasized this. Why? Because they are afraid. Indeed, the master of materialism, Ahriman, appears on one occasion in the Mystery Drama with the expression 'fear'. There you have the passage in the Mysteries,[8] where it is indicated how a person feels when thoughts begin to become mobile. But all the information in *Knowledge of the Higher Worlds. How is it Achieved?*, if followed, will lead a person to get rid of this fear of the mobile, of the living thought, to really get rid of it.

So you see, we enter a quite different world, a world at the threshold of which we must truly discard the abstract thinking that dominates the whole physical plane. The endeavour of people who want to enter the occult world with a certain convenience is always that they want to take the ordinary thinking of the physical plane into it. You cannot do that. You cannot take ordinary physical thinking into the occult world. You have to take the mobile thinking into it. All of the thinking must become agile, mobile. If you don't feel this within yourselves—and as I said, you are only not doing it properly if you don't feel it relatively soon—if you don't take into account what I have just said, then it is very easy to fail to grasp the particular nature of the spiritual world. And you must grasp it if you want to concern yourself with the spiritual world at all.

You see, it is so difficult to struggle with human abstraction in this field; for when you have grasped this mobility of thought, then you will also understand that a mobile thought cannot appear here or there in any arbitrary way. You cannot, for example, find a land animal in the water; you cannot get the bird that is suited for the air into the habit of living deep down in the water. You cannot help but accommodate yourself to the idea, when you deal with the living, that you must not take it out of its element. This is what you have to bear in mind.

I once tried in a very strict way, at first in a small area—I always try to do it this way, but I only want to give it as an example now—to show vividly with a very important thought in one example in particular how things must be if you reckon with this inner life of the thought. I gave a small lecture-cycle in Copenhagen on 'The Spiritual Guidance of the Individual and Humanity',[9] which is also available in print. At a certain point in this lecture-cycle I drew attention to the mystery of the two Jesus boys. Now let us take the matter as it is presented there. We have a lecture-cycle that starts in a certain way. Attention is drawn to how a person can already acquire certain insights when they try to look at the first years of the child's development, try to look back at these things. The whole thing is structured. Then it continues. The contribution of the hierarchies to the progress of humanity is presented—the book is printed, it is probably in everyone's hands, so I am talking about something quite well known—and then, in a certain context, at a very specific point, the two Jesus boys are mentioned. This is part of discussing the two Jesus boys, that it happens in the certain place. And if someone says: Well, why shouldn't we be able to extract this discussion of the two Jesus boys and present it exoterically torn out in this way?—that person is asking the same question as someone who asks: Why does the hand have to sit right here on the arm, on this part of the body? They might even say: Why isn't the hand on the knee? That's where it might also be. They don't understand the whole organism as a living being; they think the hand could be somewhere else, don't they? The hand cannot sit anywhere other than on the arm! So in this context, the idea of the two Jesus boys cannot be in any other place, because the endeavour is to structure the matter in such a way that the living thought lies within the account.

Now someone comes along and writes a piece and crudely extracts this idea and relates it to other ideas which are totally unconnected!

But that means nothing other than: they attach the hand to the knee! What does a person do who attaches the hand to the knee? Well, you wouldn't be able to do it on an organism but you could draw it. You can do anything on paper; you could simply draw a human figure, truncated here, and the two knees so that hands grow out of them. [This drawing has not been preserved.] So you see, someone could draw that but then they would have drawn an impossible organism; they would have proved that they don't understand anything about real life! You could also use the comparison: they have submerged the eagle, a bird that is meant for the air, into the depths of the sea, or the like.

What, then, has such a person tried to do? Well, look, what they have attempted can be done quite easily with all things that relate only to cognitions of the physical plane. One professor can write a book starting with something, another can start with something else, and it doesn't really matter: you can remove things from it and so on. But here you are not dealing with living beings but with thought machines. That is the crux of the matter.

So a person who does something like that, by removing such a matter from its context and putting it into an impossible context has proved that they are completely unfamiliar with the nature of what has filled with fire and set ablaze our whole spiritual-scientific stream since its inception because they also try to treat the spiritual in accordance with the quite normal materialistic formula. That is very important. It is very important to keep these things in mind, otherwise you will not understand from within the thrust of higher cognition. You cannot say everything in any old place. And Hegel has really already said it with regard to the exoteric, which touches a little on the esoteric,[10] that a thought belongs in its place in context. I hinted at this the other day when I tried to indicate something in this direction on Hegel's birthday.[11] So you arrive at nothing less in this way than that you immerse your thinking in life, whereas otherwise you always live in what is dead; you immerse yourself in life.

In this way, however, something is revealed which was previously not at all recognizable and which cannot be verified in any way on the physical plane, namely coming into being and passing away.

This, too, you can already see from *Knowledge of the Higher Worlds. How is it Achieved?* After all, nothing can be observed on the physical plane other than that which has come into being. The process of coming into being cannot be observed in any way, only what has come into being can be observed on the physical plane. Nor can passing away be observed, for when the object passes over into passing away, it is no longer on the physical plane, or at least it moves away from the physical plane.

So you cannot observe coming into being and passing away on the physical plane. The consequence of this is that we can say: We enter a whole new cosmic element when we discover the mobile thought, namely the world of life and that is the world of coming into being and passing away.

Speaking in occult terms, this could also be expressed in the following way: The human being was in the world of coming into being and passing away during the old moon period—but only in dream consciousness. There it was not the case that the human being first saw what had come into being with their senses, for their senses had not yet developed for sensory perception, but they were still inside things. They pictured things in a dreamlike way but the images they pictured in a dreamlike way allowed them to follow coming into being and passing away. And that is what they must first rise to again by attaining mobile thoughts. Thus the ascent to imaginative cognition is at the same time a return, only a return on the level of consciousness. We return to something we grew out of; we return properly.

So that we can say: This imaginative cognition is the return to the world of coming into being and passing away. So we discover coming into being and passing away when we return. And we cannot learn anything at all about coming into being and passing away if we do not come to imaginative cognition. It is quite impossible to identify anything about coming into being and passing away without coming to imaginative cognition.

That is why what Goethe wrote about the metamorphosis of plants and animals is so infinitely significant, because Goethe really wrote it from the standpoint of imaginative cognition. And that is why people could not understand what was actually meant when I wrote my commentaries for Goethe's scientific writings,[12] which set out again and again in all different ways that it was not at all important to measure Goethe's findings against the present scientific findings but to immerse oneself in these scientific findings of Goethe's and to see in them something tremendously superior, to see something quite different from the present scientific findings. That is why I referred to words that Goethe said so beautifully and in which he hints at what is important to him.[13] Goethe went on his Italian Journey and followed with interest not only art but also nature. If you read the *Italian Journey*, you can see how, step by step, he immersed himself in everything that the mineral, vegetable sphere and so on could offer him. And then, when he had arrived in Sicily, he said, after what he had observed there, now he would like to make a journey to India, not to discover something new but to look at what had been discovered, what had already been discovered by others, in his own way. In other words, to look at it with mobile concepts! That is what matters: to look at what others have discovered with mobile concepts. That is what is so tremendously significant, that Goethe introduced these mobile concepts into scientific life.

Therefore, for the person with an occult understanding, the following is a fact which is generally misunderstood. Ernst Haeckel and other materialistic, or as people also say, monistic scholars have spoken very appreciatively about Goethe's metamorphosis of plants and animals.[14] But the fact that they were able to express their appreciation is based on a very strange process, which I also want to make clear to you by a comparison.

Suppose you have a plant in front of you in a flower pot, or even, better still, outside in the garden, and you want to enjoy that plant. You go out into the garden to enjoy it, to put yourself into a relationship with it. And now imagine that there is a person who has no use for it. And when you ask yourself why, then you discover: it is actually life that bothers them! And so they make a very fine replica of the plant so that the plant is now like the real one but in papier-mâché. They put that in their room and now they enjoy it. Life bothered them; only now do they enjoy it!

I can't tell you what agonies I endured as a boy with such a comparison, which is also characteristic of people's attitudes. As a boy I often had to listen to someone, who wanted to emphasize the beauty of a rose, saying: Truly, it is like wax! That drives me mad! But it happens. It really happens that someone emphasizes the excellence of a living thing by saying in their turn of phrase that it is like a dead thing. That really happens. For anyone who has a sense of these things it is something terrible. But if you don't have such a sense, you really can't develop in accordance with reality.

Now then, with Ernst Haeckel the following happened. Goethe wrote 'The Metamorphosis of Plants' and 'The Metamorphosis of Animals', Haeckel reads them and Ahriman transforms the living things Goethe has written into replicas for him, into something that is actually made of papier-mâché, and that he can understand. He rather likes that. So that in what he praises, we don't have praised what Goethe really meant, but Haeckel has first transposed it into something mechanistic. The thing is that Ahriman, who transforms the living into the dead, steps between Goethe and Haeckel.

Now, as I said, this conscious ascent to imaginative cognition is a return. I already said at the beginning of the lecture: actually the imaginations are already in us; they have been in us since the moon period, and earth development consists of us having superimposed the ordinary layers of consciousness. Now we return again through what we have acquired in ordinary earth consciousness. It is a real return.

And now we can ask ourselves: How can we describe the whole thing? We can now say: It is a descent and an ascending return. Only now are we justified in drawing this line [the words on the blackboard are connected by a line, see diagram]; adding it from the outset would make no sense. And only now can we say: At the level of ordinary physical cognition, there we are at the bottom. Here we have the unconscious imaginative cognition that now sits down below in our nature, which has to do with the forces of coming into being and passing away; and on the other side, in the ascent, is conscious imaginative cognition. [Both were marked on the blackboard.]

unconscious imaginative knowledge

conscious imaginative knowledge

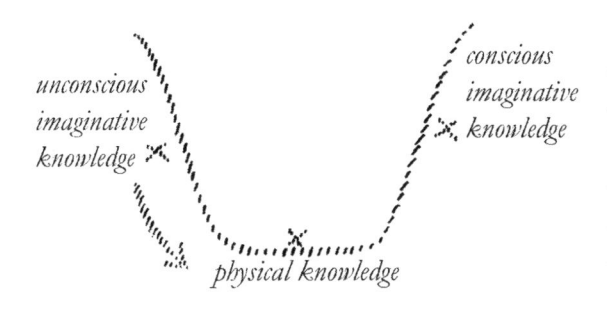

physical knowledge

If we now take Goethe in particular as an obvious example—I will only take him as an example—we can say: In Goethe's case, the point has come in the more modern age at which the outer development of humanity grasps imaginative cognition, at which it is really being introduced into science.

Now we can ask ourselves: So can we examine whether there are not quite remarkable things connected with it? Yes, they are connected with it, because basically the whole Goethean way of thinking is quite different from that of other people. And Schiller, who could not develop this way of thinking, could therefore only understand Goethe with an extreme effort, as you can see in the passage of the correspondence between Schiller and Goethe I have often mentioned, where Schiller writes to Goethe on 23 August 1794:

> ...For a long time now, although from quite a distance, I have watched the course taken by your spirit, and noted with ever renewed admiration the path you have marked out for yourself. You seek what nature is by necessity but you seek it by the most difficult path, which everyone less forceful will take care to avoid. You take the whole of nature together in order to throw a light on the individual part; in the totality of its manifestations you seek the ground on which to explain the individual.
>
> From the simple organization you ascend, step by step, to the more intricate, to finally build the most intricate of all, the human being, genetically from the materials of the whole edifice of nature. By recreating them from nature, as it were, you seek to penetrate their hidden engineering. A great and truly heroic idea, which shows abundantly how much your spirit holds the rich totality of its ideas together in beautiful unity. You can never have hoped that your life would suffice for such a goal but even to set out on such a path is worth more than to complete any other, and you have chosen, like Achilles in the Iliad, between Phthia

and immortality. Had you been born a Greek, even only an Italian, and if exquisite nature and idealizing art had surrounded you from the cradle, your path would have been infinitely shortened, perhaps made entirely superfluous. Already in your first perception of things you would then have taken in the form of necessity and with your first experiences the great style would have developed in you. Well, since you were born a German, since your Greek spirit was thrown into this Nordic Creation, you had no choice but either to become a Nordic artist yourself, or to replace for your imagination what reality withheld from it by tutoring it with the help of your thinking, and thus to give birth to a Greece from within, as it were, and in a rational way. In that period of life when the soul forms its inner world out of the outer, surrounded by deficient forms, you had already absorbed a wild and Nordic nature when your victorious genius, superior to its material, discovered this deficiency from within, and was assured of it from without by acquaintance with Greek nature. Now you had to correct the old, inferior nature that had already been imposed on your imagination in accordance with the better design that your formative spirit created for itself, and this of course cannot proceed in any other way than according to guiding concepts. But this logical direction, which the spirit is compelled to take in reflection, is not well compatible with the aesthetic one, through which alone it creates. So you had one more job, because just as you passed from perception to abstraction, so now you had to convert concepts backwards into intuitions again, and transform thoughts into feelings, because only through these can genius be productive...

He thinks of him as a Greek transplanted into the Nordic world, and so on. There indeed you can see the whole difficulty Schiller had in understanding Goethe! Many a person could learn something from this, who believes they can understand Goethe in the blink of an eye and thereby elevate themselves above Schiller, even though Schiller wasn't exactly a fool compared to those people who believe they can understand Goethe so easily!

But the distinctive thing we can discover is that Goethe also has a quite distinctively divergent view in relation to other areas, for example in relation to the ethical development of the human being, namely in the way of thinking about what the human being deserves or does not deserve as reward or punishment.

We fail to understand Goethe's work from the outset if we don't consider his way of thinking about the human being in terms of reward and punishment, which, I would like to say, diverged from all those around him. Read the poem 'Prometheus', where he goes as far as to rebel against the gods. Prometheus—this is of course a rebellion against the way people think about reward and punishment. For Goethe, the possibility exists of developing very specific concepts about reward and punishment. And in his *Wilhelm Meister* he really tried to portray this in what I might call a wonderfully probing way into the mysteries of the world. You cannot understand *Wilhelm Meister* if you don't consider this.

What is the reason for that? The reason for that is that in the field of physical cognition we cannot form any idea at all as to what punishment or reward should be applied with regard to anything human in relation to the world, for this can only come to be understood in the field of the imagination. The occultists have therefore also always said: When you ascend to imaginative knowledge, you experience not only the elemental world but also—as they put it—'the world of wrath and punishment'. So here it is not only a return to the world of coming into being and passing away but at the same time an ascent to the world of wrath and punishment. [The words 'return to the world of coming into being and passing away' and 'world of wrath and punishment' were written on the blackboard.]

That is why the particular possibility of linking what the human being is worth and not worth in relation to the universe can only be properly illuminated by spiritual science. All other 'execution' in the world is preparatory for this.

Here we are at an important point, from which I will then continue tomorrow.

Third Lecture

DORNACH, 19 SEPTEMBER 1915

YESTERDAY we led our considerations from a certain perspective to the characteristics of imaginative cognition and attached importance to emphasizing that the human being has in themselves everything they consciously bring to consciousness through imaginative cognition. I used the comparison that in a darkened room there are various objects, also people if you like, that cannot be seen with physical eyes in a dark room. Then you enter with a light and everything inside is illuminated; there is nothing new in it, everything was there before. The only difference is that things are seen and perceived afterwards and not before. It is the same with what imaginative cognition presents to us. Everything which imaginative cognition brings to consciousness is present in the human being, holds sway and works in the human being down below in the hidden depths of the soul; it is part of what lives and weaves in the human being. And what is especially important for the human being on the physical plane is that they are continually enhanced or diminished in their forces in some way or other by what in life they assimilate, experience and let sink down from their conceptual life into the depths of consciousness.

I will have something more to tell you about this matter in greater detail on a later occasion; because the process is very incompletely characterized when we say: Here [drawing] is the threshold of consciousness; here is a conception that sinks down into the subconscious and is now down there like a living being. As I said, the process is described rather incompletely. But it is our intention only slowly and gradually to ascend to the true facts in this area.

What I want to say today, then, is that we become aware of how these facts of imaginative cognition are of course—as you can see from what has been discussed—thoroughly and deeply connected with all the conditions of life of the human being, also on the physical plane from birth to death. But they belong to the unconscious or subconscious conditions of life. So that we can gain from what we have considered also the important truth that the human being as they live on earth is dependent on conditions that do not enter into the clear daytime consciousness that we have from birth to death, except when we are asleep. So we are dependent on life factors that cannot be known with the ordinary normal consciousness.

Threshold of consciousness

But in the whole way in which I have presented it, these factors of life which hold sway down there—and we said yesterday, in the etheric body—are still quite close to the human being, so close that, because they are related, they connect with that which the human being continually lets sink down from their conceptual world. For the human being can, as it were, if they transform their thoughts into recollections, themselves transform their thoughts into the substance that is down there in the subconscious. After all, it is [substantially] wholly the same as what we think. When what we think is down below, it is just such a churning, squirming world of mice as that which lives and weaves down there and which is basically living thought life. But that is the etheric body, that has come into the etheric body from the cosmos. And because it is related to our conscious thought life, it is still very close to the human being. And as it lives and weaves [today in us in the unconscious] so it was basically fully present during the Old Moon existence. The [Moon thinking]—if you imagine it as dreamlike, if you think of it as being completely immersed in the dream life—was just like when you dream but perceive in the dream the living weaving of thought. That gives you the conceptualizing on the Old Moon. The only thing that there is in addition during our existence on earth is that we have to make an effort to have thoughts, to form thoughts through our own efforts. The inhabitant of the Old Moon did not form these thoughts through their own effort. They lived in dream images, the only difference being that they were not as dead as our thoughts but were actually weaving life, image-weaving life.

You can see from what I have presented to you that when we enter into the imaginative world we gain something and lose something at the same time. The calmness, the earthly calm experience of thoughts, that is what we lose; we no longer have control over that because the thoughts themselves are living inner powers. In ordinary life we feel that we are the rulers over our thoughts; we don't have them in that way there in the imaginative world; but in return we also take hold of a life that is simply life. The thoughts we have in physical life are dead; what we grasp there, that lives and weaves. And that is what it was already like during the Old Moon existence for human beings, only they had it dreamlike, and not consciously. Then there was the ascent to consciousness [in earth evolution]. And from the conscious cognition of that which was dreamlike during the Old Moon existence, imaginative cognition emerges as the first stage of that from which spiritual-scientific cognition must be taken. So this imaginative cognition is still very much related to the human being.

Now, I said you gain something and you lose something. People would readily agree with the former, the gaining of something; but they don't agree with losing something. And that is the source of countless errors; it is the source of very, very many errors. You see, it is not so very easy if we do not make an effort to imagine what actually this dreamlike imaginative conceptualizing was like during the Moon period. When we live here on earth it is inconvenient, because of the physical period of development, to always have to form ideas and thoughts on the basis of earthly facts. That is precisely what is inconvenient about studying. We must really consider the facts, judge the facts, relate the facts to one another, and we must slowly, through our own efforts, work our way through the worlds of thought and ideas which we, as earthly human beings, control with our earthly will. Some, then, find it much more convenient if the living world of thoughts is simply given to them in such a way that they only have to wait for it: if they get 'enlightenment' from it, then it goes into their soul life, then they no longer need to develop thoughts. That is what they think; but that doesn't get them any further than they are. We stand much higher as earth human beings than as Moon human beings; because we have continued to develop. Compared with the dreamlike imagining of the Moon, as earth human beings who combine the facts and who with our rational judgement form concepts from the experiences of life we stand much higher than the Moon human beings and those who long for the return of this Moon existence, which consists of enlightenment not thoughts that have been worked on.

We can have peculiar experiences in that respect. Not that the human being, when they sink back to this Moon cognition, has no thoughts. They do have thoughts; but the latter come of their own accord, the person does not need to do the work [of thinking in facts]. That, again, seems quite convenient. We can repeatedly have a specific experience, a very important, specific experience, which must be considered if we want to understand these things properly at all.

There are people who come to have a certain visionary clairvoyance. This dreamlike imagining, this visionary clairvoyance is always a falling back into Moon nature. For the real clairvoyance which we want for the earth must be based on a higher level, on an even greater elaboration through the world of thought than the cognition of the physical plane. Sinking back is not an elevation, not an ascending development of the human being, but a descending development, becoming less intelligent than we are as normal human beings. And that is where this particular experience occurs, which we can have over and over again. There are people who have a certain visionary clairvoyance but are not actually intelligent at all. Indeed, their clairvoyance is connected with the fact that they flee intelligence, that they do not like to develop the intelligence that we have to develop as a human being on earth. It is precisely this dulling of the ordinary earthly intelligence which is very often associated with a certain degree of visionary clairvoyance, which is a Moon-like atavistic one. And then perhaps the following occurs: such people can then make a record of their pictures. These records are not thoughtless but interwoven with thoughts—the thoughts come with the images—and intellectually brilliant, very brilliant images are interwoven in them. And then the riddle can arise: yes, here is a person who describes in images, in very beautiful images, Atlantis or also other things that come to them in a visionary way and that is absolutely logically intelligent. But I have never perceived such intelligent logic in that person when they have to explain something about the things of the physical plane; then they don't have it. They have not become enough of an earthly human being. But when they are allowed to fall back into the Moon intelligence, then the intelligence comes. But then it is not their intelligence, then they are merely a medium for the Moon intelligence, then the Moon intelligence works into them. We can get wonderful descriptions of spiritual worlds from people who have sunk back a little into the Moon stage and who, when they want to use their earthly acquired intelligence, cannot understand themselves what they have actually produced, and usually do not even want to.

I said: In ascending to imaginative cognition, you have to gain something and lose something, and that most of the time people don't want to lose anything. I also pointed out that there are people who have intellect and do not want to lose it. Now these are not the ones who love visionary clairvoyance because they quite like to lose ordinary intelligence, ordinary thinking. But there is another group that does not want to lose this intelligence. They want to preserve this intelligence as it is on the physical plane, only they do not want to develop it further. They do not want to continue working in relation to this intelligence in order for the human being to come to use concepts more freely than they are used under the processes of the physical plane. And then such people get into allegorizing, into symbolizing, which after all is only an activity of the physical plane because it does not continue to develop the thinking but leaves it standing and then wraps fine words around it of all kinds of exquisite occult things. That is very important that this is also taken into account.

And you see, this was already in the awareness of those who slowly and gradually worked their way up or wanted to work their way up to the points of view that we must have today in spiritual science. Today in spiritual science we really must bring something of clear thinking to humanity, combined with the possibility of knowing something of spiritual worlds, but in clear, in completely clear thinking. It really took a long time for the possibility to arrive—and hopefully it is now here—to penetrate these matters in this way. And many people have worked their way through to this stage. After all, people of such great clarity as Goethe, for example, have come very close to complete clarity. But many have worked their way through to this stage. Just think how Jakob Böhme struggled at the point of transition to the materialistic age to work his way out of the chaotically writhing, moving, whirling and teeming concepts—which he already had—in such a way that something emerged which he presents as a profound illumination of some of the secrets of the spiritual world.

Someone else again uttered some wonderful words—let me say, as if wonderfully illuminating the horizon at the dawn of the modern age—from which we can see, or at least you can see it from the other things he achieved, how, although he was not able to penetrate with a completely clear view to what should be spiritual science today, he was nevertheless able to get as far as presenting its most important nerve. For the man I am now talking about realized in the eighteenth century: If you want to understand the human being, you must penetrate through the darkness, through the confusion of external material cognition. This is necessary even if you are at the first stage of imaginative cognition. For we have seen that what weaves down there in the depths of the soul cannot be reached at all with physical cognition. We have to penetrate the darkness. But that's not the only thing we have to do. We must also penetrate through the confusions of ordinary concepts to cognition; we must also dispel these confusions. So we must also get beyond the ordinary thinking that works on the physical plane.

And in this situation this man then coined a very beautiful phrase. The first part of this sentence is happily followed, the second part is almost never followed. But it is important to follow it. You see, this is what most people admit today who somehow want to become or be mystics in some field, that one must cast off the sensory, the material, that one must cast off the muddles of the material in order to penetrate the spiritual. But few admit that one must also cast off the forms of the spiritual that cling to thinking in concepts; for they would like to take them with them, would like to make use of them just as they do on the physical plane, would like to find the thought down there in the subconscious as a possible memory in just the same form as it has up there.

But it would be a mistake if you were to believe that the clairvoyant, when they look into the human mind, finds the thoughts there exactly as the person thinks them who has them in his head. That is not true. Down there they are transformed, they are living beings, an elemental world. The world of thoughts that the human being has here on the physical plane is not found in the spiritual world. That is why that man coined a beautiful sentence that I want to write down for you, because it can really be seen as a kind of trial in our own mind: How do we come to know anything about the worlds that lie outside the earthly world?

He said [writes on the blackboard:]

Dissipez vos tenebres materielles et vous trouverez l'homme

With this part of the sentence—dispelling the material darkness and confusion—people who want to be mystics agree. The second part of the sentence, however, people still barely understand today. [Writes on the blackboard:]

Dissipez vos tenebres spirituelles et vous trouverez Dieu

whereby for 'Dieu', because it is still coloured by religious ideas, we have to imagine the whole content of spiritual science. You see, he could not yet find the expression that we can find today.

Now you can surely imagine that when someone reads the sentence today: '*Dissipez vos tenebres materielles et vous trouverez l'homme*', that they say: Yes, fine, that's how I enter the spiritual world, that's what I want. But in '*Dissipez vos tenebres spirituelles et vous trouverez Dieu*' they will say: But what will be left for me, since I will no longer have anything?

Indeed, what is left? Precisely this remains, what today is the content of spiritual science. This is necessary: the cognitive content of the physical plane, usually believed to be the only correct one, must be dispelled just as the material darkness must be dispelled. Now take note how this is observed in our spiritual science. .. [Gap in the transcript].

These words come from the so-called *'philosophe inconnu'*, Saint-Martin,[15] who considered himself a pupil of Jakob Böhme.

Thus we find in Saint-Martin already a deep longing for that which is to come to light in spiritual science. But he calls himself *'philosophe inconnu'*, unknown philosopher, because what he carried within himself—even though, of course, the people who saw him saw his nose, saw his hands, heard the words he spoke—remained foreign to them. The actual philosopher Saint-Martin remained unknown to them, quite unknown.

So it is the acquisition of imaginative cognition in accordance with the discussions we had yesterday; a return, a conscious return to the way the human being related to the world during the Moon period. So that we can say—you will recall, we have already presented this from another side in lectures here in particular:[16] Events still prevail in human beings today—but in a supersensory way, as something spiritual and supersensory—which are actually not normal events on earth but were normal events during the Moon period. They have preserved these Moon events; they can regress in a certain sense. Then they produce cognitions in a completely different way than the earthly human being can produce such cognitions. They can come to visionary clairvoyance, have dulled intelligence, and pose precisely the riddle of which I spoke earlier, namely, that if they were induced to work in a sensible scientific way, or even to make sensible decisions with regard to the most ordinary everyday events, they cannot do it, that they would not succeed; but when they write something from out of their vision, even about the events that took place at the time of the Mystery of Golgotha, they only write down images, remain in the Moon life, but nevertheless write something terribly clever. And what they write doesn't match up at all with what is otherwise known about the person. So, theoretically they can't do anything but as a medium they write very clever things, so that we can be amazed at the cleverness. But that is not a forward development, that is a regression of the human being. This, of course, does not exclude the possibility of truths coming to light through such a person, because they in turn stand in earthly existence and are connected with earthly existence and, in addition, have this still active Moon life in them.

I have tried to depict the different types of human beings in the Mystery Dramas, and also to draw such a figure that reverts to the Moon-like, that is, who is unintelligent on the physical plane and yet can reveal correct things; in other words, who stands below the level of the normal earthly human being: that is Theodora. Theodora is a figure who is specifically meant to be a reversion to Moon consciousness. That is very clear, after all. I mean to say that it is very clearly indicated there how it is, in that it is said in the one place where Theodora appears:[17] 'Theodora, a seeress. In her, the will element is transformed into naïve seership.' That is what naïve seership means, moon seership, naturally. It is naïve seership, and that is how the character is rendered. And it is for this reason that in the final Mystery Theodora herself can no longer appear but only her soul, because she cannot participate in certain things. These Mystery Dramas in particular should be viewed very, very precisely. Perhaps the time will come when some of you will be able to understand that hardly anything has happened here in the last few days that could not already be read about in some form in the Mysteries. Had it been read as things should be read, these confusions would not have been necessary.

So to be clear: that which is experienced as the imaginative world is still relatively very close to the human being. Much less close to it, on the other hand, is that which can be experienced as the inspired world. For when we first live our way into the inspired world, it embraces those facts which did not take place during the Moon existence but already during the Old Sun existence, and which the human being has also preserved. So we penetrate into even greater depths of the human soul when we work our way through to the inspired world. And the inspired world that we initially encounter now has a [certain] distinctiveness.

You see, when the human being works their way through to the imaginative world, they come across facts that took place during the Old Moon existence. If you imagine the Old Moon in the phases where it was split off from the Sun of that time—you can read about this in *Occult Science*—the human being lived at certain times on this Moon that was split off from the Sun. And what the human being experienced there is what we first encounter when we return with the old, dreamlike, imaginative clairvoyance. But when we enter the inspired world, we do not experience in the return an existence split off from the Sun but an existence directly within the Sun; that is, the facts that the human being experienced together with the Sun. We really do experience real Sun facts. And these Sun facts, you see, they are now actually no longer related to the human being. For as the human being is now, during earth existence—if they don't look into the depths of their soul, don't look at what is in the deeply hidden grounds of their soul—they are actually more of a shell through what they are on earth. They are not a real human entity; they are more of a shell. To begin with, they have their physical form; it was created during our existence on earth in the way it appears to us on the physical plane. But forces are at work within it that cannot be seen and which even present science has not yet sought.

It was suggested to a friend of ours[18] to look in this direction with the biological material at his disposal. This friend is making a lot of effort and perhaps after some time—such things require a lot of study—he will be able to publish something to create a possible bridge over to these hidden parts of human nature. But it is necessary to investigate precisely those biological facts which are not taken into account by present science, which the present researcher who is experimenting leaves to one side, as it were. So we have to investigate the preparations for what the other researchers are not interested in at all, what they leave to one side. There is still a lot missing, of course, and a lot of new research needs to be done. It is easily possible that this will be the work of many years until it can be finished. But it would be immensely important work because it could show us what is still attainable by the means of physical science regarding what lives in human nature from the Old Moon.

A whole new embryology, a new part, a new side of embryology will result. It is necessary that this gets done at some point. But that is actually the end of it; that's all we can find when we look at the human being externally. For what can be found in the human being today externally is actually no older, not even as old as the oldest time of the Old Moon existence. But from such research to which I've just referred it will be possible to draw conclusions about processes of the Old Moon existence. They will agree with what is described in *Occult Science*. But, as I said, we don't get very far back if we look at the human being as they are today; not even to the beginning of the Old Moon existence, let alone to the Old Sun existence.

If we want to return to the Old Sun existence, then we must take much, much less of the material nature of the human being than can be taken in the science which I have just referred to. For what is involved here is that something actually penetrates into human nature which the human being on earth can bring to revelation, but does not have to bring to revelation. They can, but they do not have to bring it to revelation. When, for example, inspiration really comes to the artist, to the poet, then ultimately—if it is really inspiration—it comes from the spiritual world of Sun existence.[19] It really comes from the spiritual world of Sun existence. But our time is so terribly poor in spirit that what comes from the inspiration of Sun existence is rejected and people really only want to create naturalistically, to stick to the model, that is, to the earthly, whereas what can come from the model is only the material for what we are actually supposed to create. The arts that protect the individual artist from clinging to the model, from succumbing to the material, are architecture and music. Basically, architecture cannot replicate anything; and often does so quite clumsily, too. And music can't imitate anything either, because it is not really music if you imitate bird calls and cat's meows in the way that you copy models in painting and so on. In music, you can only take the very elevated material of the tone. But that's how it should be in every art. As much as the musician takes from the music, the painter must take just as much. What the tones are for the musician, the form, the colour, must be for the painter. The model should not give them more than the material. So the artistic cannot be taken from out of the model but springs from the inspiration that leads back to the Old Sun existence. That is why the truly great works of art are so foreign to the earth. I said that the human being can live without artistic inspiration; they can introduce it, they don't have to introduce it. The Aimoré might well say: The human being can also live without art.

But now you can—and those who are involved in these things in a deeper sense will do so sooner or later—you can raise an important, a fundamentally important question, the question: So if we have Saturn existence, Sun existence, Moon existence, earth existence, all with certain facts, and return to Moon existence in imaginative cognition, to Sun existence in inspired cognition, then from this it follows indeed that we return to Saturn existence in intuitive cognition; so if that is the case, that we have no new facts but return to the old facts, why does the human being need to evolve at all?

So someone might raise this question: Why evolution? Why, then, the whole existence on earth, which detaches us from the facts through which we have developed, so that the cognitions are moved down into the unconscious and we must first cognitively climb back to them again? Why all this?

You see, because only through this can we become true human beings, because only through this can we really complete our true nature. And this can also be seen externally if we really study such personalities who had something of these mobile concepts, of this conceptual mouse as I have mentioned to you, for example in the 'Metamorphosis of Plants' and the 'Metamorphosis of Animals' by Goethe. We have to study such characters. And such characters show at the same time that, if they are inwardly completely true, they stand in a quite specific relationship to a still different world of the soul. This is particularly evident in Goethe. Study *Wilhelm Meister*, study all Goethe's poems, and you will find that in a strange way a certain manner of judging the world, of passing judgement on the world, occurred in him. For you will find, if you engage yourself in these things, that to the same extent that the metamorphosis idea develops in Goethe, a really genuine, magnificent inner tolerance of soul also develops in him. A wonderful tolerance in the soul develops in him, a remarkable way of relating to the world and to life, a tolerance of the soul! And this is connected with very deep facts.

You see, when we look at the animal world, this animal world has the most diverse forms. If, for example, we compare the hyena, which bears its desire for carrion in its face, which bears its species in its whole posture, with the lion, with the wolf, and if we again compare these animals with the eagle and the eagle with the vulture, then compare these animals with turtles, snakes, worms, the various insects, if we take all these different animal forms, we must surely ask ourselves: How is this connected with the spiritual world?

Now you can only study that if you study the Old Moon existence. Because why? You see, during the Old Moon existence, the human being did not yet exist in their present form. The corresponding forms that were present at the human stage were the angels. With the angeloi, the angels, there existed quite different forms of judgement, quite a different way of thinking [than we have today]. The angels were then on the same level as human beings are today but they were not in such a physical body as human beings are today on earth. They were in a very soft, supple body, for the Spirits of Form had not yet collaborated to form a solid shape for bodies. Now at that time—that is, not now during the earth period but during the Moon period—these angeloi thought in concepts which, compared with our earth concepts, were much more filled with life. But these concepts have something very distinctive in addition to their vitality. They were highly saturated with impulses of mind. Stirred up under the influence of the archangeloi, the archai, the Spirits of Form, the Spirits of Movement and so on, the angels conceived the concepts during the Moon period. But they were living, impulsive concepts; much more impulsive than we find concepts in people today, who alternately become either 'happy bunnies' or 'furious bunnies', don't they?; when they put their emotions into how they judge life. There are such people, and they can be the best of people, but they will alternately be delighted, inclined to be delighted about something; they will be 'happy bunnies', or else they will be distinctly 'furious bunnies', so that their whole soul lies in what they utter and everything comes out in the concepts, doesn't it? Well, that was present to a much higher degree—directly creative—with these angels on the Moon.

Let us imagine a Moon dweller thinking in this way! He will say to himself: Well, I must now form a concept. Inspiration tells me: A wretch whose back rises from the rear to the front, who pulls a repulsive face out of a longing for carrion! This creature arises as a result, is condemned to be a hyena. Here we have the creative concept. The forms of the animal kingdom are intimately connected with this creative thinking, which creates according to the principle of good and evil. And the whole animal kingdom in its various forms is such a configuration of good and evil.

The human beings [of the earth] were not meant to learn this. One who did not want to relinquish the Moon culture seduced human beings into recognizing good and evil in the form that he experienced it during the Moon period. He ... [gap in the transcript] made judgements in that way; but human beings were to learn to make judgements differently. Such strong insertion of emotions into concepts should not go down into the deeper depths of the soul. That had to be discarded, that had to give way to a more objective, a more calm form. That is why the human being had to progress from Moon to earth evolution. And if they now continue to advance, they will become even more tolerant. Such a Moon angel, well, they hated the hyena in an unbelievable way because it was evil for them; they hated the snake, hated what was ugly and loved what was beautiful. Good and evil belonged to the realm of creative life. The human being had to get out of this habit. Human beings could not develop earthly science if they were to divide animals, as the Moon angels did, into beautiful and ugly ones—we divide differently, according to objective concepts, don't we?—into seemly and unseemly animals, into mischievous and cunning animals, and so on. The Moon angels had all that. But it would not be scientific today, for example, if it were written in a learned book: The weasel—characteristic: cunning. This may be done in a satirical poem,[20] but in science today it must be pushed away; it can't be like that today.

Thus, in order to make progress in this field, we must be able to rise to a level at which we view those things against which human beings have the most violent emotions in earthly life as scientifically as the animal kingdom is viewed scientifically without emotions today. And this is what we can see in the particular nature of Goethe's spirit. For him, human life is a calm stream to a much higher degree, which he views like natural phenomena. That is exactly the wonderful inner serenity of Goethe's view of life, that for him a part of human life also enters into the stream of natural facts. This enabled him to become so objective.

Well, starting from this point, we will have to take up the matter again and continue these reflections tomorrow.

Fourth Lecture

Dornach, 20 September 1915

In the last few days I have spoken to you of how the human being's cognition, which they must acquire as earth human beings on the physical plane, is at first a kind of dead cognition—a cognition which relates to what we must call the cognition of the next higher world in the same way as what is dead relates to what is alive. I have tried to illustrate how this dead, as it were, mechanical knowledge of the physical earthly human being comes alive when we want to rise to those levels of cognition through which the human being can learn something of the so-called higher worlds.

Dead cognition! However, even as physical earthly cognition it has not always been as dead as cognition is today but it has only become so. And you all know the time when human earth cognition became so dead. I have often spoken to you of how, if we go back to ancient times, to times of earth evolution before the Mystery of Golgotha had taken place, ordinary earthly cognition was also more alive because there was a kind of ancient heritage [of higher cognition]. Something of the ancient heritage of a higher cognition was always mixed into the ordinary earthly cognition. You can follow this in the various epistemological and religious documents of humanity. Just look at how in the Bible, in the Old Testament, where the supersensory worlds are spoken of, there is always talk either of a dream or of the inspirations of the prophets. There we always have a natural return to living cognition. The old atavistic inheritance of clairvoyance, left to human beings as a Moon heritage, had not yet been extinguished. This became extinguished at the time of the Mystery of Golgotha.

I ask you to take this sentence very precisely. For if one of you quotes this sentence somewhere in such a way that you report that I said that through the Mystery of Golgotha the old atavistic knowledge was extinguished, you are saying the exact opposite of what I have just expressed. At the time of the Mystery of Golgotha this knowledge was extinguished through the quite natural course of development of humanity, and the Mystery of Golgotha brought a substitute for what had gradually been lost, brought life into the human soul from another side. So that today we are faced with the following fact: we can go back into ancient human records on earth, where we find all kinds of scientific things even before the time of the Mystery of Golgotha. But in this science the ancient people did not presume anything that was cognition of what was supreme and most important for human beings but it was basically more subordinate things that were believed to be understood in this way. Everything that was important, everything that related to the supersensory worlds, was traced back to ancient wisdom, to a wisdom that was given to humanity, as it were, through a primal revelation. You can see this expressed in one of our four Mysteries.[21] And it was presented in such a way that this heritage was then passed on from generation to generation in the wisdom schools. As early as in the book *Christianity as Mystical Fact*[22] you will find that we tried to understand how through the Mystery of Golgotha a substitute was created for this dying old wisdom, how we might say that the primal mystery became a historical fact on Golgotha, and how, through the fact that the Cross of Initiation was set up on Golgotha for all people to see, life was to be poured into the human soul. So that since then we can say: There is our dead knowledge which the human being gains through their own effort on the physical plane, and there is alongside it something that flows into their soul through the fact that through the Mystery of Golgotha the substance which was to enter the earth aura through Christ flowed out into the earth aura and now flows into the human soul as a second source of human cognition.

So that we can say: From the spiritual-scientific point of view, the matter must be regarded in such a way that the human being's physical knowledge of the earth is a dead one but that life enters into it when the human being allows their physical knowledge of the earth to be fertilized by that which the Mystery of Golgotha can be for them. And then we have the next higher level of cognition, which we call imaginative cognition. This is already something living, something truly living. And this living cognition, this imaginative cognition, is about the things we have been discussing in the last few days.

Today I would like to emphasize once again as something important what I said yesterday, that this imaginative cognition is still related to the nature of the human soul. It is a return to the Moon period. And it is related to the nature of the human soul in such a way that, indeed, in human nature today, as I described yesterday, the old dreamlike Moon cognition can again emerge atavistically, and that some things which can also be understood through a higher clairvoyant skill can, we might say, come together with what emerges through atavism—if the Moon clairvoyant has the necessary modesty.

But further removed from the human being [than imaginative cognition] is everything that enters their soul in an inspirational way, through inspiration. For these are, in substance, the facts of the Old Sun evolution, with which the human being was connected. And that which the human being absorbed as an element of life during the old evolution of the Sun, that too is [preserved] down there in the depths of human nature. This must be illuminated through conscious cognition if inspiration is to occur.

I indicated yesterday that in real, in true art, there is an unconscious drawing forth of these things which belong to the facts of the Old Sun and which human beings have preserved as their heritage; that when what lies deep in the hidden depths of the soul is lifted up into the conscious life of the soul, it can rise to human consciousness as artistic inspiration. The human being then lives only in the consequences that come up from below; they do not live in the causes. If I have already had to indicate to you that the thought below the threshold of consciousness is very different from the thought we have when we bring something up again [into consciousness] from the subconscious thoughts through memory, it must be emphasized that what in truth lives in the depths of the artist's soul is even more different, radically different, from that which then rises up into the consciousness of the artist.

Now we must inscribe one characteristic quite acutely into our souls if we are to understand the whole of inspiration at all. You see, for the human being who is touched by the inspiration, there is no difference between an objective law of nature and that which they experience in their soul as a thought, as an experience of the soul. They feel the law of nature as belonging to them, just as they feel that which lives in their own soul as belonging to them. Let me put it this way: If the person to whom inspiration comes decides to do something, if they do something out of some motive, there is an underlying lawfulness. This lawfulness—we are initially empowered to feel it as a law of our own breast, as an experience of our own. But we feel it with the same objectivity as we feel the rising of the sun as an objective law. I can also put it like this: When I pick up my watch, I feel that it is my affair on the physical plane. With physical cognition, I will not feel it to be my affair when the sun rises in the morning. But in relation to what really comes from the impulse of the inspired world, we feel what happens in nature as belonging to ourselves.

Human interest really does extend across the affairs of nature. The affairs of nature become the human being's own interests. As long as we do not feel the life of the plant within us to be as familiar as the experiences of our own heart, there can be no truth in inspiration. As long as we do not feel a falling stone splashing on the surface of the water and making drops spray up in the same way as we can feel what is going on in our own being, for as long inspiration does not accord with the truth. I could also put it like this: Everything in the human being that lies closer to them than to nature in its fullness, that does not belong to the inspired truths. However, it would be complete nonsense to believe that the inspired person, when someone breaks their skull, would feel this just as objectively as they feel the eruption of a volcano. Subjectively, they of course make this distinction; but they do not possess an inspiration at the moment when someone breaks their skull. But for everything that in this sense belongs to the field of inspiration, their interest is extended across the whole of nature. And I have already drawn attention in the Hague cycle[23] to how the extension of interest is what matters in extended cognition in the first place. Anyone who cannot escape from what concerns them alone, at least for a short time, can naturally not come to any inspiration. They don't always need to do it, of course; on the contrary, they will do well to sharply demarcate their own interests from what should be the object of their inspiration. But if the human being thus extends their interest beyond objectivity, if they try to feel the life of the plant as it comes into being in the same way as they feel that which is going on in their own life, if that which grows and sprouts and comes into being and passes away out there is as intimately familiar to them as the life in their own being, then they are inspired with regard to everything that approaches them in this way.

But then this way of being interested is necessarily linked with a gradual ascent to such a judgement of human beings as we have indicated that the Goethean judgement of human beings gradually became. Goethe learnt to distinguish between the human being's actions and the human being's essence through his striving [for living thoughts]. And this is something exceptionally important! What we do or have done belongs to the objective world, is karma at work; what we are as a personality is constantly in development. And the judgement we make about something a person has done must basically be on a completely different page from the judgement we make about the value or lack of value of a human personality. We must, if we wish to approach the higher worlds, learn to be able to face the human personality as objectively as we face a plant or a stone objectively. We must learn to be able to empathize also with the personality of those people who have done deeds that we must perhaps condemn in the most profound sense. It is precisely this separation of the human being from their deeds, the separation of the human being also from their karma, that we must be able to accomplish if we want to be able to gain a correct relationship with the higher worlds.

And here again, if we want to place ourselves truly on the ground of spiritual science, we must see that this is one of the cases where we come into sharp contradiction with the materialistic thinking of our time. For this materialistic thinking of our time has a tendency to draw the personality of the person more and more into the judgement of their deeds. Just think that in recent times, in the field of external jurisprudence, the tendency has increasingly developed that, when a person has committed a certain act, we should not only judge the act but that we should also observe the whole of human nature; that we should take into account the psyche of a person, how they came to do [the act], whether they are inferior or perfect, and so on. And certain circles are even demanding from external jurisprudence that not only doctors should be consulted as experts regarding the assessment of offences and crimes, but even psychologists. But it is arrogance to judge the nature of a person rather than the deeds, which are solely concerned with external life.

Among the more recent philosophers, only one has shown some attention on this ground. You will also find him mentioned in my *The Riddles of Philosophy*,[24] albeit with regard to different aspects. It was Dilthey who drew attention to the fact that jurisprudence must again get away from psychological jurisprudence and everything similar.

What a person does concerns two areas: firstly, their karma. This through its causation already produces its own judgements; it is no one else's business. Christ himself did not judge the sin of the adulteress but inscribed it in the ground because it will live itself out in the course of karma. Secondly, human deeds relate to human coexistence, and the human deed should only be judged from this perspective. It is not up to the external social order to judge human beings as such.

But spiritual science will gradually rise to something other than judging; it will rise to understanding. And those psychologists who could be appointed today to function as experts when judging a person's external acts will be of no use, for they won't yet know anything about a person's soul. The assessment of a person should not correspond to judgement but to understanding; because helping and not judging should be the tendency under all circumstances. Helping, not judging! But we can only help if we have an understanding of what is going on in a human soul.

However, if we have the tendency to help in truthfulness and not in lies, we will be greatly misunderstood by the world. For the person who is to be helped will be least inclined also to judge in the right way the person who wants to help in the right way. The person who is to be helped will want to be helped in the way they think! But that may be the worst help you can give them if you help them in the way they think they should be helped. An understanding gained on the basis of the soul and spiritual life will often lead us not to do for the person we want to help precisely what they presuppose we should do for them but to do something quite different for them. Maybe even sometimes withdrawing from such a person will be the much better help than cajoling; the brusque rejection of something will be a much better, more loving help than the flattering accommodation and acceptance of what the person in question wants. Someone can be much more loving towards a person by treating them severely under certain circumstances than someone who gives in to them in every way. And there will of course be misapprehension in this field, that is quite natural. Perhaps it is precisely the person who makes the greatest effort to engage with a person's soul in this way who is most misunderstood. But that's not what matters; it's seeking understanding in all circumstances, not being a judge.

In the context of our spiritual-scientific lectures, we often had to speak of Ahriman and Lucifer. Of course, especially after the observations that have been made recently, we can see how human nature can be gripped by Ahriman and Lucifer to a greater or lesser extent. For basically life as such is a pendulum swinging back and forth between ahrimanic and luciferic impulses, only that the position of equilibrium is sought by the being of the world itself, and life consists precisely in maintaining this position of equilibrium. But now consider a great, a tremendous distinction. We can do two things: we can pass judgement that some act of a person is ahrimanically or luciferically influenced, and we can judge the person accordingly. Or we can do something else: we can realize that a deed of a person is ahrimanically or luciferically influenced and from this fact we can try to understand the person. And there is the greatest conceivable difference between these two judgements. For to judge that there is something ahrimanic or luciferic in a person requires that this judgement should never be made from any other point of view than this: that people should no more be judged according to this knowledge that Ahriman and Lucifer live in a person than a plant should be judged because it blossoms red and not blue. Any kind of judicial judgement must be excluded from the idea that anything in a person is ahrimanic or luciferic, just as the making of any value judgement must be excluded from our judgement if we want to recognize the plant, be it red or blue.

Above all, we must seek to keep cognition pure from all emotion, from all subjectivity. And we will be able to do this increasingly the more we make an effort to do so, the more we really strive to take such things as have just been said with the utmost seriousness.

Goethe, for example, was concerned, especially in his most mature period, to present events between people as if they were natural occurrences. Not, of course, from the point of view as if a mechanical necessity were inherent both in a human context and in a natural context. There can be no question of that. But the position of the human soul in relation to the events in human life will gradually become such that, with the same objective love as we look at natural events, we will also allow the events in human life to apply with regard to cognition. This provides the inner tolerance that comes from cognition itself.

In this way, however, we acquire the possibility of gradually allowing that to flow into cognition which otherwise must not flow into cognition at all: namely the terminology which arises out of feeling and the will. When I explained psychoanalysis to you,[25] we concluded one day in particular by having to speak damning words about it; but we first showed that this followed from the matter itself. And why could this judgement be passed? Here I may also say something subjective. Why did I presume to pronounce a seemingly entirely subjective judgement about psychoanalysis? Because I made an effort—I am saying something subjective, but then it means that things are perhaps most easily understood—to study psychoanalysis in the way that I study something that is very pleasant for me and that I like a lot. That is: to show the same objective love to one as to the other. And to this we must gradually work our way, really work our way; otherwise we seek nothing but sensation in cognition, we seek only what is pleasant in cognition. But we never have cognition if we seek only what is pleasant in cognition!

For our physical life, the sun-like never enters the consciousness of the human being in any other way than by pleasing them or repelling them. Only feelings enter from the sun-like, and we must meet the sun-like with our understanding; we must penetrate down into that which is otherwise foreign to the human being. We said that the moon-like is related to the human being, but the sun-like is no longer related to the human being. We must take down, carry down our understanding into regions we do not otherwise penetrate if we want to make what is sun-like in inspiration accessible to us.

The real cognition of the higher worlds does indeed demand preparation in the whole mood of our soul and without this mood in the soul we cannot penetrate into the higher worlds. I do not mean now merely to penetrate clairvoyantly but also to pursue things with understanding. We cannot understand the things told in *Occult Science* if we wish to absorb them in the frame of mind we usually have for something outwardly neutral, that is to say for something mathematical or the like; but we can only absorb them if we first prepare ourselves for them in our minds. The person who wants to absorb inspired cognition with the ordinary understanding of the physical plane is like the person who believes that they can crawl into a plant with their physical body and thus be inside its life. That is why the attempt was always made to prepare human beings before giving them knowledge of the higher worlds, to prepare them gradually so that the mood of the soul was such that such cognition of the higher worlds could have an effect on the mind in the right way. They inevitably had an effect on the mind, for this particular way of facing the higher world requires a certain exertion of the mind, a certain cohesion, a gathering of the inner soul forces; it requires that above all we should not be surprised that a certain inner effort is necessary in order to face the cognition of the higher worlds in the right way.

Hence it is necessary for the human being to create a counterbalance, a proper counterbalance, such that it allows them to tip the scales the other way, as it were, in their soul. We have to consider the matter very carefully.

If you make an effort in the soul—and you must if you really want to grasp the spiritual worlds, even only those things which are given from the spiritual worlds; you can't follow a lecture about the spiritual worlds if you don't listen carefully, if you don't make an effort with your soul—if you really try hard to understand what is said about the spiritual world, you feel that you have to make an effort. You shouldn't then be surprised about that. You shouldn't have to say: Well, that is very demanding. Because it is natural that it is very demanding! But if it is so demanding, then, as long as we are human beings on earth, a consequence will naturally result. And this consequence is that egoism is aroused in the human being. The more the human being feels themselves within themselves, the stronger is their egoism. Take simply the most common phenomenon: as long as we go through the world in good health, we are unegoistic with regard to the physical body; the moment we fall ill, when everything hurts, we become selfish in relation to the external body. That is quite natural. And it is simply nonsensical to demand of the ill person that they should not be selfish in relation to their illness. That is simply nonsense. And if someone says: I may be ill, but I accept my illness selflessly, that is of course just a pretence and untrue words.

But it is the same when we go through this effort in the soul which is necessary in order to work our way up into the higher worlds, to climb up. There you also get into the egoistic element. We should not deceive ourselves but rather, if we want to penetrate this world, we should hold the truth up to ourselves. We have to say to ourselves: You are working yourself into a mood of egoism if you want to enter the higher worlds, because you have to feel these efforts within yourself.

I would like to compare this way of working our way into the higher worlds with something. I would like to compare it with a particular kind of artistic activity, such as was present in our friend Christian Morgenstern. This certain singular way—I have often highlighted it—was different with Morgenstern than with other poets. When he worked his way into serious matter it happened with him in a different way from other poets; it carried him personally up into the region of seriousness to a much greater degree. Therefore he needed a counterweight, something like in the Gallows Song:

> *Ein Wiesel* (A weasel)
> *saß auf einem Kiesel* (sat on a pebble)
> *inmitten Bachgeriesel.* (amidst a trickling brook.)
> *Wisst ihr weshalb?* (Do you know why?)
> *Das Mondkalb* (The mooncalf)
> *verriet es mir* (revealed it to me)
> *im stillen:* (quietly:)
> *Das raffinierte Tier* (The cunning animal)
> *tat's um des Reimes willen.* (did it for the rhyme.)

These light poems, these satirical poems, that's what he needed as a counterweight, for balance. Those who can always poetically pull a 'long face', who look up sentimentally into the higher worlds, those are not the true poets. The true ones are those who need the counterweight, the antithesis.

Now, however, we do look everywhere, do we not, for the possibility of understanding that which must accompany the striving up into the higher worlds as the phenomenon of egoism? You must not judge egoism when it occurs in such a region because you have to understand it like a natural phenomenon. You must not possess the egoism of always wanting to be rid of egoism because then you are not real. For example, we create the counterpart in relation to some things [through the exercises] in *Knowledge of the Higher Worlds. How is it Achieved?*; initially the inner counterparts. But also in what we have created as eurythmy there is a kind of counterpart in this specific way of bringing the etheric body into its appropriate movements and gaining an understanding of this whole language of the human being. It will encourage young people in particular in a natural way to live their way into the spiritual realm.

But something that must be emphasized on this occasion is that one element should be particularly sought after by the person who really wants to gain a right relationship with the spiritual worlds; that is the element—don't be surprised at this, but it must also be clearly expressed for once, or at least expressed more clearly than has otherwise always happened—that is the element of humour. It is really necessary not to be humourless with regard to the striving for the higher world! Such a humourless stance is what produces such terrible excesses. For if the person who imagines themselves to be Homer or Socrates or Goethe were to realize how infinitely ridiculous they should feel in this role, then this would help them tremendously in curing their views! But only those who keep humour away from their untruthful, sentimental lives can fail to think of such things. For if a person should really, well, let me say have the 'misfortune' to have been Homer, and by a correct recognition in a later incarnation come to know that this was the case, then this realization would really appear to them first of all in a humorous light. Especially if it is true, it would first of all appear to them in a humorous light. You would truly laugh at yourself first of all!

It is difficult to talk about this chapter in the right way, especially in brief. But keeping the soul free and open to humour is a good way to take the serious matter really earnestly. Otherwise you debase yourself; the serious matter turns into a lie through sentimentality, and sentimentality is the worst enemy of real earnestness for the serious things of life. I can even imagine that someone who—as a foreign lady once said—only ever wants to face the serious nature of spiritual-scientific cognition 'with a face down to the belly', might have found it objectionable that I have been talking these days about thoughts that act like a mouse in the hand. But you free yourself from the seriousness of the facts by trying to present them in such a form. For you can easily falsify the facts if you approach them with mere sentimentality, because then in sentimentality you already feel sufficiently elevated to the higher worlds and do not believe that you should also ascend to the spiritual worlds through flexible, elastic, fluid understanding. And truly, it is easier to speak of the elemental world being conquered when you are 'unselfish, quite unselfish', easier to get some hazy idea of the elemental world in this way, than really to make the matter so palpable that you have the transition of the thought from a dead object to a living being. Such clear characterization is what we should strive for. So that we gradually train ourselves to ascend into these spiritual worlds without any sentimentality.

Don't worry, the seriousness will come. The effort arises precisely from the difficulty of acquiring spiritual science. And what matters is that we gain the strength to understand the position of the spiritual-scientific worldview within present-day materialism in the right way, and through this strength to become a proper member of the spiritual-scientific movement. We gain this strength in no way other than by trying to understand clearly in the right way how these spiritual worlds can be clothed in words, in ideas, taken from the physical world, even though the spiritual worlds themselves are so dissimilar to the physical world.

Inspiration as such deals with those inner facts in human nature which are inherited from the evolution of the Old Sun, which are connected with all that makes a person capable of performing in the world that which is from heaven, that which is truly from heaven. For this, however, the human being must not only reflect on that which can be acquired in the individual life within the work of the soul which is present between birth and death; but the human being must reflect on that which is in the hidden depths of their soul so that the divine worlds work into their organization. The person who is to be a poet in the world must have the brain of a poet, that is, their brain must be prepared for this from the spiritual world. The person who wants to be a painter must have the brain of a painter. And in order to lend a person a painter's brain or a poet's brain, those forces and impulses must work in human nature which were already substantially there during cosmic evolution in the Old Sun period and were connected with human nature when the human being themselves was not yet nearly so condensed as they are on earth, when the human being themselves had only reached the density of air. Consider that during the Old Sun period human beings consisted only of warmth and air. In that which works in the human being in warmth and air lies, as hereditary material from the Old Sun period, that which can prepare the human brain in such a way that it can be a painter's brain, that it can be a poet's brain.

But from this you can see how, as a result of these reflections on what is observed in the human being and what goes out from the microcosm into the macrocosm, we must say: The human being is one with their environment through that which is the heritage of the Old Sun; because air and warmth are just as much outside as inside. I have often pointed out: the amount of air I have in me now is outside me in the next moment; it always goes out and in, exhale, inhale. The air has my form, and at the moment I exhale the air it is the same air; it is then just outside, outside the human being. But as truly as my bones are myself, as truly the shape of the air is something which is part of my own being from the moment of inhalation to the moment of exhalation. As truly as the bones are part of me from my birth to my death, so the air current is part of me from the moment it is inhaled to the moment it is exhaled. It is me just as my bones are me, it is just that the air stream being me lasts only from inhalation to exhalation, and my bones being me lasts approximately from birth to death. These things are different only in terms of time; the air human being dies on exhalation and is born on inhalation. And as truly as our bones are born before our physical birth and gradually deteriorate slowly, as truly something is born in us when we breathe in, as truly something dies in us when we breathe out. That which is born in us when we breathe in dies when we breathe out; that itself belongs to the heritage from the Old Sun, that was predisposed at that time.

We see how the human realm expands into the cosmos, how the human being merges with it. But we should learn to understand how the human being lives inside the spiritual realm. Our time does not even have the talent to conceive in the most primitive way such togetherness of the human being with the spiritual realm. We have to return to that as well. It would not have occurred to a human being of ancient times to create such words as are created today when it is necessary to create a word for some composite substance. Now, at the most, chemists seek to find appropriate names according to hypothetical premises, if something is to be named according to the principles of chemistry. These names are very unpleasant for people; sometimes they have an awful lot of syllables! Get those who are chemists among our friends, for example, to teach you about it! But where names are not given according to these principles, the names are not connected with the things.

That was not always so. I spoke to you about inspiration today; I showed you how inspiration leads back to the Old Sun heritage of the human being. On the Sun, however, the human being had come as far as breathing. That is to say, that which is now the breathing, and which lives in the air element, was predisposed at that time. So there must be a relationship between the breathing of the human being and inspiration. You only have to consider what the word inspiration originally actually means. In this word, the intimate relationship of breath to 'inspiration' is already expressed, for it is basically the word for inhalation. Those who want to deny the spirits need only look at the development of language.[26] We have already indicated this from another side: we would indeed find the spirits of language, but we would also find how these spirits of language work in human nature! Then we will find how we are embedded in the spiritual worlds, how the spirits work with us, how in everything we do in life the spirits are involved. And we will feel in a real way: our self expanded to the great self of the world. What is theory will become feeling. And that is the way to really enter the spiritual worlds.

But we also really need to engage with these things. We must take them in their details; we must try to take them really seriously, to be serious about much of what has just been said about the relationship of the human being to the spiritual worlds in relation to the simplest circumstances.

This is what I would like to put to you particularly at the end of these lectures, which were intended to show you from a certain perspective how a descending current exists in the human being and an ascending current, and how the human being stands within the ascending and descending currents.

And when Faust opens the book and utters the words:

> 'How heavenly forces ascending and descending
>   Pass golden pails from one to another!'

you have what I have been trying to convey to you these days: this ascending and descending of the heavenly forces which Faust at first gawps at and cannot comprehend. But it is expressed in a way in this Faust poem that we can already see in *Faust*[27] the direction in which modern times must strive. It must be no surprise to us that we want those things with our spiritual science which human beings should strive for. We have to realize that spiritual science must become a spiritual asset of humanity. And once we have reached the point of being involved in working on the coming into being of a new spiritual asset, we must do everything to realize it, to achieve this goal of humanity.

And with that, I consider these reflections to be concluded for the time being.

II

THE RELATIONSHIP BETWEEN SPIRITUAL SCIENCE AND NATURAL SCIENCE

Discussion of the pamphlet *Science and Theosophy* by F. von Wrangell as an example of how texts can be discussed in branches

First Lecture

DORNACH, 26 SEPTEMBER 1915

Today I am going to give neither a lecture nor a reading, but I am going to discuss some things of the kind that I believe are still lacking in our branches. I will build on the brochure *Science and Theosophy* by F. von Wrangell,[28] published in Leipzig by Max Altmann in 1914.* In doing so, I would like to show in particular how the discussion can build on such a text.

The title *Science and Theosophy* obviously touches on a question which is important for us to think through, for we will very often be in the position of hearing the objection against our movement that it is not scientific or that the scientist doesn't really know what to do with it. In short, to deal with science in some way will certainly very often be necessary for one or the other among us because they will have to face this objection and perhaps also be pointed to some particular things in the process. Therefore it will be good to build on the observations of a man who is of the opinion that he stands entirely within the scientific spirit of the present time and of whom, when you have read through the pamphlet, you can easily say that he deals with the relationship of science and theosophy in a very perceptive way, and in such a way that he creates a relationship which many will try to create who stand precisely within the scientific enterprise of our time. And we, or at least a certain number of us, must be able to think along with such people who want to create a relationship between science and theosophy.

---

* The quotations inserted in this and the following lectures reproduce the entire text of Wrangell's pamphlet.

Since, moreover, the pamphlet is written with a favourable view of theosophy, we need not initially lapse into polemics, into criticism, but can attach to the author's thoughts some things that arise from the specifics of our spiritual striving. Of course, some of us, if we were writing such a pamphlet, might even avoid the title 'Theosophy' after the various experiences we have had in such an investigation. This is a question that can perhaps be examined more closely in the course of reading the pamphlet itself.

The pamphlet is divided into individual, easily comprehensible chapters and bears as its motto a saying by Kant, which reads:

> It is not correctly spoken when people always say in the lecture halls of wisdom that there cannot exist more than one single world in the metaphysical sense. [Kant]

Taken out of context like this, we can certainly not learn a great deal from this statement by Kant. The author of this text, however, wants to refer to Kant with the thought that Kant wanted to say with this statement that the worldview created by external science does not have to be regarded as the only possible one. Here Kant's opinion is perhaps not entirely accurately interpreted by the author of this little text, for Kant basically means something else in his context. Kant means: when the human being thinks, thinks metaphysically, they can think of different real worlds, and the question is then why, of these different conceivable possible worlds, the one in which we live exists for us; whereas for the author of this little text the question is: Is there the possibility of having other worldviews apart from the materialistic worldview? Of course he is of the opinion that a different, a spiritual worldview must also apply to this world of ours.

Then the text begins with its first essay, which bears the title:

Preliminaries

> A powerful spiritual movement has currently taken hold of the European cultural world, in contrast to the materialistic intellectual current that was the dominant one in the leading intellectual circles around the middle of the nineteenth century.

So, in a sense, the author looks at the goings on of intellectual work around him and finds that things have changed from what they were around the middle of the nineteenth century; that around the middle of the nineteenth century scientific salvation was found precisely in materialism, while now—in the period in which this booklet was published, 1914—a powerful spiritual movement has taken hold of European culture.

Now he goes on to say:

> What are the inner reasons for this counter-current? It seems to me that they lie not only in the metaphysical needs of people but also, at least in part, in the frequently awakened consciousness of the danger facing the ethos of humanity which is connected with the rule of a materialistic worldview.

So the author of this little text is one of those who not only believes that the twentieth century has awakened a metaphysical need in humanity but also believes that there is a certain ethical danger in the fact that people's minds are being taken over by the materialistic worldview.

> With increasing speed, the materialistic current of thought is pouring through numerous channels from the intellectual heights into the low places of human society and there it is displacing the religious convictions based on reverence which provided the firm support for the moral life of the masses. It is becoming increasingly clear to many that the victory of the materialistic worldview inevitably leads to a materialistic view of life, bringing about a corresponding way of life which sees the only reasonable measure of life in the exploitation of our brief lifespan for as much enjoyment as possible.
>
> In earlier times, too, when a firm moral edifice based on tradition and authority succumbed to the corrosive criticism of reason, the pursuit of crude sensual pleasure seized humanity and led it along ruinous paths that distanced it from what we feel is its proper destiny.
>
> This is not contradicted by the fact that among the men who, animated by an unconditional love of truth, make the results of their research and thinking known to their fellow human beings, regardless of what consequences this may entail—that among these men many, if not most, occupy a high level of moral greatness and are driven by noble, selfless motives, fully convinced that they are thereby serving humanity.

So here the author points out that certain dangers for the moral life of human beings must arise as a consequence of a materialistic worldview, and he says: This danger cannot be countered solely with the objection that those people who theoretically recognize a materialistic worldview as their own, and as the right one, themselves occupy a high level of moral conduct.

The author touches here, from his own observation, on a point to which I have repeatedly referred in our spiritual science, I may well say, from a higher point of view. If a person says that such an eminently theoretical and materialistic spirit as Haeckel, for example, occupies the ground of high moral ideals in life and also shows in his life a higher moral conception of life, and that therefore the materialistic worldview does not necessarily entail a materialistic way of life, then they forget one thing—and I have pointed this out in various lectures I have given[29]—namely, they forget that in the development of humanity feelings and thoughts move at different speeds.

If you survey just a short section of the historical development of humanity, you will find that thoughts move relatively quickly. From the fifteenth and sixteenth centuries onwards, materialistic thinking, the expression of human theoretical reflection in materialistic thought, developed rapidly and all sciences were gradually permeated theoretically by materialistic forms of thought. The moral life, which lives in feelings, has developed less rapidly. At least people still reveal in their old sentiments and feelings that feeling hasn't followed on so quickly. That is why people today still live in the spirit of the moral feelings that resulted from the previous worldview, and that is why there is a dichotomy today between materialistic thinking and what is still, in the old spirit, a non-materialistic life and a non-materialistic way of living. But the time is approaching when the consequences will be drawn from the materialistic theoretical worldview, so that on the threshold there stands what can be described as the moral life being flooded by the consequence of the materialistic worldview. So you can significantly deepen your understanding of the different speeds that feelings and thoughts have if you look at them in terms of spiritual science.

Now it says further:

> But if the end result of this intellectual work is one that seems to us to be in contradiction with the determination of the human being, then the question is justified as to whether there is not a fundamental error in the seemingly so solid structure of critical reasoning?

The author is thus convinced that immorality must follow from theoretical materialism and that he can expect salvation for humanity only from morality. And so he asks himself whether a materialistic worldview, which must necessarily lead to immorality, not only shows up faults but has faults in itself, if looked at critically. And so he goes on writing:

> Does this error manifest itself only through feeling, or can it also be discovered through reason? This question has also preoccupied me and in the following I will try to clarify it for myself. I hope that my reasoning will also interest some readers who, like me, are convinced that it is more effective to fight an error of reason with its own weapons than to call only feelings into the fray against it. In order to describe my scientific stance, I will mention that by training I am an astronomer, that my independent work is in the field of theoretical meteorology and physical geography, and that from my early youth I have moved almost exclusively in academic circles and that respect for rigorous science based on critical thinking has, so to speak, become second nature to me.

With this, though, the author can justify that he has something to say about the relationship between science and theosophy because he shows that he knows science in a certain point and that his judgement must therefore be worth infinitely more than the judgement of someone who, for example, reads Kant and says that this is all nonsense; we theosophists do not need to read Kant, and who thus only reveals that they themselves have perhaps not seriously read and thought through even five lines of Kant. It further says:

> I am firmly convinced that a worldview which cannot stand up to strict critical reasoning is of no lasting value, no matter how much it may appeal to the feelings.

These introductory words should inform the reader about the task I have set myself in this text and the perspective from which I have intended to approach it.

The next essay describes in a few sentences what a materialistic mechanical worldview is, the worldview which developed in the last half of the nineteenth century in such a way that there were and still are many who consider what the author describes here in a few sentences to be the only scientifically possible worldview. Let us consider what the author writes:

The basic assumptions of the materialistic mechanical worldview

Let us begin by considering the most central basic assumptions of a materialistic mechanical worldview. They can be summarized in the following tenets:

1. All events that we observe through our senses and perceive through our thoughts proceed according to laws, i.e. every state of the cosmos is necessarily conditioned by the state that precedes it in time and just as necessarily results in the states that follow it. All changes, i.e. all events, are inevitable consequences of the forces present in the cosmos.

Now, what the author is trying to analyse here as the basic assumption of the materialistic mechanical worldview has also been said many times in the course of our lectures. But if you compare what the author says here with the way it is said in our lectures, you will notice the difference. And for those who want to enter into our spiritual-scientific consciousness, it is good if on occasion they make themselves aware of this difference.

Anyone who reads through this first point, in which the materialistic mechanical worldview is characterized in a beautiful, perceptive and scientifically knowledgeable manner, will see: this is very good; this captures the materialistic mechanical worldview. But when we try to characterize such things in the lectures that are given for the purpose of our movement, it is in a different way that we specifically attempt to do so, and it would be good to think about how we do such things differently in our case.

Mr von Wrangell reproduces what can be called the materialistic mechanical worldview, does he not? He says a few sentences of his own making in which he summarizes his impressions of the matter. You will have noticed—if you presume to notice such things at all—that I usually don't do it this way, but quite differently. As a rule, I start from something that is there, that is really there as a result of a historical process. And so, when I wanted to characterize this point, I did not simply say such words starting with myself, but I chose any of the significant, and indeed the good, authors to say, in the words and in the manner of such an author, what the matter in question is.

Thus I have often attached to the name Du Bois-Reymond that which could serve as a basis for my lectures. This may often, if you do not see the whole thing in context, have led you to believe that I wanted to criticize Du Bois-Reymond. But I never want to criticize; I only want to single out a characteristic representative so that it is not me who has to speak but he speaks. This is what we might call the sense for the facts we require, the spirit in which we do not make assertions but let the facts speak for themselves. For example, I have often told you that Du Bois-Reymond gave a speech on the cognition of nature at the Leipzig Naturalists' Meeting in 1872.[30] He also spoke at the time about the way he had arrived at his view of the world from his scientific research.

Du Bois-Reymond is a physiologist according to his special field of research. His main work is in the field of nerve physiology. He has often spoken out about the naturalists' view of the world in eloquent words. Thus he also spoke about the limits of the scientific worldview, about the limits of the knowledge of nature at this Leipzig naturalist meeting of 1872, and in doing so he also spoke about the Laplacean mind. What is it? Du Bois-Reymond characterized it at the time. This Laplacean mind is the one which is versed in the mathematics, physics, biology, chemistry and so on of the present and forms a worldview from these sciences. Such a Laplacean mind thus comes to form a worldview based on the so-called astronomical understanding of reality.

What is the astronomical understanding of reality, we might now ask; what is astronomical understanding? We can make it clear to ourselves in a few words.

The astronomer pictures the sun, the planets, the moon, the earth; they picture the planets revolving around the sun or moving in ellipses around it; they picture the force of attraction, gravity, acting on the planets; they picture a force of momentum, and out of this momentum they picture that the planets revolve around the sun.

In this way, the astronomer has in mind that they can follow what is going on around them in the cosmos as the great events; that they could follow them out of the material entities that are to be seen in space and out of the forces that they exert on each other in space. Through the entities exerting material forces on each other, things are set in motion; that is, things are set in motion when you imagine the solar system like this and look at it like this. You have a picture of the things spread out in space and the events that happen over time.

Now the person who wants to form a worldview in the sense of Du Bois-Reymond which has kept pace with the time, says the following. We must assume that all matter consists of the smallest parts, of atoms. Just as a solar system consists of the sun, the moon and the planets, so also the smallest piece of matter consists of something similar, like the sun with the planets. And as the sun exerts forces, and as the planets emit forces between themselves and act on each other, so do the forces among the individual atoms. This sets the atoms in motion. So we have a movement inside every material particle. The atoms, like the sun and the planets, are in motion. The movements may be small movements, but they are such that we can compare them with the great movements that are performed by the heavenly bodies outside in space, so that if we take the smallest piece of matter that we can see, something is going on inside, like that which the astronomer imagines outside in the universe. And then natural science came to imagine all this in such a way that wherever something is really in motion, this is due to the fact that the atoms are guided by their forces.

In the second half of the nineteenth century, thermodynamics, as founded by Julius Robert Mayer, Joule, Tyndall and Helmholtz, and further developed by Clausius and others, particularly contributed to the formation of this worldview. Thus it is said when we touch a body and feel heat: that which we have there as the sensation 'warm' is only appearance. What really exists outside is that the smallest parts, the atoms of the substance in question, are in motion; and we know a state of heat when we know how the atoms are in motion, when we have, to use Du Bois-Reymond's words, an astronomical understanding of it. The ideal of the Laplacean mind would be to have attained the point when we say: What do I care about heat? My view of the world depends on finding out the movement of atoms which through their movement cause everything we have in terms of heat, light and so on. This Laplacean mind thus forms a worldview that consists of space, matter with its active forces, and movement. So Du Bois-Reymond, in that lecture he gave on the limits of the understanding of nature at the Leipzig naturalists' meeting, sets up this ideal of the Laplacean mind and he asks: What would such a Laplacean mind be able to do?

You see, his ideal is the astronomical understanding of the world. If a mathematician takes the picture of our solar system as it is at any given point in time, they only have to put certain numbers into their formula and they get a picture of how it was an hour ago, three hours ago, ten years ago, centuries ago. How do we go about calculating whether a solar or lunar eclipse occurred at a certain time in the first decade of our era? For that you have formulas developed according to the current state of science. You only need to insert the corresponding numbers into the formula, so you can calculate each individual state. You can calculate when a solar eclipse will occur, say in 1970 or in 2728. In short, you can calculate any state preceding or following in time. And now the Laplacean mind would have to have the formula that encompasses this whole solar system. So anyone who had this Laplacean mind, which encompassed the atoms that are in space and all the states of motion, could—and Du Bois-Reymond also says this—calculate today from the broad formula that they have about the atoms and their present states of motion, for example, when Caesar crossed the Rubicon. They only need to insert what is necessary into the formula. It would only depend on how the atoms stood at that time, and the fact would have to follow: Caesar crossed the Rubicon. If you put certain values into the formula, a certain picture of the present state of the atoms should emerge, and then you would be able to recognize, for example, the Battle of Salamis. You would only have to go on from differential to differential and you would be able to reconstruct the whole Battle of Salamis. This is the ideal of the Laplacean mind: an understanding of the world that is called astronomical. Other things may be added on occasion about these things. Now I just want to mention a little experience for those who are observing these things. As a boy I once got hold of a school programme. Such school programmes are printed, after all. Inside there is usually an essay written by one of the teachers.[31] This essay was not that easy for me to understand at the time, because it had the title 'The force of attraction considered as an effect of motion'. There I was already dealing with an author at the time who had, so to speak, also set himself the ideal of the Laplacean mind; and he set out many other things in the same direction.

If you put all this together, you will see that I did not try to speak in accordance with the mere idea of an astronomical-materialistic view of the world, but to let the facts, the personalities speak for themselves, so that in a certain sense I really strove to cultivate a style of presentation that eliminates the personal. For when I told you what Du Bois-Reymond spoke on a special occasion, I let him speak and not me. My task is only to follow up what these persons have said; I try to let the world speak. This is an attempt to eliminate yourself, not to tell your own views, but facts. When reading this point of Wrangell's, we should realize that our spiritual science, even in the way it is presented, strives for a sense of facts, a sense of not merely dabbling in objectivity, but the sense of immersing ourselves in the facts, of really immersing ourselves in them.

Now you will recognize what I have extracted from the facts if you let the following lines of the booklet sink in again: 'All events that we observe through our senses and perceive through our thoughts proceed according to laws, i.e. every state of the cosmos is necessarily conditioned by the state that precedes it in time and just as necessarily results in the states that follow it. All changes, i.e. all events, are inevitable consequences of the forces present in the cosmos.'

And now it says further:

> It does not affect the essence of the question whether we—for the sake of better clarity—call the vehicle of the forces 'matter' or, according to the practice of monists, imagine the concept of 'energy' as the only effective thing which, although it presents various forms of appearance to the human senses, basically represents an unchangeable sum of latent or actual possibilities of movement.

Such a sentence, too, I would only put in the rarest of cases, and only when other things have already been summarized. Remember that I also once spoke about what is expressed in this sentence.[32] It says: 'It does not affect the essence of the question whether we—for the sake of better clarity—call the vehicle of the forces "matter" or, according to the practice of the monists, imagine the concept of "energy" as the only effective thing...'. I wouldn't say that, but I would really point to the students of Haeckel and Büchner, who above all look at the matter that is distributed in space. These were, as the Swabian Vischer put it, the 'collectors of matter'.[33]

Then came the person who is now the chairman of the Monist League: Ostwald.[34] He gave a lecture at a naturalist meeting, I think it was the one in Kiel—I have already spoken of it—on overcoming materialism through energetics, through energism. He pointed out that it was not the material that mattered, but the force. So he replaced matter with force. Remember how I quoted his own words that he used at that time. He said in essence: If a person receives a slap in the face from another, for that person it is not a matter of the substance but of the force with which they receive the slap. Nowhere do we perceive the matter, but the force. And therefore force or, not only in a certain paraphrase but a certain transformation, energy, was substituted for matter. But this energism, which now calls itself monism, is nothing other than a masked materialism. Again, I tried to show you with an example how there really was once a time when the 'collectors of matter' were replaced by the 'collectors of energy'.

I did not try to present a theoretical proposition but to characterize it from the reality. And that must be our aspiration in general. For it is only through this that we come to develop a sense of what is real in the spiritual, that we have a sense of what is real in the physical and do not chew on our own assertions.

So the author of the booklet says: 'It does not affect the essence of the question whether we—for the sake of better clarity—call the vehicle of the forces "matter" or, according to the practice of the monists, imagine the concept of "energy" as the only effective thing...' Warmth is one way, the tool, as it were, of getting slapped in the face, light is the other way. And if you look at the different sense organs, you have to say that the slaps each have a different effect. For example, when they fall on the eyes, the same slaps act as light phenomena. That is also the theory. Just look again at the words: 'It does not affect the essence of the question whether we—for the sake of better clarity—call the vehicle of the forces "matter" or, according to the practice of the monists, imagine the concept of "energy" as the only effective thing which, although it presents various forms of appearance to the human senses, basically represents an unchangeable sum of latent or actual possibilities of movement.'

What the author means here by the expression 'latent or actual possibilities of movement' can be made clear to you in this way: imagine here some kind of a stopper, and on top of it a tube, a glass tube, with water inside. This water weighs down on the bottom here. The moment I pull the stopper away, the water runs down. In the latter case, we are dealing with an actual movement; before I pulled the stopper away, the same force was there, only it was not actual but dormant. Everything of the water that then flowed down and became actual, that was latent before, not actual.

> The course of all events is unalterably given, and the human being, too, is just as unfree in their thinking, feeling, volition as, for example, the stone is as it falls.

That is the necessary consequence of the worldview of the Laplacean mind, that when I put my hand there, that is an image of the moving atoms, and if the Laplacean mind can still calculate the image, as I have indicated, then that excludes the freedom of the human being, that is, the Laplacean mind excludes the freedom of the human being.

This is the first point that Mr von Wrangell makes on the basis of the materialistic-mechanical worldview. The second point is the following:

> 2. The inner experiences which take place in the consciousness of the human being (their feelings, thoughts, will impulses) are not essentially different from other processes in nature which the human being observes through their senses. These inner experiences are only by-products of material processes within the human brain and nervous system.

In this second point, then, it is expressed that when I think, feel and want, this is only a by-product of the inner processes that the Laplacean mind chooses. So we are not dealing with independent thoughts, feelings and will impulses, but only with by-products. If you follow what I have said, for example, in the lecture 'The Legacy of the Nineteenth Century'[35] and in similar other lectures, if you study some of what is contained in *The Riddles of Philosophy*, then you will see how many intellectuals in the second half of the nineteenth century formed this view as a matter of course, that the human being is actually nothing other than the structure of material processes and their energies, and that thoughts, feelings and impulses of will are only by-products.

As the third point of the materialistic-mechanical worldview, Mr von Wrangell states the following:

> 3. After the physical death of the human being, the existence of the human individual ceases definitively, since the so-called spiritual life of the human being is bound to their physicality and cannot exist without it.

Everyone can recognize this point as a consequence of the first point. The first point is what matters. The second and third are necessary consequences.

In the next small essay, Mr von Wrangell talks about what he calls:

Examination of these basic assumptions

What are these basic assumptions of the materialistic worldview based on? Are they indisputably proven facts or only more or less probable hypotheses? The most important and momentous of the three assumptions mentioned earlier is the first one about the necessary course of all events. It is not only regarded by materialists as beyond all doubt, but also by many spiritualists who accept the independent existence of spiritual entities and believe in the continued existence of the human being's spiritual being, their 'soul', after physical death, but who accept the immutable laws within the spiritual world as well as within the world of the senses. First of all, then, let it be stated that this idea of absolute, unconditional laws, i.e. the necessity of everything that happens, even in the spiritual sphere, excludes the concept of morality, of good and evil, for to act morally is to choose the good when evil could be chosen.

In this small chapter Mr von Wrangell tries to make it clear that there can be no morality if the materialistic-mechanical worldview is the only correct one. For if I have to do in every moment of my life what is only a by-product of the atoms, then there can be no question of freedom, nor can there be any question of morality, for everything is done out of necessity. Just as we cannot say that the stone that falls to the earth is good and the one that does not fall to the earth is not good, so we cannot say of the actions of people that they are good or not good. With the criminal, everything is done out of necessity; with the good person, everything is done out of necessity. Hence there is something correct in the words: 'First of all, then, let it be established that this idea of the absolute application of laws without exception, i.e. the necessity of everything that happens, even in the spiritual sphere, excludes the concept of morality, of good and evil; for to act morally is to choose good when evil could be chosen.' But we cannot choose when everything is bound in materialistic necessity.

The next chapter is headed:

Freedom and Morality

> As soon as there is no freedom of decision, there can be no talk of morality in the sense in which this concept is understood by people and as it corresponds to our inner feelings. We may well speak of more or less useful, unfree actions and impulses, but a moral judgement of unfree actions or feelings has no justification, no meaning. With the removal of freedom, accountability also falls away. This undoubted connection between freedom and morality cannot be held as an argument against the concept of the application of laws; it is merely to remind us of the logical consequences associated with the assumption of unconditional necessity.

So Mr von Wrangell is trying to make it clear here that it necessarily follows from the materialistic-mechanical worldview that freedom and morality cannot actually be referred to.

Now he has a scientific mind, and a scientific mind is used to really, in an honest way, drawing the consequences from premises. Our time overlooks many things that would immediately seem absurd to it if it had really already absorbed the scientific conscience, if it did not stir up and throw together all kinds of things without a scientific conscience. Mr von Wrangell does not do that, but he says: If we accept the materialistic view of the world, we must no longer speak of freedom and morality; for either the materialistic worldview is correct, and then it is a nonsense to speak of freedom and morality, or we speak of freedom and morality, and then it makes no sense to speak of the materialistic-mechanical worldview.

But since Mr von Wrangell is a scientist who is already used to drawing the consequences from his premises—that is an important fact—he is not used to having things so sloppy in his thinking; for it is sloppiness in thinking for a person to say, I am a materialist, and not at the same time deny morality. He does not want to be guilty of such sloppiness of thinking. On the other hand, he also has the habit that you have when you become a scientist, namely to say: May the world go to ruin; what I have scientifically recognized must be true! Therefore you cannot say that you simply throw away the materialistic view, but if the materialistic worldview is true, it must be accepted and then you are faced with the sad necessity of having to throw morality overboard. So it is not just a question of asking: Where are we going with morality?—he says that this is not enough—but the materialistic worldview must be examined, irrespective of the consequences this has for morality.

So the materialistic worldview must be tackled in a different way. The next chapter is called:

The riddle of the universe

> Indeed, we can say that the question of whether the human being is responsible for their actions, i.e. whether they have the possibility of regulating their will impulses according to motives that are not clearly determined by their bodily organization, that this question about freedom or lack of freedom of the will for us human beings encloses the whole riddle of the universe. For if this question has to be answered in terms of the necessity of all events, which applies absolutely and without exception in the whole universe, then materialism is the only correct view and the world, with all its agony and suffering, is a mechanism running without purpose, without a recognizable beginning, but with the eternal death of the whole as its final goal.

When we began our spiritual-scientific movement, I had occasion to read some poems by the poet Marie Eugenie delle Grazie, who, we might say, has come to terms with a materialistic-mechanical view of the world and even as a poet really draws the consequences from it. That is why she has fashioned poems like 'A dirty vortex is existence'.[36] That is the conclusion you have to reach if you are not sloppy in your thinking, if you let your thinking affect your feelings. And it is only because people are so sloppy in their thinking and so cowardly that they do not ask themselves the question: What will become of life under the impact of the materialistic-mechanical worldview? But surely you must show that it is intrinsically incorrect, otherwise you would simply have adopted the consequence of delle Grazie.

Mr von Wrangell continues:

> The great minds, the deepest thinkers have tried to solve this most important of all questions, and it seems presumptuous to want to say

something new about it. But it cannot be a question here of a generally valid answer but at most an indication of the train of thought which led to a subjective solution of the riddle. Such an indication can sometimes be a help to a similarly attuned soul.

Mr von Wrangell thus points out that the greatest minds, poets and thinkers have endeavoured to solve this question and that it is unnecessary to want to say anything new about it. It could at most be an indication of the train of thought that led to a subjective solution to this riddle; in other words, an indication of his own train of thought.

In the next chapter he examines the origin of our notion that the preceding always has the following as its lawful corollary. It is called:

Origin of laws

> From this point of view it seems justified to raise the question: From where do we derive the idea that all events are subject to absolute laws? Is it an immediate, intuitive truth that underlies all thinking, or has humanity only gradually come to this conception through long and arduous mental work; a notion that now appears to be a self-evident truth to the Europeans who are feeding on the cultural heritage of the past?

So Mr von Wrangell is asking here: Is it the case that human beings have always believed in these absolute laws, or have they only come to believe in them in the course of time? Only then can we understand what the impact of this idea is; for if human beings have always believed in it, there must be something self-evidently true about it; but if human beings have had to work their way through to this idea, it is possible to examine how they arrived at it. In this way you can get an idea about the validity. He goes on to say:

> The latter is the case. It is acquired, not original knowledge. On the contrary, the human being's original, immediate consciousness gives them the idea of inner freedom limited by external conditions, of arbitrariness in their decisions of will. The idea of conformity with laws is only gradually derived from experience.

Well, you can see that from countless lectures of mine, how slowly people came to this idea of conformity with laws, from the old clairvoyance to the time when the idea of conformity with laws arrived.

In truth, the idea of conformity with laws is only four centuries old because it basically stems from Galileo. I have often explained that. If you go back before Galileo, there is no idea at all that everything is pervaded by such a conformity with laws.

Mr von Wrangell says: 'This is acquired, not original knowledge... The idea of conformity with laws is only gradually derived from experience.' Well, I would like to know whether the child is compelled by their inner astral conditions to reach for the sugar, that is, whether it is natural to them, or whether the child thinks they already have a choice. I have previously told something like an anecdote,[37] which I would also like to quote here. It was in my student days; I used to walk up and down the concourse of Vienna's Südbahnhof station with a fellow student. He was a diehard materialist and firmly held the view that all thinking is just processes in the brain, like the advance of the hands on the clock. And just as you could not say that this was something separate but was connected with the mechanical materials and forces present in it, he was of the opinion that the brain also made these astronomical movements. That was a Laplacean mind; we were eighteen or nineteen years old at the time. I once said to him: But you never say 'my brain thinks', you say 'I think'. Why do you keep lying? Why do you always say 'I think' and not 'my brain thinks'? Well, this fellow student had taken his knowledge, the ideas of volition and compliance with laws not from experience but from complicated theories. He did not believe in inner arbitrariness, but he said 'I think' and not 'my brain thinks'. So he was in perpetual contradiction with himself.

The next chapter is called:

Freedom of will cannot be proven by experience

> Can this contradiction be resolved intellectually? It makes sense that proof of the freedom of will of human beings or other beings based on experience cannot be produced. For this, it would have to be proven that in an actual case the same being made two different decisions under the same circumstances.

Mr von Wrangell thus says that one cannot prove the truth of the freedom of will of human beings by external experience because you can only make one decision. If you wanted to prove it, you would have to be able to make two decisions. Well, I have also already said that people do not refer to experience at all in this question but construct an experience. For example, a donkey was once imagined which had a bundle of hay on the left and on the right, the same tasty bundle of hay of the same size. The donkey, which is getting hungrier and hungrier, has now to decide whether to eat from one bundle of hay or the other, because one is as tasty as the other and as big as the other. And so it does not know whether to turn this way or that. In short, the donkey does not reach any corresponding decision and starves to death between the two bundles of hay. Such things have been constructed because people felt that they could not get to the point of observing freedom through experience. Mr von Wrangell draws attention to this and then asks the question:

> But can freedom of will be refuted by experience? To answer this question, let us first recall some epistemological truths!

In order to answer this question, Mr von Wrangell now speaks about some epistemological truths in the next little chapter. This chapter is called:

Epistemological review

> Human beings have direct consciousness only of themselves. They feel desires which they seek to satisfy and which trigger impulses of will in them; they receive impressions which they soon convince themselves are dependent on certain sense organs of their body. When they close their eyes, they receive no light and colour impressions; when they plug their ears, they weaken their sound sensations or lose them altogether. Similarly experience shows them that the nose conveys the sense of smell, the mouth in its parts covered with mucous membranes conveys the sense of taste. Only the sense of touch does not seem to be bound to any particular part of the body, but can be exercised through the entire skin. The normal healthy human being, when awake, has five different senses which convey impressions to them, each sense its specific kind of impressions.

Here Mr von Wrangell is influenced by the popular understanding of the senses. Anyone who heard a small cycle of lectures,[38] which I then entitled 'Anthroposophy', will have seen that we cannot get by with five senses at all, on the contrary, that we have to assume twelve senses. Among these twelve senses is also the sense for the thinking of others, for the I of others, and therefore anyone who has correctly observed our spiritual-scientific movement can recognize the defectiveness of Wrangell's assertions. Although they are not incorrect, they are only partially correct. We cannot say: 'The human being has direct consciousness only of themselves.' That is incorrect. Because then we could never perceive other I's.

In recent times, there has been a very complex view that is held by all kinds of people. Perhaps we might cite the philosopher and psychologist Lipps as a characteristic personality among those who advocate it. They are not aware when they meet a person that they have an immediate impression of their I but they say: When I meet a person, they have a face; that makes certain movements and they say certain things, and now you are supposed to be able to conclude from what they say and do that there is an I behind it. So the I is something ascertained, not something directly perceived. In contrast, a new school of philosophy, which has its good interpreter in Max Scheler, takes a different view. This has already observed that you can have a direct impression of the other person's I. And what Husserl, the philosopher, wrote of the I in a more rigorously academic way, and then Scheler somewhat more popularly, namely in his more recent essays, shows that the more recent philosophy is on the way to recognizing that a direct consciousness can also know something of another consciousness. So we could say Mr von Wrangell is infected by popular epistemology when he says: 'The human being has direct consciousness only of themselves.' And further: 'They feel desires, which they seek to satisfy and which trigger impulses of will in them'. And then he describes how human beings perceive the world through their senses.

I have also already written about this sensory physiology. Read *Lucifer-Gnosis*[39] and you will see that I tried to make clear the impossibility of this sensory physiology with the simple seal comparison. I said at the time: This sensory physiology is already materialistic from the outset. It assumes that nothing can enter us from the outside because it secretly conceives of the outside in a materialistic way. But it is the same as with the signet and the sealing wax: the signet always remains outside the sealing wax; nothing of the material part of the signet passes over into the sealing wax. But the name 'Miller' which is imprinted on the seal is completely transferred from the signet to the sealing wax. If we place the main value on that which is mentally expressed in the name Miller, and not on the material, from which nothing passes over, we can see that what is put forward on the part of sensory physiology means nothing at all. But these are such gruesome teachings hammered into brains, the thing being that most do not follow them, even if they want to become spiritualists. You can read about this in more detail in my book *The Riddles of Philosophy*, in the chapter: 'The World as Illusion'.

Then Mr von Wrangell continues:

> Since the human being is unable to conceive that an existing state can change without a cause, they assume that the sensory impressions they feel are brought about by causes they place outside their own directly felt selves. They call these external causes of their inner sensory impressions 'things' and, in their totality, 'the world' or—epistemologically—the 'non-I', in contrast to the directly felt 'I'.

That is clear; you just have to get used to the fact that there is a bit of epistemological language.

> Thousands of experiences and the agreement in this respect with beings they recognize as similar to themselves—their fellow human beings—teach them that these 'things', the 'non-I', can exist also independently of their consciousness.

Otherwise, the human being would have to believe that when they turn their eyes away not only from living things but also from inanimate things, these things cease to exist.

> If, for example, they lose consciousness during sleep, when they awaken they find that things continue to exist in their 'reality', that is, in their ability to evoke sensory impressions in them. The human being also recognizes their own body as belonging in a certain sense to the world 'outside them'.

This is good when it is emphasized, because we not only have things that are internal, but also things that are external.

> They can receive sensory impressions from their limbs, as from other things; for example, they can see their hands, touch them, and so on, and also distinguish here between the inner process of their sensory impressions and their outer cause, which in this case they recognize as one of their body parts. That it is their body, that is, that this thing has a very special connection with their 'I', with the thing that feels and thinks—they soon convince themselves of that, especially through the sense of touch which shows them that when they bring their own body parts into contact with other things, they feel the contact immediately, whereas they do not feel it immediately when other objects are brought into contact with one another.*

It is very good to be made aware of something like this. So this is how Mr von Wrangell answers the question as to how the human being comes to recognize their own body in a specific thing among the things that are in the surrounding space. Those who think sloppily simply say to themselves: Thinking about such things is nonsense; it is would-be scientists who think about such things. But Wrangell says: When these two chalks bump together, it doesn't hurt, but when I bump into something with my body, it hurts. That is the difference. And because one hurts and the other doesn't, I describe the one as belonging to me and the other as not belonging to me. It is good to know that we have nothing but the consequence of this consciousness.

Now, you see my dear friends, I intended to conclude the discussion of this pamphlet today. But we have only got as far as page 10. An attempt was to be made regarding the way the connection can be found between what is written in the world and what belongs to our spiritual science in a stricter sense. But the next chapters are just too interesting: Formation of concepts; Notions of space and time; The principle of causality; Applying the notion of arbitrariness to the

---

*In the pamphlet itself, this is still followed by the footnote:

'"The externalization of sensibility in highly sensitive persons" observed by de Rochas is a particular abnormal phenomenon which deserves detailed study.'

world around; Observation of uniformly progressing phenomena; The essence of all science; Astronomy, the oldest science; Uniform movement; Measuring; The principle underlying clocks. It is so interesting that perhaps we will continue the discussion tomorrow at seven o'clock after all.

Second Lecture

DORNACH, 27 SEPTEMBER 1915

Yesterday, following on from a characterization of the materialistic-mechanical worldview by Mr von Wrangell, I also spoke of the poet Marie Eugenie delle Grazie as an example of someone who really takes the materialistic worldview seriously; I might say takes it at its word. Now we might well raise the question: How must a person who has elemental, strong feelings for everything human which has been instilled in people through historical development, how must such a person feel if they take the materialistic-mechanical worldview as being true? This is roughly how—25 to 30 years ago now—Marie Eugenie delle Grazie approached the materialistic-mechanical worldview. She called Haeckel her master and assumed that, in a sense, the Laplacean mind was right in its conception of the world. But she did not express this worldview theoretically but, on the assumption that it is true, she also let human feeling speak. And so her poems are perhaps the most telling testimony to the way in which the feeling human heart can behave in our time in relation to the materialistic-mechanical worldview, what can be felt, sensed, when it is taken as a prerequisite. And in order that you may have a rather vivid example of the impression made on a human heart by the materialistic-mechanical view, we shall start by reciting to you some of these delle Grazie poems.

[Recitation by Marie Steiner:]

> At midnight
>
> When tired and half intoxicated
> By the day's colourfully changing life

The earth dreams in blissful peace,
The moon's bluish radiance
Floods the desolate streets
And blessed oblivion
Gently spreads its wings—
In these blessed hours,
So full of bliss and slumber—
Why, loudly beating heart,
Is it just you who can't find peace?
Why, hot and fevered brow,
Does the army of tormenting thoughts,
Robbing slumber and scaring dreams away,
Swirl just through you?

The stars move calmly
In the sky above,
And motionless the city lies,
The vast, vast huge metropolis—for behold,
It's midnight and both poor and rich are given pleasure
Without difference by the dream god's beckoning cup,
Heavy and poppy-wreathed...
Only you groan
And whimper into your pillows at midnight,
O wretched one, and weep and brood—for
It is a demon who, dark and yet enchanting,
Hovers around your bed and demon whispers scare away
Dream's fairy-tale messengers from close around,
So that their lovely roundel dissipates wanly
And the night terrors of madness encircle you.
And even if with shining eyes
The bewitching lady fantasy beckons with golden wings,
The poppy wreath and rejuvenating beauty's fiery potion
Of delight—your evil foe drives also this comforter
Away with his satanic grin
And gazing into your eyes, bewitching, stays
For so long, wretch, at your bedside,
Until you spread your arms, press him to your heart
And wanting, slavishly gasp just for him,
A victim who willingly submits herself.
Then he spreads his black demonic wings
And shakes his locks in splendour of the night,

With frozen kisses driving love and faith from out your soul,
Trickles the poison of despair into your breast
Mauls with convulsive, twitching predatory claws
Your heart, embracing you with fervour like a vampire would
And whispering with an icy smile: 'Cognition is my name!'

2.

Nature, your begetter, holds you fast
With iron bands,
Chaining you to dust and decay;
Nature, the beckoning monster,
Presently smiling and with sunny sweetness
Spurring you on to furious existential joy, presently
Giving birth to horror and distress,
Whipping you with the rod of woe,
But always crushing and enigmatic, always
Medusa and Sphinx at the same time!
Through your pulses chases
And races in feverish beats
Her merciless law,
The eternal law of destruction;
She gave you the will and strength
To destroy yourself—but save
Yourself you never, ever can!
On her triumphal chariot we all
Draw—wheezing, sweaty and yet
Blissful too: for as a mirage hope
Sways before us and happiness and every illusion
Created by her in mockery of us,
Which we, the army of slaves poisoned by longing,
Call ideals!—So in eager haste
And a great chase we storm along, until treacherously
Our strength leaves us, our breath fades and further away
Than ever our goal hovers on golden clouds,
Until helpless and gasping we
Collapse—then demonically she exults,
Then she calls out her cruel: 'Evoe!' and guides
The iron spokes of her biga
Over a thousand victims, crushing them!

3.

What cruel demon must
Have written the tormenting urge for love
Into our beating hearts?
What treacherous hellish delusion
Tells it to quiver with longing and foolishly
To crave and thirst for divine delight,
Consuming itself for something infinite
In feverish embers
And building over the seething swamp
Of finiteness the most enticing fairy realm
Of dreams—ah! lamenting and unresolved
This anxious question fades into eternity...

Charmingly the divine
Smiles and waves to us
In those puzzling hours—
Yet we also want to snatch it,
Bind it, also see it in
The garment of transience
And call out, chaining a second, foolish I
To our fate: 'Found—Found!'

Yet only gods and fairy-tale heroes are refreshed
By the nectar of eternal folly,
The little people are guided by reason,
And Reason, the gluttonous ogress,
She only nourishes and fortifies herself
With shattered ideals!
Disenchanted and shivering awakes
The heart and the sober everyday soul,
Smiling at the dream that once intoxicated her...
The shining star of divinity,
She could not rip it from the sky,
Proud like a Titan—no, she reached
And stretched, more foolish than a foolish child,
After its dull reflection
In the puddle of her own kind...

4.

Among the living there goes
And passes from mouth to mouth
A short word whispered in fright—
Its brazen sound, it makes
The rosy cheeks pale,
The jubilant hymns of delusion,
The dazzling lying tales
Of existence are torn away, and
Fade away with it for eternity.

The crown of thorns of suffering,
The rosaries of happiness
And diadems of glory—
All of them, all are entwined,
Overgrown and entangled
By pale death's asphodel!
For whom his wings rustle,
They tremble, and for whom his hollow voice resounds,
They have lied for the last time...

Decay and mould ferment
In our veins, decay guides us
According to its law, and what lives and breathes there,
Decay created it,
Decay destroys it too!
A dirty vortex full of mystery and madness revolves around
Life, and our pygmy kind, it revolves
With it: in blind weakness, droll dignity
And powerlessness...
All-conquering and free, the ogre Death
Rules on his own: with flashing sword he mows down
The glistening lie of existence
And speaks, for eternity
Pointing to dust and decay,
The one, eternal truth: 'There is nought!'

It is precisely from such an example, I believe, that we can see where the materialistic-mechanical view of the world must lead. If this worldview had become the only dominant one and people had retained the possibility of feeling, then such a mood as that which speaks from these poems would have had to take hold of people in the widest circles and only those who would have wanted to go on living without feeling, only these unfeeling people would have been able to avoid being seized by such a mood.

We do not learn to know the course of the world and to see through it in the right way by those merely theoretical thoughts with which people usually construct worldviews for themselves, but we only learn to know the supporting power of a worldview when we see it flowing into life. And I must say that it made a deep impression on me when, a very long time ago now, I saw the mechanical-materialistic worldview enter the brilliant soul—for it may be called a brilliant soul—of Marie Eugenie delle Grazie.

But we must also consider the preconditions that led a human heart to confront the mechanical-materialistic worldview in this way. After all, Marie Eugenie delle Grazie is already, by her descent, what I would call a cosmopolitan figure. She has blood of all kinds of nationalities in her veins from her ancestors. She had already become acquainted with the sufferings of life in early childhood, and she had also learned in early childhood how to reach up in order to find something in addition to that which forms the outer meaning of life, something which carries this life through a higher power to something higher; because a Catholic priest,[40] who died some years ago, became her teacher. The genius of delle Grazie was demonstrated by the fact that in her sixteenth, seventeenth year she had already written a book of lyrical poetry, a comprehensive epic, a tragedy and a small novella.[41] No matter how much one might criticize these poems in one direction or another, genius is expressed in them in a captivating way. These poems came into my hands back then, when they were published in the eighties of the last century, and at the same time I heard talk of delle Grazie through various acquaintances. I heard, for example, that the aesthetician Robert Zimmermann, who wrote an aesthetics and a history of aesthetics and was an important representative of the Herbartian school of philosophers—the Herbartians are now extinct—and who was already an old man at that time, said: Delle Grazie was the only real genius he had met in his life.

Through various circumstances I became personally acquainted with delle Grazie and became friends with her, and we talked a lot about philosophical matters and other things. It was a significant lesson to see on the one hand delle Grazie's teacher, the Catholic priest who, professionally steeped in Catholicism, had come to a worldview that he only expressed with irony and humour when he spoke more intimately, and on the other hand delle Grazie herself. From the very first conversation I had with her, it was apparent that there was something profound about her with regard to the world and life. As a result of her upbringing by the priest she had become acquainted with Catholic Christology, with all the possible bright aspects that one could get to know if one was close to Professor Müllner—that is this priest—who for his part had also looked deeply into life. All this had taken shape in delle Grazie in such a way that she connected everything that life brings in terms of evil and wickedness, pain and suffering with the view of the world that had initially been given to her by this priest—you must bear in mind that I am talking about a seventeen-year-old girl—so that from this arose the idea of a poem, which she discussed with me in a long conversation: she wanted to write a 'Satanide'. She wanted to show how suffering and pain are in the world on the one hand, and on the other hand the worldview that was handed down to her.

Now, into such a soul fell the materialistic-mechanical worldview. The latter is very persuasive, unfolds a huge force of logic, so that people can only escape it with difficulty. I later asked delle Grazie why she had not written the 'Satanide'. She told me that since, according to the materialistic-mechanical view, she did not believe in God and therefore not in the opponent of God, Satan, either, she could not write the Satanide if she was to stay true to her feeling.

But she had a tremendous power of human experience and she then elaborated it in the great two-volume epic *Robespierre*,[42] which is completely permeated by such moods as you have heard. I heard her read aloud many of the cantos herself while they were still in the making. Two women once became nauseous while this was happening. They couldn't listen to the end. This is characteristic of how people veil things for themselves. They believe in the science of materialism, but if you were to show them the consequence, they would faint.

The materialistic worldview truly makes people weak and cowardly. They look at the world through a veil and still want to be Christians. And that in particular subsequently seemed to Marie Eugenie delle Grazie to be the worst thing in existence. She said something like this to herself: Everything is just swirling atoms, jumbled atoms. What are these jumbled atoms doing? They cluster together—after they have clustered together into cosmic bodies, after they have made plants grow—they cluster together into human beings and human brains, and in these ideals arise through that clustering of atoms, ideals of beauty, of all kinds of greatness, of all kinds of divinity. What a terrible existence it is, she said to herself, when atoms swirl, and swirl in such a way that they make people believe in the existence of ideals. The whole existence of the world is deception and mendacity. So say those who are not too cowardly to face the ultimate implications of the materialistic-mechanical worldview. Delle Grazie says: If it were at least truthful, this world of jumbled atoms, then we would have jumbled atoms in front of us in our minds. But in this way the jumbled atoms still deceive us, lie to us as if there were ideals in the world.

So when we have learned to recognize what consequences the human mind must draw when it relates in honesty to the materialistic-mechanical worldview, then we have again one of the reasons for working on a spiritual worldview.

Those who always say: We have everything, we have our ideals, we have what Christianity has brought so far, they must be answered: Has it not been the way we have behaved that has brought us to the powerful mechanical-materialistic worldview? Do you wish to continue like this? Those who want to demonstrate the unnecessary nature of our movement because this or that is put forward from other sides should reflect that despite these other sides having worked for centuries, the mechanistic-materialistic worldview has become great. It is simply a matter of striving to grasp life where it occurs in truth. What matters is not what we think but that we look at the facts and let the facts teach us. I have often mentioned that I once gave a lecture in a town[43] about Christianity from the standpoint of spiritual science. Two priests were also there. They came up to me after the lecture and said: That's all well and good what you're saying, but the way you present it, only a few people will understand it; more correct is how we present the matter, because that is for all people. To which I could say nothing other than: Excuse me, but do all people really come to you? That you believe it is for all people, that doesn't decide anything about the matter, but what does is what is real, and so you will not be able to deny that many people no longer come to you. And it is for these that we speak, because they too must find the way to Christ. That's how you speak when you don't take the easy way out, when you don't simply think your own opinion is good, but let yourself be guided by the facts.

That is why it is not enough either, as you saw yesterday, to read the sentences of such a text as Wrangell's, one after the other, but that you build on it what can be built on it. I would like to give you an example—and this can be done in various ways—of how different writings can be discussed in our branches, and how what lives in our spiritual science can emerge clearly by measuring it against what is discussed in such pamphlets.

The next chapter in Wrangell's pamphlet is called:

Formation of the concepts

>That which surrounds the human being takes many different forms. Each thing is distinct from the other. Even if several things agree in some of their properties, that is, if they evoke the same or similar sensory impressions, they nevertheless differ in at least one attribute: every thing that I perceive through my senses occupies a certain part of space at the time.

>For greater clarity in this multifaceted world, humans group similar things, that is, things with similar characteristics, together under common names. For these mentally generated concepts, they form words. They also designate the same or similar properties, such as red, hard, warm, hot, etc., by words.

Here Mr von Wrangell speaks about the formation of concepts in a way that is very popular and is very often presented in this way. People say to themselves: I see a red flower, a second, a third red flower of a certain shape and arrangement of petals, and since I find them the same, I form a concept about them together. A concept would therefore be formed in such a way that I group together what is the same in different things. For example, the term 'horse' is formed by my combining in a certain way a number of animals that have certain similarities into a single thought, into a single conception. I can do the same with properties. I see something with a certain colour shade, something else with a similar colour shade and form the concept of the colour 'red'.

But if you want to get to the heart of the matter, you have to ask yourself: Is this really the way to form concepts? I can only give some indications right now, otherwise we would never get through the text, because you can actually always attach the whole world to any thing.

To illustrate how Mr von Wrangell represents concepts being formed, I will choose a geometrical example.* Suppose we saw different things in the world and we found something with a boundary like this one time, something with a boundary like this another time, and something with a boundary like this the third time, and so on countless times. We often see these boundaries, which are so similar to each other, and now we would form the concept of 'circle' according to Mr von Wrangell's definition. But do we really form the concept of a circle in accordance with such similar delimitations? No, we only form the concept of a circle when we do the following: here is a point that has a certain distance from this point. There is a point that is again the same distance from that point, and there is another point that is the same distance, and so on. I look for all points that have the same distance from a certain point. If I connect these points, I get a line that I call a circle, and I get the concept of a circle when I can say: The circle is a line in which all points are equidistant from the centre. And now I have a formula and that leads me to the concept. The inner work on it, the inner construction actually leads to the concept. Not until someone knows how to

---

* Here there was obviously a demonstration on the blackboard; there is no record of the drawing.

make concepts in this way, how to reconstruct what exists outside in the world, do they have a right to speak of concepts. We do not find the concept of a horse by looking at a hundred horses to find out what is the same about them, but we find the essence of the horse by reconstructing it, and then we find what has been reconstructed in each horse.

This moment of activity when we form conceptions, concepts, is often forgotten. In this chapter, too, it has been forgotten to consider the moment of inner activity.

The next chapter is called:

Conceptions of space and time

> The sense of touch in combination with vision creates the idea of space. The direct experience of the succession of sensations leads us to the notion of time. Space and time are the forms of thought in which our conceptions of the world outside of us are formed, as far as we perceive it through our five senses.
>
> The conception of movement, as the change in the position of a thing in space within a period of time, is likewise an original conception, given at first by the movement of our own body.
>
> When things that we perceive through our senses evoke the same sensory impressions in us within a certain period of time, we gain the idea of 'being', of existing. If, on the other hand, the impressions received from the same thing change, we gain the idea of 'happening'.

So in a neat way, as the saying goes, Mr von Wrangell seeks to gain conceptions about the concepts of space and time, of movement, being and happening. Now it would be most interesting to study how everything in this chapter is nevertheless, I would like to say, 'rather scant'. It would be quite good for many—I do not want to say for you in particular, my dear friends, but for many people—if they would consider that a very perceptive man, an excellent scientist, forms such conceptions, makes every effort to form conceptions about these simple terms. At the very least, we can learn a lot from it about conscientious thinking. And that is important; because there are so many people who don't even feel the need before thinking about anything, the cosmos, to first ask themselves: How do I arrive at the simple ideas of being, happening and movement? That is usually too boring for people.

Well, a deeper look would show that the concepts as formed by Mr von Wrangell are nevertheless rather scant. For example, Mr von Wrangell says without further ado: 'The sense of touch in conjunction with sight produces the idea of space.' Just consider, my dear friends, if you do not use the blackboard to draw a circle but draw the circle in your imagination, what does the sense of touch have to do with it, what does sight have to do with it? Given that, might we still be able to say: 'The sense of touch in conjunction with vision creates the conception of space'? We cannot. However, someone might object that before we can draw a circle in our imagination, we must have gained a conception of space, and this is gained through the sense of touch in connection with sight. Surely it is a question of considering for a start what kind of conception we form at the moment when we touch something through the sense of touch. If we think of ourselves as gifted only with the sense of touch and that we touch something, we form the idea that what is being touched is outside us. Now take this sentence: 'The thing touched is outside us.' In the 'outside us' lies space, that is, when we touch an object, we must, so that we can carry out the touching in the first place, already have space within us. It was this that led Kant to assume that space precedes all external experiences, thus also the experience of touching and seeing, and likewise with regard to time, that it precedes the multiplicity of processes in time; that space and time are the preconditions of sensory perception.

Basically such a chapter about space and time could only be written by someone who has not only studied Kant thoroughly but also knows the whole course of philosophy in general; otherwise you will always have slightly scant concepts in relation to space and time. It is the same with the other concepts, the concepts of 'being' and of 'happening'. There it could easily be shown how the concept of being could not exist at all if the definition given by Mr von Wrangell were correct.

For he says: 'If things that we perceive through our senses evoke the same sensory impressions within a certain period of time, we gain the conception of "being", of existence. If, on the other hand, the impressions received from the same thing change, we obtain the conception of "happening".' We could just as well say: If we see that the sensations change in the same thing, then we must presuppose that this change adheres to something that has existence, occurs in something that has existence. We could just as well claim that it is only through change that being is recognized. And whoever wanted to claim that we only arrive at the concept of being when the same impressions are evoked within a certain time—just think!—if we wanted to arrive at the concept of being in this way, then it would be possible that we could not arrive at the concept of being at all; there would be nothing at all that could be connected with the concept of being.

We can learn from this chapter 'Concepts of Space and Time' in particular how, with great acumen and extraordinarily honest scholarship, we can find concepts that are tenuous in all sorts of places. If we want to form concepts that can stand up to life a little, then we must have obtained them in such a way that they have been tested by us at least to some extent with regard to their value for life.

You see, it is for this reason I said I had only found the courage to speak to you about the last scenes of *Faust*[44] because for more than thirty years I had lived again and again in the last scenes of *Faust*, testing the concepts in life. This is the only way to distinguish valid concepts from non-valid ones; not logical speculation, not scientific theorizing, but the attempt to live with the concepts, to examine how the concepts prove themselves by introducing them into life and letting life give us the answer, that is the necessary path. This presupposes, however, that we are at all times inclined not merely to surrender to logical conceits but to join the living stream of life. This has a number of consequences; above all, that we learn to believe that if someone can produce seemingly logical proofs for this or that—I have mentioned this many times—they have by no means yet produced anything that relates to the value of the matter.

The next chapter is called:

The principle of causality

> The principle of causality that underlies our thinking forces us to assume that if something happens, i.e. a change takes place, a cause must have brought it about. All rational thinking is based on the 'principle of sufficient reason'. Every thing has a reason for being; every change in what exists is brought about by a reason.
>
> This principle is not an empirical proposition; it precedes all experience, indeed, it makes it possible in the first place because without the presupposition expressed in it, no coherent thinking is possible.

Mr von Wrangell here adopts the standpoint of the so-called principle of causality. He says: All rational thinking must assume in everything that confronts us that there is an underlying cause. We can agree to some extent with this principle of causality. However, if we want to measure its significance for our life-filled view of the world, then we must field much, much more subtle concepts than this formal principle of causality.

For you see, in order to be able to state a cause or a complex of causes of a thing, much more is necessary than merely following, as it were, the thread of cause and effect. Basically, what does the principle of causation say? It says: A thing has a cause. The thing I am drawing here [there is no record of the drawing] has a cause, this cause has a cause in turn, and so on; we can carry on like this beyond the beginning of the world, and we can also do the same with the effect. Certainly, this is a very reasonable principle, but you don't get very far with it. For example, if we look for the cause of a son, we must certainly look for causes—complex causes—in the father and mother, in order to be able to say that these are the causes of the child. But it is undoubtedly also the case that such causes can be there but have no effect, namely when a woman and a man don't have children. Then the causes are there but have no effect. With the cause it is important that it is not just a cause but that it also causes something. There is a difference between 'being a cause' and 'causing'. But even the philosophers of our time do not yet allow themselves to be drawn into such subtle distinctions. But anyone who takes things seriously has to deal with such distinctions. In reality the issue is not that causes are there but that they cause something. Concepts that exist in this way need not yet correspond to reality but one can indulge in a great fantasy with them.

Goethe's worldview is fundamentally different from this in that it does not go to the causes but to the archetypal phenomena. That is something quite different. For Goethe traces something that exists in the world as a phenomenon—let us say that certain series of colours appear in the prism—back to the archetypal phenomenon, to the interaction between matter and light, or, if we take matter as representative of darkness, between darkness and light. In the same way, he goes into the archetypal phenomenon of the plant, the animal and so on. This is a worldview that faces the facts and does not merely continue spinning concepts logically, following the thread of logic, but groups the facts in such a way that they express a truth.

Try to read what Goethe wrote in his essay 'The experiment as mediator between subject and object' and also what I was able to publish as a supplement to this essay, and also try to read what I said in my Introductions to Goethe's scientific writings in *Kürschner's Deutsche National-Literatur*,[45] then you will see that Goethe's view of nature is based on something quite different from that of modern natural scientists. We must take the phenomena and group them not as they are there in nature but so that they speak their secrets to us. To find the archetypal phenomenon from the phenomena, that is the essential thing.

That is also what I wanted to indicate yesterday when I said that you have to go into the facts. What we think about the mechanical-materialistic worldview matters little. But if you can show how, in 1872, one of its representatives stood before the assembled natural scientists in Leipzig and said: To trace all natural events back to the movements of atoms is the task of natural science—then you are pointing to a fact, we might say to an archetypal phenomenon of historical development. Tracing historical development back to archetypal phenomena is shown by pointing to what Du Bois-Reymond has pronounced, for this is an archetypal phenomenon in the process of the materialistic-mechanical worldview.

If we proceed in this way, we learn no longer to think as if we were in a glass compartment, but to think in such a way that we become an instrument for the facts that speak their secrets, and we can then test by our thinking whether it really conforms to the facts.

Truly, not in order to make a name for myself but in order to recount my own experiences as far as possible, I will mention the following. I prefer to talk about concepts that have been experienced rather than all kinds of thought-up concepts. Those who want to believe that what I am about to say is said in order to gain prestige may believe it, but it is not so.

When I tried to present Goethe's worldview in the [eighteen] eighties, I said on the basis of what you find when you live your way into it: Goethe must once have written an essay that expresses the most intimate part of his scientific outlook. And I said, after recreating the essay, this essay must have been there, at least in Goethe's mind. You will find this in my Introduction to Goethe's scientific writings. You will also find the recreated essay there.[46] I then joined the Goethe Archive[47] and there I found the essay just as I had created it. So you have to go with the facts. Those who seek wisdom let the facts speak. However, that is the more inconvenient thing because you have to deal with the facts, you don't have to deal with the thoughts that happen to come.

The next chapter is called:

Applying the notion of arbitrariness to the world around us

> Since our sentiment is that from which we, as the immediately given, proceed in all thinking, we also judge that which we address as the external world initially according to what is going on within us.

If I were to read *Truth and Knowledge*[48] to you, I could show you which is the right thought, the right understanding, and how here again there is a slightly scant thinking. I would like to know, firstly, how there would ever be mathematics if we started from our sentiments in all our thinking. Then we would never be able to arrive at mathematics. For what is our sentiment supposed to be in the question: What is the sum of the squares of the two legs of a right-angled triangle in relation to the square of the hypotenuse? But Wrangell says: 'Since our sentiment is that from which we, as the immediately given, proceed in all thinking, we also judge what we address as the external world first of all according to what goes on within us.' You can't do much with this sentence. Let us see further:

> We have the awareness that those changes in the surroundings which we ourselves consciously bring about by movements of our limbs are brought about by inner processes which we call will impulses. This is why the unbiased person initially assumes similar causes for other changes in the surroundings, i.e. they assume that they too are caused by will impulses from beings that are similar to them. The mythologies of all peoples are the expressions of this anthropomorphic bringing to life of nature, and the belief in spiritual beings, which even now serves for many people to explain many events in the surrounding world, has the same origin. Lastly, the observation of the child shows that they even attribute a will, similar to their own, to inanimate objects. They bump into the table and scold the table for such naughtiness.

I have often said: The child bumps into the table and hits the table because it places a will in it. It judges the table as being like itself because it has not yet developed the conception of a table. It is exactly the reverse that is the case, and the next chapter also suffers from this confusion:

> *Observation of uniformly proceeding phenomena*
>
> If, therefore, many events are at first attributed by the human being to free will impulses, daily observation nevertheless shows them that with regard to some phenomena they can count with certainty on a regular repetition familiar to them. They know, for example, that after the sun sets in the west it will reappear in the east the next day; that light and warmth are associated with it. They know that the regular course of the seasons influences the life of plants, etc. This knowledge enables people to organize their actions accordingly. They soon find that the more closely they observe nature, the more regularities they discover in it, the better they are able to put themselves in harmony with it.

If we want to speak of regularities in nature in this way, then we must not disregard the fact that we speak of such regularities in quite different ways. I drew attention to this in *Truth and Knowledge*. Let's say, for example, I get dressed in the morning, go to the window and see a person passing by outside. The next morning I get dressed again, look out the window again, and the person passes by again. The same thing happens on the third morning and again on the fourth. I see a regularity there. The first thing I do is get dressed, then go to the window; the next thing is that I see the person walking out there. I see a regularity because the processes repeat themselves. So I form a judgement and it would have to be: because I get dressed and because I look out of the window, that's why the person outside passes by. We don't make such judgements, of course, because it would be mad. But in other cases it seems that we do; but in reality we don't do it even then. But we form concepts, and from the inner construction of the concepts we find that there is an inner regularity in the phenomena. And because I cannot construct a causality between my getting dressed, looking out the window and what is going on outside, I do not recognize any causality. You can find this in greater detail in *Truth and Knowledge*. You will find there all the premises, including the one presented by David Hume, in order for us to learn something about the regularity of the world from repetition.

The next chapter is called:

The essence of all science

> This is probably the beginning of all science, the essence of which is to summarize facts of experience in a clear way in order to extract rules from them that enable the human being to know in advance what will happen. That is why every science contains a descriptive part, the clear compilation of facts, and a theoretical part, the extraction of rules from these facts and the conclusions to be drawn from these rules.

Goethe objected to such conclusions: Did Galileo need to see many phenomena like the swinging church lamp in the cathedral of Pisa in order to arrive at his law of free fall? No, he recognized the law after seeing this phenomenon. That's when it hit him. It is not from the repetition of the facts, but from the inwardly experienced construction of the facts that we learn something about the essence of things.

It was a basic error of recent epistemology to assume that we can obtain anything like the laws of nature by summarizing the facts. It so blatantly contradicts all real obtaining of the laws of nature, and yet it is repeated over and over again.

The next chapter:

> *Astronomy, the oldest science*
>
> If we look around in the immeasurable realm of what we perceive through our senses, we will find no group of phenomena in which the regularity of events is so conspicuous, so easy to discover and express, as the apparent movement of the heavenly bodies. It is therefore understandable that astronomy is the oldest of all sciences based on sensory perception.
>
> It is above all the regular, apparent movement of the stars, repeated day after day, which captivates the attentive observer, stimulates them to observe and urges them to form a vivid conception. In the cloudless regions of the Near East and North Africa, the external conditions were particularly favourable for the study of celestial phenomena. Following their direct sensory impression, the ancient astronomers assumed that the countless fixed stars, which remain unchanged in their reciprocal position, were attached to a transparent but solid celestial sphere, in the centre of which rests the earth. The celestial sphere rotating evenly around an axis gave a vivid conception of the perceived process.

So the chapter is called 'Astronomy, the oldest science'. Now we should actually first go into what the oldest astronomy was like. For here we must consider above all that the oldest astronomy did not look at the regularity but at the will of the spiritual beings who cause the movements. The author, however, has today's astronomy in mind and stamps it as the oldest science. Sometimes it is really necessary to pursue the truth in the method you use in a completely unvarnished way, that is, with an unvarnished method. And when the chapter here on page 13 is called: 'Astronomy, the oldest science', I compare that—because I stick to the facts and don't speculate—with what is written on page 3. There it says 'that by training I am an astronomer'. Perhaps someone who is a mathematician or physiologist would come to a different conclusion; so we should not forget what is written on page 3. It is of great importance to point to the subjective motives in a person much more than is usually done; because these subjective motives usually begin to explain what needs to be explained. But in terms of subjective motives, people really are quite peculiar. They want to admit to themselves as little as possible of subjective motives. I have often mentioned a gentleman whom I met and who said that in doing this or that, it was above all important for him not to do what he wanted to do according to his personal preference, but to do what corresponded least to his personal preference, what he had to regard as the mission imposed on him by the spiritual world. It was of no use to explain to him that he must also count finger licking as part of his spiritual mission when he said to himself: I do everything according to the mission imposed on me by the spiritual world. He masked it, however, because he liked it better when he could present as a strict sense of duty what he was so terribly fond of doing.

The next chapter:

Uniform movement

> When we speak of uniformity in the movement of an object, we mean that the object in question passes through equal sections of space in equal segments of time.

Remember the lecture on speed,[49] I once gave here. [In this volume.]

> However, mere perception is not enough to determine this; one must be able to measure both sections of space and segments of time. Only when we are able to express both sections of space and segments of time in numbers through measurement, that is, through comparison with an unchanging, uniform quantity chosen as a unit, only then can the actual uniformity of a movement, as well as the effect of a certain cause, which is always the same in terms of magnitude, be proven experientially.

This is where the learned scientist begins to speak. You need only look around a little to see what craving pervades scientists to strive for objectivity by measuring what is independent of the subjective human being, by striving to apply objective standards. This happens most objectively when we really are measuring. That is why real science is considered to be that which is obtained through measurement. That is why Mr von Wrangell speaks of measurement itself in the next chapter.

> *Measuring*
>
> Every measurement operation is based on the assumption that the unit chosen, for example a metre, a gram, a second, etc., is invariable. We cannot prove this unconditionally of our measurements, but we can be sure that our measuring operations are correct within certain limits that we can recognize. Let us give an illustrative example to explain what has been said: We want to compare the length of two objects and measure them with the same metre stick, assuming that it retains its length. However, we know that all bodies change under the influence of temperature, humidity, etc., so our metre stick may also have become longer or shorter. Without knowing the size of the presumed change, we have, however, a reasonable belief that the change cannot have reached the magnitude of, say, 1 mm in such a short time. We can therefore be sure that we have not made an error in this measurement that exceeds 1 mm for every metre measured. Through such a measurement operation we have gained an empirical fact—in our case the ratio of two lengths—which is valid for us within the limits of accuracy to be established by critique.

This is a very nice little chapter, where it is made clear how measurement can initially tell us something about proportions.

The next chapter:

> *The principle underlying clocks*
>
> It is similar with measuring periods of time. The instruments used for this purpose, clocks, are essentially based on the conviction that the same causes produce the same effects. The ancients mostly used water clocks (clepsydras) for this purpose, in which the outflow of water from a container was kept under as uniform conditions as possible (the water level kept at the same height, the outflow tube of a certain shape, etc.), and the magnitude of the period of time was deduced from the amount of water that flowed out. Our pendulum clocks are based on the perception that, all other things being equal, the speed of a pendulum swing depends on the length of the pendulum. By ensuring that the length remains as constant as possible, that the resistance is as low as possible, and that the force which overcomes it acts evenly,

one achieves the even running of a clock. There are methods to check this movement, whereby one can indicate exactly by how much at the maximum the clock has moved too much or too little in the course of, for example, one day.

You see, this chapter is so good because you can bring to mind in simple terms how we cut corners in life, so to speak. We can easily see this if we stay with the old clocks, the water clocks, for the time being. Suppose a man who had used the water clock said: It took me three hours to do this work. What does that mean? Everyone understands that kind of thing, you'd think. But people do not consider that in doing so they are already relying on certain preconditions. For the person concerned should actually have said, if he had expressed facts: While I was working, so and so much water flowed out from the beginning to the end of my work. Instead of always saying: From the beginning to the end of my work, this much water flowed out, we have compared the flow of water with the course of the sun and have used an abbreviation, the formula: I have worked for three hours. We then continue to use this formula. We think we have something factual in mind, but we have omitted one thought, namely, so and so much of the water has flowed out. We only have the second thought as an abbreviation. But by giving ourselves the possibility of such a fact becoming formulistic, we are moving away from the fact. And now think for a moment that in life we don't just combine a job and a formula, but that we talk in formulas in general, really talk in formulas. Just think, for example, what it means 'to be diligent'. If we go back to the facts, there are a tremendous amount of facts underlying the formula 'to be hard-working'. We have seen many things happen and compared them to the time in which they can happen, and so we speak of 'being hard-working'.

A whole army of facts is contained in this, and often we utter such formulas without reflecting on the facts.

When we return to the facts, we feel the need to put our thoughts in a living way and not to speak in nebulous formulas. I once heard a professor lecture,[50] who began a course on literary history by saying: When we turn to Lessing, in order to consider his style, let us first ask ourselves how Lessing used to think about the world, what his way of working was, how he intended to use it, and so on. And after questioning like this for an hour, he said: Gentlemen, I have led you into a forest of question marks! But now imagine a 'forest of question marks', imagine that you want to go for a walk in this forest of question marks; think what that feels like! Well, from this man I have also heard the saying that these or those people throw themselves into a 'bath of fire'. I always had to think what people look like when they throw themselves into a fire bath like that. You often meet people who do not realize how far they are removed from reality. If you delve into their words, into their conceptions of words, and try to make clear to yourself what their words mean, then you will find that everything dissipates and scatters in the wind, because what people say in this way is not at all possible in reality. So you can learn quite a lot, really quite a lot, in these perceptive chapters on 'Measuring' and on 'The principle underlying clocks'.

I cannot now say with certainty when I will be able to continue to discuss the subsequent chapters of this booklet. Today I would just like to say still that of course I only wanted to highlight examples and that of course this can be done in a hundred different ways. But if we do this, we will ensure that we are not cocooned in our spiritual-scientific movement, but that we really extend threads into the whole world. For that would be the worst thing of all, my dear friends, if we were to cocoon ourselves.

I have pointed out that the thinking is of particular importance and significance, and that is why it is important that we take some of the things that have come before our souls in the last few weeks in such a way that we think about them, do not take them in the most one-sided way and wish to put them into practice in our lives. When, for example, 'mystical eccentricity' has been mentioned,[51] then this has been done with good reason. But if you now think in turn that you should no longer speak of spiritual experiences, then that would be the greatest nonsense. If spiritual experiences are true, they are realities. The important thing is that they are true and that we stay within the spiritual boundaries. It is important that we do not go from one extreme to the other. It is more important that we really try not only to accept spiritual science as such, but that we also become aware that spiritual science must be integrated into the fabric of the world.

Certainly it would also be wrong to believe that we should no longer do spiritual science at all, but only read such pamphlets in the branches. That would be another incorrect interpretation. You have to think about what I meant. But the great harm I have indicated, that many just copy everything down instead of listening, is prevented in that we do not just copy everything down but listen. For if, when copying down, only such stuff is produced as really happens when copying down lectures, and if we believe that we certainly need such copied-down lectures, well, my dear friends, then I must say that, first of all, we show that we attach little importance to what has appeared in print, for there is really plenty of material that has already been printed; and secondly, it is not at all necessary that we are always scrambling for the very latest. This is a habit adopted by people as a result of journalism, and we must not cultivate it among ourselves. Thoroughly working through what is available is something fundamental and meaningful, and we will not spoil listening closely for ourselves by copying everything down but will have the desire to listen closely. Because scribbling everything down seldom results in anything other than spoiling the attention we might develop while listening. Therefore, I believe that those of us who want to work in the branches will, if they think they have no material, find the opportunity to have such material after all. You will no longer need to tug at the sleeve of everyone who has scribbled them down to get transcriptions of lectures just so that you can always read out the very latest. Truly, it depends on a serious approach, and the fact that not much serious work has been done in this direction is evident in many phenomena, even if indirectly, from which we are actually ailing.

So, my dear friends, I don't know for sure yet, but when I can manage again, I will continue perhaps on Saturday the discussion of Mr von Wrangell's excellent, perceptive pamphlet, which I have chosen because it is written by a scientist and has a concurring rather than a negative content.

Third Lecture

DORNACH, 2 OCTOBER 1915

So we continue today with our consideration of the pamphlet *Science and Theosophy* by F. von Wrangell. Before doing so, I would like to briefly recapitulate some thoughts that could be related to the various chapters so far.

First of all, I would like to mention why the points of view in this pamphlet can be of importance for our consideration. I have already said that in the present day we are living in circumstances which can put those who stand on the ground of spiritual science in the position of having to defend spiritual science against the various attacks to which it is exposed. Now, in our present time, a defence will be particularly necessary when the attacks come from science for the reason that science, which has developed in a certain form for three to four centuries, can with a certain right claim to establish a worldview, and actually does make this claim. So as a spiritual scientist you can hear it said: Well, if spiritual science has nothing to say about the objections of science, then it proves to be poorly founded; because anyone who wants to represent a worldview today must be able to defend it against the objections of science. Therefore it is particularly important to take note when a scientist appears and discusses what he has to say about the relationship between genuine scientific thought and theosophical teachings, and spiritual teachings in general.

The previous considerations have shown you that it can be particularly important if words are spoken in support of spiritual teachings precisely from the point of view that is determined by a consciousness that has engaged in astronomical and similar scientific research. I have pointed out how a representative of the modern worldview, Du Bois-Reymond, invokes the so-called Laplacean mind, the astronomical knowledge of the world; I have shown what the modern human being imagines by the Laplacean mind, by the astronomical understanding of the world. It is therefore necessary to show how far a comprehensive worldview can be built out of such astronomical conceptions.

Then I said that it was important that this pamphlet pointed out that from theoretical materialism, from the theoretical materialistic-mechanical conception of the world, practical materialism must of necessity gradually follow. I then showed how spiritual science must also adopt this standpoint, even though in our present day the objection is often raised that theoretical adherents of the materialistic-mechanical view of the world do not deny the validity of ideal, ethical motives, but on the contrary profess them.

We then saw in the pamphlet in a beautiful way what kind of worldview results for those who want to place themselves exclusively on the standpoint of the mechanical-materialistic worldview. I sketched out this image of the world to a certain extent, and particularly emphasized—which is also emphasized in the pamphlet—that anyone who sees the mechanical-materialistic image of the world as all-embracing cannot regard the inner experiences which take place in the consciousness of the human being as essentially different from other natural processes—that is, as anything other than by-products of mechanical-materialistic processes—and that if such a mechanical-materialistic view of the world is established, there can logically no longer be any question of the survival of an inner core after death.

The pamphlet then moves on to examine this basic assumption. In particular, it points out how freedom and morality relate to basic mechanical-materialistic conceptions; how the concept of freedom and responsibility cannot possibly still be held if we completely subscribe to the materialistic-mechanical view of the world, and how the actual question or riddle of the universe arises from this, namely that it is necessary to obtain such a conception of the world within which the ideas of freedom and responsibility can have a place.

Then it is pointed out how we have only gradually arrived at the idea of a general application of laws spread out, as it were, as a network over all phenomena, and also how it is impossible ever to disprove free will by experience, because, as we have seen, free will can never be thought to be so interwoven into this network of materialistic-mechanical processes as it would have to be if one were to profess this very image of the world alone.

Then, in an epistemological discussion, it is shown how the human being enters into a relationship with the outside world through their senses; how to conceive of the formation of concepts, of conceptions, the formation of the conceptions of space and time. It is pointed out how the principle of causality ought to be a general principle of the worldview, but how it has only gradually entered the worldview because it was originally assumed that similar real motives were present in things as they are present in human beings themselves; so that development would show that the human being did not originally proceed from a mechanical causality, but basically only worked their way towards the mechanical-materialistic view from a different view about the connection between phenomena.

Then it is pointed out how, in more recent times, scientific observation has attempted to achieve objectivity. Now the very particularly important principle of materialistic-mechanical science, the principle of measurement, is explained, and we shall see in a moment how this principle of measurement has further consequences also for the more complicated parts of present-day science.

Now I would like to draw your very special attention to what is written in the pamphlet about measuring. Truly, I would like to ask you to use it as a starting point to obtain an understanding of the character of the modern scientific approach precisely through this discussion about measurement. We have seen how the principle of measurement is then applied to the principle underlying clocks. I would now like to make a few remarks particularly about the principle of measurement, in order to show you how you could use this chapter of Wrangell's pamphlet *Science and Theosophy* as a kind of leitmotif to tie in with what you can find in the various arguments about the modern scientific approach, precisely with reference to the character that is required of a real scientific approach in the present day.

We have seen what the nature of measuring is, and we have also found an indication of how measuring in a certain respect introduces a kind of uncertainty in spite of all the objectivity in the observation over which it extends. We can point out this uncertainty very simply by saying the following: When we have simple measuring, measuring lengths or spaces, we base it on a base unit, a measuring stick. If we have to measure a length, we have to do it in such a way that we determine the relationship of the length to a measuring stick. The length must be given in the sensory world and our measuring stick must also be realized in the sensory world. Now you find a remark in the pamphlet that points out that something is introduced that makes measuring uncertain. Measurement is based on comparing something with the measuring stick; we compare how often the measuring stick is contained in what is to be measured.

Now, however, a slight warming for example results in heat expanding the measuring stick. So let's assume that the measuring stick has been heated and has thus become a little longer. Of course—since we are measuring in a space that shows approximately uniform heat, otherwise we would have to envisage further complications—the thing to be measured would be extended in the same proportion as the measuring stick. But if the measuring stick and the thing to be measured are made of materials that do not expand to the same extent, so that the measuring stick expands less or more than the thing to be measured, then we are already dealing with inaccuracies in measurement.

So we can highlight two things. One is: the observation becomes independent of our subjectivity, of the observer. We compare what is to be measured with the measuring stick, that is, we compare something objective with something objective. This is the basis of a good part of modern science, and basically it also constitutes an ideal of modern science. The other is if we simply looked at things around us according to our subjectivity. For example, you only need to imagine the following. Imagine you have a vessel with water in front of you; now move your one hand close to the stove and hold the other hand into a pool of ice; then put both hands into the water. You will have a very different feeling in each hand, even though the water is the same temperature. To the warmed hand the water will appear cold, to the cold hand it will not appear cold at all. In this way, the subjective extends over everything objective. This is only a crude example, but you can see from it how the subjective always underlies all observation. Measuring detaches the content from the subject, from the observer. Therefore there is an objective truth, a cognition, detached from the subjective. That is important. And because in more modern times greater and greater efforts have been made to become independent of the subjective with regard to our view of the world, measurement has become a kind of ideal.

You see, measuring becomes so objective because the measuring stick is independent of us, because we eliminate ourselves and insert the measuring stick in our place. Those who remember the lectures I gave in Berlin[52] on the different standpoints we can adopt towards the world will see that something similar also underlies spiritual science itself. I said there: As long as we stand on the ground of external reality, we confront the world and create an image of the world for ourselves. But as soon as you enter the spiritual world, you basically have to look at what you are observing from different viewpoints—but now the viewpoint is meant spiritually. I mentioned twelve standpoints, and it is only when you take these twelve standpoints that one standpoint always corrects the other. This also makes us independent of subjectivity in a certain way.

You see from this how science and spiritual science move in tandem, how that which lies as a necessary developmental motive in science, objectivity, must also be striven for by the spiritual scientist, though not by asserting all twelve standpoints. The twelve different standpoints correct each other. Thus measurement is the detachment from subjectivity. But on the other hand the point is made how even in measuring, accuracy can only be achieved within certain limits, and it is pointed out by Wrangell in the next chapter:

Limit of error during measurement

> It is also possible to specify the limit of accuracy, or more correctly the limit of error, in time measurement, as in length measurement. Within these limits, the fact obtained is objectively correct, but it never achieves error-free correctness.
>
> In this, all facts taken from sensory perceptions differ from intuitive truths of the thinking, such as the formal laws of logic and all truths of mathematics.

Thus while measurement is rightly put forward as the tool which, when the limit of error is taken into account, gives a certain accuracy in relation to an image of the world, it is at the same time pointed out how this accuracy, which can be achieved in relation to the external sensory world, can never be error-free accuracy. It can never provide the same kind of truth that we have in the so-called intuitive truths of thinking, in the formal laws of logic and in the truths of mathematics.

The next chapter is a further elaboration of what I have already said:

Absolute validity of logical and mathematical truths

> The logical truth, for example: a part is smaller than the whole,

—that is a mathematical truth. It cannot be said with absolutely equal certainty how many times a part is contained in this line [presumably a line on the blackboard was pointed to]—

> or: if two things are equal to a third, they are also equal to each other, is not subject to any restriction;

—these are absolute truths; but they are also not gained through external perception, but through thinking—

> every person of sound mind acknowledges its compelling necessity. This is also the case in mathematics; if certain basic assumptions have been agreed upon, all other theorems of mathematics follow with compelling necessity without any restriction. If, for example, we agree on what is called a straight line, what is a right angle, what we call parallelism, the propositions of geometry follow from this with absolute certainty.

It is necessary to come to an understanding on these matters. It is necessary to agree on what a right angle is, what a straight line is, what parallelism means. Once it has been agreed that parallel lines are those that are equidistant from each other at all points that lie vertically above each other, or once it has been agreed that parallel straight lines are those that, no matter how far they are extended, never intersect, then parallel lines can be used to gain insight into further theorems of mathematics. I now want to tie in something seemingly quite remote.

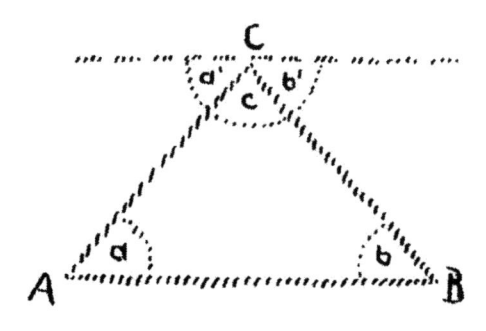

Let's say we have a triangle here: we have discussed many times that the three angles of a triangle together are 180 degrees. Well, what are 180 degrees? A hundred and eighty degrees is if you think of a point here and a straight line drawn through that point. A hundred and eighty degrees is contained in the arc around this point, which is a semicircle. So it should be possible to arrange these three angles a, b, c in such a way that, if you put them together in a fan shape, they form a straight line. This can be illustrated very easily by drawing the parallel to the straight line A B through the point C here. Then it follows, once we have agreed on the parallel, that the angle 'a' must be equal to this angle a, and the angle 'b' must be equal to b. Now the three angles lie next to each other in a fan shape and form 180 degrees. I should still introduce intermediate links, but you will see that the truth that the three angles of a triangle together are 180 degrees is built on this. That is to say, there are certain basic truths of mathematics that result from thinking activity itself, about which we have to come to an understanding, and from which the whole of mathematics then follows.

> A person who has the ability to follow the line of reasoning is as convinced of the eternal validity of the final proposition as he is of his own existence.

There can never be any doubt that the angles of a triangle together are 180 degrees. For those of our distinguished friends who know something about it, I emphasize that we disregard spatial geometry, which would take us too far today.

> Spatial science (geometry) establishes certain relationships between area content and its linear size, as well as between parts of space and the corresponding linear size.

This is the simplest idea. Because if you draw a rectangle for yourself, the area of this rectangle is the area that I am shading. State the length of the base line a, that of this line b—this is how you get the area when you multiply a by b; that is, you compose the area from linear size and linear size.

> These relationships were discovered by thinkers through intuition and logically linked with already known truths (that is the mathematical proof). The correctness of the proof is not tested by experience, but is directly recognized by intuition.

It is very important that you should engage with this matter; how in this respect mathematical reasoning and mathematical cognition in general differ from all cognition that relates to external sensory objects. We can never have the latter without approaching the external sensory object. So you have to take into account all the inaccuracy that comes into play. However, you do not need to draw mathematical constructs at all if you want to carry out a proof, but they are a consequence of autonomous thinking. Drawing is only an illustration for sluggish thinking that does not want to work within itself. But in and of itself, you could think of doing mathematics without any visualization in the inner imagination.

> We must never overlook this deep, fundamental difference between facts taken from experience, which always have sources of error due to the limitations of our senses, and logical or mathematical truths, which have absolute validity for us humans as soon as we have recognized the basic assumptions as correct.
>
> If a conclusion is drawn from any empirical fact by a chain of mathematical or logical propositions, the former is only correct within the limitations under which that empirical fact was observed; only with this limitation can the final result obtained be accepted as a scientifically proven fact of experience; this is often overlooked.
>
> Such empirical facts, when applied to phenomena of the sensory world, can lead to correct practical and also theoretical results, and often they reach such a high degree of probability that this probability seems to us equivalent to certainty, but epistemologically it is not.

The next chapter is called:

All laws of nature are taken from experience and therefore have only conditional validity.

> When we speak of laws of nature according to which, when certain conditions exist, certain phenomena necessarily occur—or in other words: certain causes necessarily have certain effects—these laws are taken from experience and can therefore only be proved to be correct within certain limits of accuracy.
>
> Let us illustrate this with a few examples: The astronomer says that the earth rotates around its axis at a uniform speed; what does he mean by that?

So you can recognize certain mathematical truths inwardly, but you cannot recognize inwardly that the earth rotates on its axis. So what does the astronomer mean by this?

> First of all, this means: 'We have substantial reasons to believe that the apparent daily rotation of the starry sky is an optical illusion and is caused by the rotation of the earth's sphere around its axis; the duration of such a revolution we call a "sidereal day". In order to measure the duration of a sidereal day (that is, one revolution of the earth on its axis), we have to compare it with a duration of time that we regard as unchanging. As such a unit of time we choose the period of oscillation of a pendulum of a certain length connected to a clock. Experience shows us that the better the conditions are fulfilled to ensure the regular running of a clock, and the more accurately we make the observations of the stars by which the duration of one revolution of the earth is determined, the more constant proves to be the relation between the number of oscillations of the pendulum and the number of revolutions of the earth. With the current state of the art, the rotation of the earth has proven to be uniform within the possible error limits, which can only reach a small fraction of a second. We cannot claim absolute uniformity, indeed we have reasons to doubt it.'

We do not need to address the last sentence; it can be the subject of a later reflection.

What is it now that is actually subject to external observation? Firstly, the phenomenon that we have as day and night on earth, and secondly, the comparison with the oscillations of a pendulum clock. And since we find from other premises that the pendulum swings uniformly, and that we can compare the uniform swinging of the pendulum with what we perceive in relation to the earth, we must conclude from this that the earth also turns uniformly about its axis.[53] Another explanation is given in the next chapter in relation to chemistry.

Chemical laws

> It is similar with chemistry. The whole edifice of this science rests on the proposition: chemical compounds can only occur in very specific quantities by weight of their indivisible constituents,

—as an example of this, a footnote states: 'For example, one unit by volume (say one litre) of oxygen combines only with two units by volume of hydrogen to form water.' So one atom of oxygen combines with two atoms of hydrogen to form a molecule of water. I have often spoken of this combination of oxygen with hydrogen to form water. Then the footnote goes on to say: 'Since an atom of oxygen is 16 times heavier than an atom of hydrogen, we can also say: one unit by weight of hydrogen combines with 8 units by weight of oxygen to form 9 units by weight of water. If there is more oxygen in the mixture than 8 times the amount of hydrogen by weight, the excess remains as "free" (uncombined) oxygen; if, on the other hand, there is less oxygen, the excess hydrogen remains uncombined.' So only in this very specific ratio does oxygen combine with hydrogen to form water; in the water they are present in this ratio. There is no other way for them to combine.

> or technically speaking: the elements only enter into chemical compounds in whole multiples of their atomic weights.

This sentence now contains the whole hypothesis of the atom. What is stated here is correct for the whole of sensory perception, for the observation of quantities by weight and relationships by volume. But if we assume that the oxygen and the hydrogen consist of the smallest parts, no longer divisible atoms, then we must assume that the same specific relationship also occurs between the atoms. And since we can no longer divide the atoms, when oxygen combines with hydrogen, that is, when one smallest part of one combines with two smallest parts of the other, the same weight ratio must exist. If we take the atomic weight of oxygen and the atomic weight of hydrogen, we get a weight ratio; that is, one atom of oxygen combines with two atoms of hydrogen, with the oxygen atom being eight times heavier. The whole multiple of the atomic weight goes into the compound. What do we have to do to discover something like that? You have to weigh something, which is also a measurement. So you take the sensory facts and from the result of weighing you get this law that the individual substances do not combine in an arbitrary way, but in a very specific ratio.

> However, the empirical facts from which this law is taken are never completely accurate (because all weighing and measuring is subject to errors of observation); if the law nevertheless expresses an absolute, this is intended to say the following: the more precisely the apparatus used for chemical analysis is constructed, the more careful the methods for breaking down aggregate compounds into indecomposable elements, the better the composition of the substance from elements can be represented by a combination of multiples of the corresponding atomic weights of these elements.
>
> Since the chemist is aware of the possible limits of error of their measuring operations, they know whether the final result of their analysis is in accordance with the above law within these limits of error or not. If they find a greater deviation, they are so convinced of the correctness of the law that they assume the presence of a still unknown element to explain the deviation they have found, or they look for an unnoticed source of error. Thus they consider the law to be absolutely correct in practice, although they are theoretically aware of the conditionality of this empirical law.

That is to say, if it were found from other empirical facts that two or three elements combine according to a certain ratio, and if another ratio were seen in the substances in which these are contained, then it would have to be assumed that there is something else in them.

The next chapter is called:

Physical laws

> When physics states the law of conservation of energy, it means that if we convert a certain amount of kinetic energy into heat and

compare the numbers expressing the amount of kinetic energy in its units and expressing the amount of heat generated in calories (units of heat), we get a ratio called the 'mechanical equivalent of heat'; the more precise the measurements are made and the better it is ensured that the entire movement is converted into measurable heat, the more precisely the ratios obtained in different tests agree with each other. That is the actual result of the experience.

Here we have a whole theory of physics before us in a single sentence. What leads to this theory can already be shown by the very simple fact that when we run a finger over a surface, it becomes warm. You can check that for yourself. This energy, this muscle energy of your own that you are expending, is not heat at first; but heat occurs and energy is lost. What happened here? Your energy has been transformed into heat. If you press here, for example, a certain amount of heat is generated; if you apply a different energy, heat is also produced. Now, you might think that it arises erratically; but that is not the case. The question as to what the relationship is between the expenditure of energy and the heat that is generated from it has been the subject of important research. In 1842, Julius Robert Mayer—who was treated rather badly by his peers at the time, although today he is considered a scientific authority of the first order—first drew attention to the fact[54] that the relationship between energy and the resulting heat is something constant. And he also tried to give the ratio. In his treatise, written in 1842, it is still stated imprecisely. Subsequent scholars then established and stated the exact number through their research. Helmholtz, who disputed the priority of the discovery,[55] set out to prove that there was such a ratio, a constant ratio, between the energy expended and the resulting heat. Equal amounts of energy give equal amounts of heat, and the ratio that exists between heat and expended energy is as constant as the ratio to the constants is constant. This is called the 'mechanical equivalent of heat'. That's how you get a law of physics.

> The physicist goes beyond experience when they replace the observational results, which always differ from each other, with a simple common formula. They are entitled to do so as long as they are aware of the conditions under which the formula is valid.

A formula is already created by the fact that I say: When energy is transformed into heat, there is a certain relationship between energy and heat. But even though there are many cases that have been investigated, the cases that will be investigated the day after tomorrow have not yet been investigated today. So when the physicist states a formula in such a context, they must be aware of the scope within which such a formula can be valid.

> Similarly all laws of nature can be shown to transcend experience in their simplification.

So that basically you are already going beyond experience if you do not stop at the description of the individual case.

Let us now consider the next chapter in relation to the whole of its thrust; it is called:

> *Cognition progresses from the simple to the complex*
>
> The phenomena of the sensory world, as they confront us, are so complex that, in order to fathom their connection, the human being is compelled first to limit their attention to the simplest and only then, step by step, to expand the field of what has been comprehended. The apparent, uniform, circular motion of the heavenly bodies offered in its simplicity the possibility of applying the absolute truths of mathematics to empirical facts of observation and thereby predicting future events by calculation.

For future lunar or solar eclipses, as I mentioned last time, this is based on observing the stars, putting their movements into formulas, and then inserting certain variables into these formulas. This makes it possible to indicate the day when, say in 1950, there will be a solar eclipse.

> This successful activity developed the capability of presenting large groups of phenomena in a clear, generally valid, mathematical form. In the geocentric world system, the concept of natural events governed by laws was expressed in a sublime way. Around the earth, resting in the centre of the world, the crystal brightness of the celestial sphere with the countless stars attached to it rotated with unchanging uniformity. Only seven celestial bodies: the sun, the moon and the five planets visible to the naked eye, have their own movement, for the illustration of which various combinations of circular movements

were used. Finally, the meaningful but complicated so-called Ptolemaic system with its cycles and epicycles arose.

The earlier world system was geocentric,[56] which assumed that the earth was at the centre of the world and that the other stars somehow revolved around it, and this was how the world mechanism was observed. The movements could also be calculated mathematically. It is not relevant that people held a view of the world that is no longer valid among astronomers today.

> With the increasing accuracy of the observations and the expansion of knowledge, the difficulties grew in representing the observed facts in this way with mathematical accuracy, until finally the boldest and most momentous of all scientific hypotheses—the Copernican hypothesis—solved the difficulties.

It happened like this; today, the situation is considerably different. It was assumed that the earth was at the centre, that the starry sky moved around and that the planets had their own motion. It was assumed that such a planet moved in a circle, which itself moved in a circle. It had to be imagined in epicycles. It was necessary to have a very complicated understanding of space, which complicated the whole worldview. Now a principle came into human thinking that contributed significantly to the Copernican worldview gaining a foothold. This was the principle that has never been invoked more often than then: nature does everything in the simplest way. But that, it was said, she had not done in the simplest way. And here it was Copernicus who simply turned things around. He said: Let's try to put the sun in the centre and let the other celestial bodies move around it. And so another astronomical picture of the world emerged, the Copernican one. I have already mentioned to you that it was not until 1822 that the Church allowed[57] a Catholic to believe in this system.

> The earth diminished from its position of rest at the centre of the world to a satellite of the sun, revolving around it like the other planets at breakneck speed, turning like a spindle on its axis—this is a conception so contrary to appearances and the teaching of the Church that its endeavour to nip the heretical doctrine in the bud is understandable.

> The reasons which urged the acceptance of this hypothesis could at first be fully appreciated only by those who were aware of how much more simply the results of the observations were explained by this hypothesis than if the earth were assumed to be at rest. Admittedly, the distances separating us from the fixed stars had to be imagined to be unfathomably large.

Now comes an argument which is important, but which we must make the subject of special consideration at this point:

> Incidentally, full proof of the correctness of the Copernican hypothesis was only provided two and a half centuries later by the discovery of the so-called 'aberration of light', and even later by the measurement of some stellar parallaxes.

From what stellar parallaxes and aberration of light are, you will see that the Copernican worldview was indeed subject to some uncertainty until these discoveries.

> The mathematical method which had been strengthened by the study of the movements of the stars was gradually applied also to the phenomena of earthly, lifeless nature, which were closer to us and therefore presented themselves in a more complex way. Statics, the theory of the equilibrium of forces, was already developed by the ancients; then, not until the revival of the exact sciences, dynamics, the mathematical theory of movement. Galileo investigated the laws of falling bodies; he recognizes them intuitively, expresses them in formulas, tests and proves them through meaningful experiments that enable more precise measurement.

There it is pointed out how it is basically a penetration of external phenomena with mathematical ideas that science aims for. The Ptolemaic worldview also aimed to extend the mathematical part like a net. When you see a star, you must already have grasped the mathematical concept of the circle if you are to say: The star moves in a circle. So you connect the mathematical with what you see empirically. This is also done in a large part of mechanical science, for example in statics, which is concerned with investigating the conditions under which the equilibrium of forces is brought about, whereas dynamics investigates the conditions under which movements can be controlled and so on.

So we see how sciences are formed by infusing what is externally empirically perceived with mathematics.

> Newton eventually applies the earthly laws of falling bodies to celestial phenomena. He proves mathematically that the same force that propels the apple to the earth—the mutual attraction of two masses of matter—forces the moon to revolve around the earth, and the planets, together with the earth, to describe their orbits around the sun whose elliptical shape, discovered by Kepler, corresponds to the requirements of mechanics.

Newton's famous apple anecdote[58] is considered here, who once sat under an apple tree and saw an apple fall down. Now you may ask: Why does the apple fall down? For the naïve person, this is not really a scientific question; this is where the scientific person reveals themselves, in that something that is not a question for the naïve person becomes a question for them. The naïve person finds it quite natural that the apple falls down. But it could also remain hanging, and it would do so if a force were not exerted by the earth; the earth attracts it to itself. If you now imagine the earth and the moon going around the earth, you will realize that the moon would have to fly away if another force did not act against it. Just remember what boys do; maybe girls too, but I don't know. Suppose you have an object; tie it to a thread, hold the thread at one end and move it around in a circle. Try to cut the thread and the object will fly away. The moon also goes around like that. But why does it not fly away? At every point it aspires to do so. If we suppose that the earth were not there, it would certainly fly away; but because the earth is there, it attracts the moon, and it attracts the moon in such a way that the moon does not go to A but goes to B, after a certain time.[59]

The earth must always attract it in order to hold it in a circle. This is the same force, Newton said to himself, as that which acts on the apple that the earth pulls down towards itself. It also uses it to keep the moon in its orbit. This is the same force with which celestial bodies attract each other in general and keep themselves in their orbits. We see the force in the falling apple; the same force, the general force of attraction, gravity, is in the celestial bodies. The rest about the calculation, how such gravity works, how it decreases with distance and so on, these are details. It was precisely with this Newtonian theory of gravitation that a very important chapter of the scientific worldview was initiated, a chapter that was basically established right up to our own time. It is only in our time that this is being challenged to some extent. I have, after all, drawn your attention to how a so-called theory of relativity is challenging this. But we will talk about that another time.

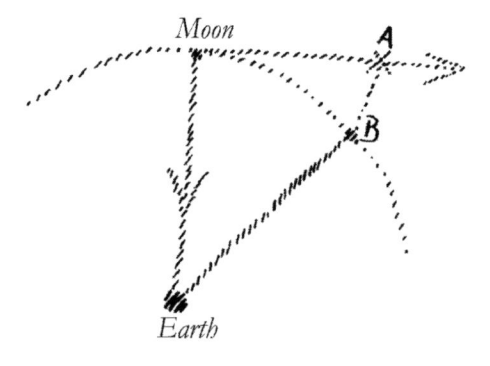

> It was not until the discovery of the laws of gravity that the worldview became a unified one, encompassing the entire cosmos. The sublime idea of a cause (force) working everywhere and with necessity, measurable in its effects, therefore suitable for objective examination, accustoms the human mind to look everywhere for such examination and always to strive to trace phenomena back to as few basic assumptions as possible.
>
> The progress of European science depends substantially on the application of this principle.

Indeed, much revolves around the application of this principle. I have already drawn your attention several times to how, as a twelve-year-old boy, I was surprised by a treatise in the school programme,[60] in which an attempt was made to explain phenomena in a way other than by gravitation. That caused me a lot of headache at the time, because I was not yet very familiar with the formulas, with the integral and differential formulas with which the treatise was interspersed. But I can nevertheless tell you what it was all about, if I leave all that out.

Think of the earth here, the moon there. [Draws. See below.] That is, the earth acts on the moon through empty space; so it has an effect over distance. Now there was a lot of thinking about whether such an effect could really take place over distance. Many were of the opinion that a body cannot act where it is not, and others said that a body is where it acts.[61] Schramm [the author of the treatise mentioned] says:[62] The whole theory of gravitation is mysticism, for it assumes that one cosmic body extends into the invisible in order to attract another. Whether it is a cosmic body or a molecule, it makes no difference. So they were there at a certain distance. Now he claims the following: the cosmic bodies are not there alone. Space is filled with bodies. There are many more bodies. But they are not at rest either, they are in constant motion. If we now imagine that these bodies are all in motion, then they are continually bumping into this body that we are imagining here; bodies bump into each other here as well; but there are also bodies bumping from the inside, so that the body is bumped from all sides. And now he calculates the number and effect of these impacts. You can see very easily that here are smaller areas to be knocked, and here larger areas. But because there is less impact here than out there, the bodies are forced together. You have here the result of the force of attraction, composed of different impacts by the fact that they take place in different numbers. So there is drumming there, there is drumming there; so there must be fewer impacts from the inside to the outside than from the outside to the inside. The bodies therefore have a tendency to come together. They are driven together by the individual impacts.

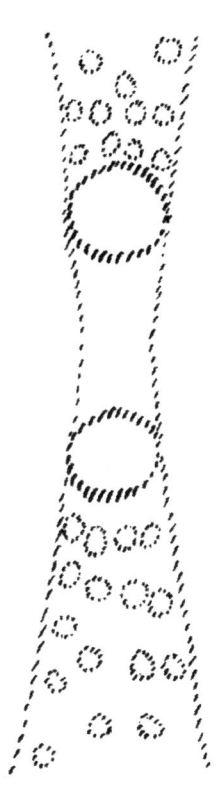

This man [Schramm] tried to replace gravitational force with another way of drawing together. He tried to eliminate the mysticism in the theory of gravitation.

A treatise was written by Paul Du Bois-Reymond in which it was mathematically proved[63] that such collisions are never possible which are equal to the phenomenon of gravitation.

This is how science goes about its work; it tries to arrive at principles from uncertain premises, then to overturn them again in order to return to the old principles. If Paul Du Bois-Reymond's arguments are correct, we must return to what is older. So we come back to what was to be rejected. This is an interesting case that can show you how science works.

> The progress of European science depends substantially on the application of this principle. In this way it was gradually possible to unify within inanimate nature ever more and larger areas of manifestation, to trace the phenomena of mechanics, heat, light, sound, electricity, magnetism and chemical affinity back to transformations of a quantitatively indestructible something which we call energy, and whose measurable magnitude is expressed by the product of the moving mass with the square of the velocity.

That is to say, attention is drawn here to the fact that if we form a worldview in this way, we arrive at the assumption of an energy that is in space. I have already pointed out what the naturalist Ostwald said,[64] that it is not the slap that matters but the energy that is applied. And so, hypothetically speaking, you can have a material body here: [It was evidently drawn.] How do you perceive it? Only by the fact that a different spatial expansion can be noted here than in the surrounding area.

But that is also only a pushback, just as you, when you see a body, cannot perceive anything other than what acts with a certain force on the eyes. So matter can be replaced by energy. What we call matter can only be energy everywhere, and so observation and the mathematical law according to which movements proceed provides the basis that the law of energy can be expressed by the product of the moving mass and the square of the velocity. But to discuss this would take us too far; it can be done at some later time.

> Up to now no authenticated fact is known which contradicts the basic assumption of the mechanical view within inanimate nature; on the other hand innumerable conclusions logically or mathematically derived from it have been confirmed by empirical examination, and indeed the lawful linkage of events and the indestructibility of mass and energy[65] is confirmed all the more surely, the more exactly the examination is undertaken, the smaller the possible errors in the measurements are.

It is pointed out here that a certain comprehensive physical law can be inferred from observation. The easiest way to come to this law is to say: We have a certain energy. We transform it into heat. Heat in turn—we see this in steam engines and so on—can undergo another transformation, it can be converted into another energy. This transformation takes place in corresponding ratios. That is to say, we are led to the so-called law of the conservation of energy, that is to the law which is expressed thus: In the universe there is a certain sum of energy. It transforms itself. When a certain amount of energy, let's say heat, is transformed, energy disappears on one side but on the other side there is different energy. So there is a transformation of energy. This is a law that plays an important role and for which in recent times the attempt has been made to extend it to the entire worldview. And that brings us to the next chapter:

Extension of the mechanical conception to the organic

> However, this has only been proven numerically within the inorganic world in so far as we receive impressions of it through our five senses. It is understandable that this conception of the application of laws should also be applied to organic, animate nature.
>
> But the question is, to what extent are we entitled to do so?

So that means, if we compare these energies, apply the law of energy, that you can apply it to everything that is inanimate, inorganic nature, and now try to encompass organic nature with the same law. That is why the next chapter is called:

Difference between inanimate and animate bodies

> What is the difference between an animate and inanimate body?
>
> We call a body animate when material changes take place in it not only according to physical and chemical laws, but when, in addition to these forces which alone act in inanimate nature, other forces also act which are peculiar to every species and every individual and which condition the growth, reproduction and death of every living individual being.

It is the characteristic of living beings that they grow, reproduce and die. We do not find this with the inorganic. But now there is a tendency in the mechanical-materialistic worldview to apply the same principles that are applied to the inorganic world to the animate beings, to the organic.

> Whether we ascribe these laws to a 'life force' or to some other hypothetical cause, the fact is that the gap between the organic and the inorganic has not yet been bridged and that the more precise the observations are made, the more certain it becomes that living things only arise from living things.

Now a sentence follows that can be found quoted numerous times; here it is put as:

> The opposite assumption, that the animate is only another arrangement of the inanimate, is for the time being a hypothesis not confirmed by any fact.

But I have also mentioned something else, and it is important to consider the latter with reference to this point of view. For it might be thought that the validity of a spiritual worldview depends on it not being possible to prove how a living thing comes into being from inorganic substances. Yet there was a long period that was grounded in the spiritual worldview and yet believed that a homunculus could be produced in a laboratory. So the spiritual worldview has not always been made dependent on it not being possible to make living things arise from lifeless things. It is part of our time to emphasize that living things only arise from living things, and that the spiritual worldview attaches to this. I have often said how Francesco Redi, as late as about 200 years ago, stated the proposition: 'Living things can only come from living things', and proved it incorrect that the animate can arise from the inanimate. It is also important that science points out that there is a gulf between the organic and the inorganic. Ferdinand Cohn emphasized at the Natural Scientists' Meeting in Berlin,[66] that the laws used to prove the inorganic are not sufficient to prove the organic. We might cite Bunge from Basel; and Julius Wiesner,[67] the botanist, says: The further botany progresses, the more it becomes apparent how a gulf exists between the inorganic and the organic. Wrangell therefore says:

> So, if we want to remain within what is scientifically established at present, we must distinguish between two essentially different groups of phenomena: the animate and the inanimate.

The next chapter is called:

> *Consciousness*
>
> We humans encounter another phenomenon through inner experience: consciousness with its expressions, which are: feeling, thinking, volition.
>
> We have no compelling reason to suppose that the plant also thinks and wills, and, without leaving the ground of experience, are justified in still making the distinction within the organic kingdom between the unconscious vegetable and the conscious animal.*

We have often talked about how there are people who want to blur the distinction between the vegetable and the animal, who claim that plants attract and devour living beings. You also know a creature like this that attracts creatures that come near and then devours them: that is a mousetrap. And yet we need not assume that a mousetrap has an animal soul in it.

> All phenomena that are connected with consciousness we call 'spiritual phenomena'.

We would have to say more precisely, 'All phenomena which we bring to consciousness', for in spiritual science we must also call spiritual that which is not astral body and I. When you are only in the physical body and etheric body, we are not dealing with consciousness but with spiritual activity.

> Thus the world, as far as we become aware of it by means of our five senses and our faculty of thought, appears to contain three essentially

---

* Here the footnote still follows in the pamphlet: 'Those who do not recognize any fundamental difference between plants and animals only retain the distinction for the sake of greater clarity.'

different principles: matter, which is immutable in its mass and in its properties, life, which obeys its own laws, and the spiritual.

I would also like to point out that even philosophers outside of spiritual science, such as Eduard von Hartmann and others, have spoken of an unconscious spiritual part, so that we ... [Gap in the transcript]

> In science, which has the inorganic as its object, the assumption proves itself, as we have already said, that cause and effect stand in a numerically fixed relation to each other, that all that happens within this world of the inanimate follows the strict law of necessity.
>
> Biological science, which sets itself the task of investigating the phenomena of life, proceeds, in accordance with the nature of every science, from the same assumption. Since, however, in the case of many phenomena of life, measurement, hence numerical testing of the lawful course of changes (i.e. of events), is not applicable, the rule of the necessary, unalterable linkage of cause and effect cannot be perfectly proven in the field of biology. But there is nothing to be said against it, and the intrinsic probability, as well as the analogy with what we know for sure, speaks in favour of it. In any case, this assumption must be the basis of all scientific research, because its task is to discover these laws.

Now, I have pointed out in various lectures how in more recent times efforts are being made to trace numerical constancy right up to animal and human phenomena. Rubner, for example, tried to prove how much heat energy is contained in the food[68] that a certain animal receives; and then he tried to prove how much heat the animal develops in the occurrences of its life. From the resulting constant number it follows that the heat absorbed with the food reappears in the activity. The activity was transformed food.

Another researcher extended this to the psychological sphere by testing a number of students. The principle of applying numerical ratios is quite good. This can be applied to all these phenomena. We will talk tomorrow about how that is quite correct. But logically the matter is usually kept very short-sighted, for someone could, after all, according to the same logical laws by which Rubner proceeds, examine how the monetary values or the equivalents for them which are carried into the bank, and likewise all those which are carried out, correspond. They have to correspond to each other, after all. If we were to conclude from this that there are no people in the bank who do this, that would certainly be wrong. If we examine the food that is introduced into the organism and the energy that comes out again and find a correspondence between them, we should not suppose that the soul is not involved.

Then comes another chapter:

The spiritual phenomena

> If we look at spiritual phenomena, they are, for ordinary sensory observation, linked to certain material conditions, and this could give rise to the materialistic view according to which spiritual phenomena would not exist at all without the material basis of a living being with its brain, nerves etc.

This assumption arose to such an extent that Du Bois-Reymond said in one of his speeches that if you wanted to speak of a world soul, you had to show where the world brain was.[69] He said: If you want to speak of a soul of the world, you must show where there is a brain of the world. That is how much it has been reinterpreted in terms of materialism, because when you observe the human being in the physical world, you see that everything psychological is bound to the brain.

> Most people have always had an inner aversion to this view, and the belief in the independent existence of spiritual entities and their interaction with the world of the senses with which we are familiar has been expressed in the most diverse forms of religious and spiritualist ideas.
>
> Very many facts which are supposed to be direct confirmations of such a view are certainly based on deception and delusion.

We have also been through some of these deceptions and delusions in recent times here. It is of great importance that anyone who stands on the ground of the spiritual-scientific worldview is free from deception and delusion.

> In recent times, however, well-authenticated factual material has been brought together which makes the assumption of a spiritual world appear to be the most probable hypothesis for its explanation, so that

it would now be unscientific to simply reject the latter out of hand—as it was done only a few decades ago.

And now this is discussed further in the following chapter:

The occult capabilities of the human being

> If numerous facts that can be perceived with the ordinary senses already suggest, if not demand, a spiritualistic interpretation, then it must be added that many credible people claim to possess, in addition to the five senses, other organs of perception not developed in most people, which allow them to enter into direct contact with the spiritual world.
>
> That the five senses of the human being do not exhaust all the possibilities of perceptive abilities must be assumed a priori and is confirmed by some phenomena in the animal world. There is therefore no justification for denying it, but it is a scientific duty to examine the facts in question carefully, without prejudice, which is also now being done by many outstanding representatives of the exact sciences.
>
> For very many people who have occult experiences themselves or hear of them from credible persons, the existence of spiritual worlds is a proven fact, and the possibility of gaining insight into the riddles of the world by penetrating them is not subject to doubt.
>
> Since time immemorial, doctrines have developed from such supposed or real insights, sometimes spreading as secret teachings among a select few, sometimes appearing as openly taught religious systems. Of the great world religions, the European cultural world is most closely interwoven with Christian teachings.

Now it is important that we use such a debate to build on it how spiritual science positions itself in this regard. Spiritual science today, when it takes into account all that human development has gone through up to the present day, takes the standpoint not so much to emphasize that there are already other organs of perception apart from the human being's five senses—you know, if you look back on much of what we have discussed, that there are other organs—but to emphasize that other organs of perception can be formed. *Knowledge of the Higher Worlds. How is it Achieved?* describes what we have to do so that such organs can be formed. It is important that the spiritual science of today claims the same general applicability as other science, maybe in a different sense but still in a certain sense. The other science tries to obtain knowledge that applies to all people. Spiritual science seeks to train such organs of perception that can be developed by all human beings. If the scientist can examine what is asserted, the person who trains the spiritual organs can examine what spiritual science asserts. Ordinary science reckons with those capabilities that are already there, spiritual science with those that can be developed.

Now let us look at the principle according to which these capabilities are developed. How these capabilities are developed is described in detail in *Knowledge of the Higher Worlds. How is it Achieved?*. Now I just want to briefly state how such capabilities are to be understood.

When a symphony is played, there is actually nothing more than oscillations of the air in the room. These oscillations of the air can also be calculated mathematically. And if we made enough calculations, we could express all the movement that takes place in the instrument and in the air mathematically as the sum of the facts comprising the movement. We could abstract completely from the symphony we are listening to and say to ourselves: I don't care about Beethoven's symphony; I want to be a mathematician and investigate what states of motion apply. If we proceeded like this, we would cut out the symphony and have only the states of motion. But you will have to admit that the symphony is also still there. It cannot be denied and is something other than the mere image of the states of motion. What happened there? After all, Beethoven in a certain way only caused such states of motion to arise. But that does not yet give a real symphony.

If you now imagine that a human being applies all those capabilities which are otherwise applied to comprehend the outer physical world in order to obtain such laws as the intuitive laws of mathematics and logic are, that is, the laws which the human being develops by being a thinking human being; and if they treated themselves in this way by means of these laws as the composer does with the states of motion of the air; if they do not accept the capabilities of mathematics and logic and other capabilities as they are, but work on them inwardly, then something arises in them that is something different from the empirical capabilities of logic, mathematics and empirical research. Compare this and the treatment that the composer gives to the air with what we do inwardly and look at what emerges, then you have the possibility of saying: Here we have a human being who has the capability of empirical research, the capability of forming mathematical and logical judgements, that is just like a sum of the states of movement that are in the instruments and in the air. But if you treat them again in a certain way, the result is a symphony, a musical work of art. The laws by which we treat ourselves are just such as are given in my book *Knowledge of the Higher Worlds. How is it Achieved?*. Then something arises that is still in development, that is a consequence of human activity. And just as the person who has a musical ear not only perceives the oscillations from the instruments and the air, so the person who has developed the inner senses not only perceives the sensory, the mathematical, not only the logical world, but they also perceive the spiritual world. Such nurturing of something new on the basis of what is already there leads us to work our way into a spiritual world. Thus, for spiritual science, it is a matter of recognizing that the capabilities that the human being already has can be developed, just as the movements of the instruments and the air can be developed. It is on the basis of this capacity for further development that the human being can develop towards a conception of the world that gives them something that they do not perceive without this further development. The essential thing about spiritual science is that it points to the possibility of the further development of certain capabilities; not to the existence of those that are already present, but to their further development. And then it is correct when Wrangell says that in the various systems of religion the same thing is referred to as in the secret teachings.

The next chapter is called:

Essence of the teachings of Jesus

> If we regard what is common to all the countless interpretations of Jesus' teachings as the essence of Christianity, it consists in the 'good news' that the Creator and Controller of the universe is a loving Father to the human being whom He created in His image, that love for God and our fellow human beings is the highest moral commandment, that the soul of the human being is eternal and that after death a lot will be prepared for it which corresponds to the moral conduct of the human being during their life.

In the way that we have worked on the essence of Christianity with the instrument of spiritual science, it must be said that what is pronounced here is the content of Jesus' teachings, but not the essence of Christianity. The essence of Christianity consists of a development that has taken place in time, in that the human being Jesus was implanted with the Godhead, that is, that a being which until then had not been connected with the earth connected itself with it through the familiar process, whereby time is thus divided into a pre-Christian and a post-Christian era. Such an understanding of the appearance of the Christ being on earth is part of the essence of Christianity.

> The conspicuous aberrations into which the organized Christian communities, the historical Churches, have fallen have brought their dogmas into opposition with some firmly established scientific achievements, and have thus brought about the conflict between faith and knowledge, religion and science, which is corroding the spiritual life of the European cultural world.
>
> This situation explains the interest that has turned to other religious systems that claim not only to be in harmony with science, but also to extend it.
>
> Among these teachings, theosophy deserves special attention. Since the European cultural world was made aware by HP Blavatsky of this teaching, which originated in India, it has found various representations.

Whenever the word 'theosophy" is uttered, it is important to draw attention to what spiritual science is and what the theosophical worldview is.

Tomorrow I think I will be able to finish. But I still have to discuss in what way Blavatsky's teaching originated in India and in what way it did not originate in India, and I have to go into some things that separate spiritual science from much of what is called theosophy. Of that, then, tomorrow.

Fourth Lecture

DORNACH, 3 OCTOBER 1915

We now continue with the interpretations which we have related to the Wrangell pamphlet *Science and Theosophy*. We stopped at the chapter 'Essence of the teachings of Jesus', according to which the essence of the teachings of Jesus should consist 'in the "good news" that the Creator and Controller of the universe is a loving Father to the human being whom He created in His image, that love for God and our fellow human beings is the highest moral commandment, that the soul of the human being is eternal and that after death a lot will be prepared for it which corresponds to the moral conduct of the human being during their life.'

We had to point out that the teachings of Jesus can be described in this way, but that the essence of Christianity in the spiritual-scientific sense is not understood if we do not realize how the appearance of Christ in Jesus of Nazareth and the Mystery of Golgotha are facts which must be understood by those who want to gradually find their way into the essence of Christianity. These facts belong to the essence of Christianity. Christianity, as I have often said, is not merely a doctrine, but encompasses a reality, and understanding this reality, which can be expressed as the 'Mystery of Golgotha', is part of understanding the essence of Christianity.

It is then pointed out that the various religions have created a conflict between faith and science: 'The conspicuous aberrations into which the organized Christian communities, the historical Churches, have fallen have brought their dogmas into opposition with some firmly established scientific achievements, and have thus brought about the conflict between faith and knowledge, religion and science, which is corroding the spiritual life of the European cultural world. This situation explains the interest that has turned to other religious systems that claim not only to be in harmony with science, but also to extend it. Among these teachings, theosophy deserves special attention. Since the European cultural world was made aware by HP Blavatsky of this teaching, which originated in India, it has found various representations.'

From the spiritual-scientific point of view, it must be pointed out in particular that what spiritual science is of necessity to modern humanity must not be called a teaching originating in India, but that it has developed purely out of itself, out of the impulses of the present cycle of development. And if outsiders repeatedly point to a relationship between our spiritual science and Indian teachings, it is only because the concept of repeated earth lives has remained so alien to the West that everyone who hears of repeated earth lives immediately thinks of India, because there this teaching has become dogma within the religious ideas. The only important thing is to emphasize again and again that what is our spiritual-scientific content is built up from the needs of the present itself and is not a doctrine originating from here or there, but should be grasped and understood on its own terms.

Finally, it must also be said with regard to Blavatsky that she was at first quite independent of any East-facing cultural current with her teachings, as she expressed them for example in *Isis Unveiled*; that what was written by her in the initial periods belongs entirely to European spiritual culture. Only it then happened, through various machinations, that Blavatsky became more and more attracted to things Indian. In this way she imposed a kind of Indian signature on the current that originated with her and swore by her, which must in turn be removed again because it would be impossible to accomplish even the slightest thing in more modern culture in the right way with any old system of religion. This is extremely important; it also remains important for the consideration of the particularly interesting chapter of our pamphlet in which the theosophical teachings are compiled. The chapter is called: 'Essence of theosophical teachings'. Mr von Wrangell does not describe here what spiritual science is directly as such but what he has found in the literature of the various worldviews that call themselves theosophical. I will read this chapter and then we will link our reflections to it. So:

Essence of theosophical teachings

The most central assumptions common to the various presentations and views of theosophy can be expressed as follows.

    1. Apart from the world perceivable through our five senses, there are other spiritual worlds, of which each higher world acts on the lower ones.

    2. There are people who have other means of perception besides the ordinary five senses, so-called 'occult senses'.

    3. Thoughts, feelings, impulses of will, in short, what we call 'spiritual phenomena' in human experience, are—even if they have not expressed themselves in the sensory world as words or deeds—living entities, capable of effects in the spiritual worlds and indirectly in the sensory world.

    4. The soul life of every human being leaves imperishable traces in the higher worlds, which in its entirety is called the 'Akasha Chronicle' by occult researchers and can be investigated by some people (initiates) who are qualified to do so.

    5. The living human being is not a simple being consisting of the animate body but the physical body is only the instrument by means of which the actual being of the human being, their indestructible 'I', can enter into a relationship with the physical world. These relationships are mediated by intermediate constitutional elements: firstly, the 'etheric body', which is the bearer of the unconscious, vegetative life and shapes the material substances of the body according to its own laws; secondly, 'astral body', carrier of desires, passions, urges.

    6. The 'I' of the human being, bearer of their self-consciousness, is endowed with freedom, i.e. they can direct their desires, impulses of will, thoughts, etc., set them a goal and direction.

    7. Depending on whether the 'I' makes use of the external opportunities offered to it in life in accordance with the eternal laws and the purpose of the world as a whole, or neglects to do so, it shapes its 'karma', i.e. the degree of contentment or pain to which it is entitled in the world as a whole.

8. After bodily death, the immortal 'I' of the human being passes through various spiritual worlds, carrying with it the sum of the eternal values it has gained in earthly life. After a period of time that differs for each individual being, the 'I' begins its return journey from the higher worlds to the lower ones, enriched by the insights gained in those worlds, and begins, through reincarnation, a new life on earth which is shaped according to its karma and according to the aspirations of its changed 'I'.

9. World events are regulated in accordance with the purpose of the whole by spiritual beings which intervene in events—promoting or inhibiting according to their nature or direction of will.

10. These entities are hierarchically structured in accordance with their sphere of action and power and, like everything in the world, are subject to development from the lower to the higher.

11. The supreme law of all world affairs is 'free sacrifice out of love'. The Deity encompassing the universe, following this law, sacrificed itself through manifestation in the external world by endowing the spiritual entities originating from it with the ability of free impulses of will. The cosmos brought into being by this act is left to develop.

12. This development leads through eons from the unconscious to the conscious comprehension of the supreme cosmic law and through its realization to the reunification of the individual with the whole.

Let us now go through the individual points. Under 1. it says: 'Apart from the world perceivable through our five senses, there are other spiritual worlds, of which each higher world acts on the lower ones.' We can agree with that. Under 2. it says: there are so-called occult senses. I already said yesterday that it is necessary to emphasize that spiritual science takes the view that through special treatment of the ordinary faculties, spiritual faculties of perception can also be developed in the human being, and that in the present cycle of development it is these systematically developed faculties that are most important. We can also find such abilities in humans which still originate from earlier times. They can be awakened because they are present in almost every human being but they must be developed as described in *Knowledge of the Higher Worlds. How is it Achieved?*. It is therefore not good to say this in the way Mr von Wrangell says, but we should say: It is possible that the human being, just as they develop their five senses through prenatal development and develop them further in the existence outside the mother, they also develop inner powers in the purely spiritual sphere; develop abilities to see purely spiritual worlds. Such abilities are the conscious transformations of older abilities which were appropriate for earlier epochs on earth and which awaken in every human being of their own accord, either through external cause or during systematic training by the methods described in *Knowledge of the Higher Worlds. How is it Achieved?*. The expression 'occult senses' should be avoided, for we cannot say that the human being acquires occult senses but it is quite a different way of perception. We should not call senses that which organizes itself from what is called the Lotus Flowers, but at most sensory abilities.

Under 3. it says: 'Thoughts, feelings, impulses of will, in short, what we call "spiritual phenomena" in human experience, are—even if they have not expressed themselves in the sensory world as words or deeds—living entities, capable of effects in the spiritual worlds and indirectly in the sensory world.' Well, this has often been described very precisely, especially recently, where I have described the transition of the perception of thoughts into the experience of living thoughts. And it would be even better to say: Those things which appear in the human being as thoughts, feelings and impulses of will are, as they appear to the human being in the soul, the image of beings of the higher worlds, the elemental world and the still higher worlds, so that we actually have true reality in what we first have as thoughts, feelings and impulses of will in the same way as we have true reality in the sensory perceptions. It lies behind the one as much as the other.

Point 4. says: 'The soul life of every human being leaves imperishable traces in the higher worlds, which in its entirety is called the "Akasha Chronicle" by occult researchers and can be investigated by some people (initiates) who are qualified to do so.' This has often been described, and it is of very special importance that we take this into account, that when we enter the Akasha world we immediately enter a living world and not a world of dead images.

Then, under 5., attention is drawn to the human being consisting of different constitutional elements of their being. You know how to state that much more precisely than it is stated here.

As it stands with the sixth point, concerning freedom, we have often spoken of the human being on their path being led towards freedom, that the human being becomes ever freer and freer.

Point 7 about karma, you know that very well too.

Point 8 says: 'After bodily death, the immortal "I" of the human being passes through various spiritual worlds, carrying with it the sum of the eternal values it has gained in earthly life. After a period of time that differs for each individual being, the "I" begins its return journey from the higher worlds to the lower ones, enriched by the insights gained in those worlds, and begins, through reincarnation, a new life on earth which is shaped according to its karma and according to the aspirations of its changed "I".' You can learn exactly, to a certain degree, what may be said about this from the lecture-cycle *The Inner Nature of Man and Our Life Between Death and Rebirth*.[70]

Point 9: 'World events are regulated, in accordance with the purpose of the whole, by spiritual beings which intervene in events—promoting or inhibiting, according to their nature or direction of will.' You know this too.

Point 10 says: 'These entities are hierarchically structured in accordance with their sphere of action and power and, like everything in the world, are subject to development from the lower to the higher.' It is not good if everything is generalized again in this way. The idea of development also has a limited validity. I have often said that it is necessary to form new thoughts when we ascend to the higher worlds. Thus we can say that in ascending to the higher worlds we first penetrate regions where time still plays a role; but then we enter regions that can be described as regions of permanence. In these, time no longer plays a role. There is no other way to say this than to point out that the law of development only applies as a symbolic one, as I have done in my *Occult Science*.

Point 11 says: 'The supreme law of all world affairs is "free sacrifice out of love". The Deity encompassing the universe, following this law, sacrificed itself through manifestation in the external world by endowing the spiritual entities originating from it with the ability of free impulses of will. The cosmos brought into being by this act is left to develop.' Point 12: 'This development leads through eons from the unconscious to the conscious comprehension of the supreme cosmic law and through its realization to the reunification of the individual with the whole.' All this can be seen in greater detail in the context of spiritual-scientific research, and you can probably see that this compilation is made for outsiders. I hope that each of you could make a similar compilation, which could probably be even more accurate than is the case here, since it would then paraphrase actual spiritual science.

Now Mr von Wrangell tries to recapitulate and characterize the points made once more by saying:

> All the occult researchers in European culture agree on these basic teachings: HP Blavatsky, Mrs A Besant, Leadbeater, Dr Hartmann, Dr R Steiner and others. The same teachings are said also to apply in the Indian occult schools from which HP Blavatsky took them.

But here we now know that spiritual science—as it gradually represents itself in its pure form to the world—must not be mixed with other things; for it can really only fulfil its mission if it takes into account the essentials of the western cultural world and therefore also of western scholarship. But there can be no question of this in the case of personalities like the late Dr Franz Hartmann, nor can there be any question that the form which theosophy has taken under the leadership of Mrs Besant, or even under Leadbeater, has anything to do with the western cultural world as it naturally makes its cultural demands.

And here I would like to refer those who, as seekers, are beginning to develop a certain interest in our spiritual science and who attach great importance to our spiritual science detaching itself from that which otherwise often prevails in the world as theosophy to a very nice and kind article written by Dr Rittelmeyer in the journal *Christentum und Gegenwart*. Truly, I mention this article not because Dr Rittelmeyer also says some things about me in it. Those who know me better know that I do not mention the matter for these reasons but because our cause and especially our building[71] are spoken of with a certain affectionate understanding, and are characterized with affectionate consideration in one direction or another. It seems important to me to highlight one passage from this article that I received this morning:

> Apart from working together on the building, what holds the different nations and people together and brings them together is Steiner's lectures. I was kindly allowed to attend several of these lectures. They were mainly about Christ and represented an extraordinary effort to grasp the world-historical fact of Christ from various angles as the deepest and innermost cultural event. The time will probably come when this inner struggle for Christ will be made accessible to a wider circle. For just as in Steiner the old theosophical movement is working its way out of the dogmatic and mediumistic into the scientific, so in him it is also making the significant transition from the Indian into the Christian.

So it is important for those who want to develop an interest from out of western culture in what spiritual science aims to be that we do not wish to rehash ancient Indian teachings, but that we want to create something out of the spiritual world that is suitable precisely for our cycle of time.

Perhaps I may refer you further to the article after all. I can probably do that with reservation; because after the many things that are said about our movement and about my writings, something can also be said for once that does not berate us but responds with some understanding. The article is in number 10 of the journal *Christentum und Gegenwart* from October 1915, which is published in Nuremberg, Ebnergasse 10, Buchhandlung des Vereins für innere Mission. As I said, when you read this article, do not misunderstand this pointer. But after I said that it would be good to get to know the ideas that the spiritual life outside associates with us, you might also be interested if something appears occasionally that does the opposite of what usually happens with our movement. The article is called: 'Two Buildings of a German Future (Dornach and Elmau)'. Elmau was founded by Dr Müller.[72] It is with great understanding that this article in particular points out what distinguishes the Dornach building from the building in Elmau. Perhaps I may read out this passage. I shouldn't read out another passage because there is too much talk about me; but perhaps I may read out the following:

> Even if you see Dr Müller only a little and only at times when he is weary, you always get the impression how much he is personally serious about the life he talks about and how much unceasing inner effort for this life is present in his soul. The 'Mainbergers' themselves—well, of course there are all kinds of people among them and not all of them likeable, as is also the case among the 'anthroposophists', but time and again you meet people who make you glad that there are such people, men and women, for whose inner life and striving you gain every respect. It would be highly interesting to compare the kind of inner work people do on themselves in Dornach and in Mainberg-Elmau. What a telling difference, even outwardly, between the folk costume-like women's garments in Elmau and the stole-like, serious, but in part very tasteful women's garments you see in Dornach! Or when you become aware that both in Dornach and in Mainberg-Elmau emphasis is placed on free natural bodily movement, that in Elmau this is expressed in the cultivation of the old German dance, while in Dornach there is a serious search for 'eurythmy', that is for a form of bodily representation of the spiritual, initially for example in the recitation of poetry in which the actual inner experiences of the body in human speech are also expressed outwardly. Many Christians who still have the old disregard for the body in their blood will understand the one as little as the other.

Basically, what Rittelmeyer is saying here is that they want to rehash the old in Elmau and we want to create something new here. We can be quite satisfied with that. It is very pleasing to see that there are after all some people who have an understanding of the spiritual-scientific movement, while it is smeared before the world in such an unpleasant way by those who do not want to learn about it.

Now Mr von Wrangell goes on to say:

> The occult faculties, like the sensory faculties in the earthly life of the human being, are said to be of very different degrees. The highest level of initiation attainable at the present time enables

the human being, in an awake state and in full possession of their spiritual faculties, to go with the 'I' at will into higher spiritual worlds, up to that world where the Akasha Chronicle provides information about the past of the world as a whole and each individual human being.

So, on the whole, we can very much agree with the presentation. It is only necessary to know what our spiritual-scientific movement wants in particular and to focus sharply on this. For it is indeed necessary that it should not be confused with others who are also concerned with the spiritual worlds, but who lump everything together in one big mishmash and talk of deepening into the divine and so on. It is important to keep this firmly in mind.

This is followed by the chapter:

Secret Doctrines

The results of the knowledge gained by the occult researcher were previously only communicated in occult schools but are now partly revealed in writings and lectures accessible to everyone. These communications naturally in form and content bear the stamp of the occult researcher's personality. Since they are stated to be based on occult observations, their truth can only be independently verified by people who possess the same degree of occult gifts and the same power of judgement. For judgements must first be derived from the observations made in the spiritual world and these conclusions must be translated into the language of the earthly sensory world in order to be able to communicate them to fellow human beings.

On the other hand, it should be pointed out that although the content of the spiritual worlds can only be explored if those abilities are present of which we have spoken, basically really anyone can examine what has been explored. For the world that everyone can observe is in a certain sense a reflection of the spiritual world into which we can look through the faculty of spiritual observation. And if a person just looks at the world around them with really open eyes and asks themselves: Is that which is explored in the world of spiritual reality by the occult researcher in accordance with what is happening in life, then they can—even without developing occult abilities—judge everything. It is not that you cannot form a judgement, when people say you have to 'trust' the occult researcher, but that you do not want to engage in any verification. What is said by spiritual science proves itself in life and in the world, and everyone can verify it. Those who say they cannot verify these things are basically saying: I don't want to engage with whether you can verify the teachings of spiritual science in life and in the world; I don't want to engage with this wakeful perception, I want to sleep with my reason and my power of judgement. And because people are so fond of sleeping with their reason and their power of judgement, that is why they say: You cannot verify it.

But, again and again, I want to impress upon the world, so to speak, that it is important that spiritual science is not accepted on authority but can be verified by what happens in the sensory world. It is only because science still observes in a sensory way that it does not engage in a spiritually awake consideration of life. That is why the correctness of what the spiritual researcher says is not accepted. And that is why I try not to lean on any authority, not to lay claim to any faith, but I endeavour again and again to show by this or that in outer science, in philosophical strivings, how people stand before the spiritual world and only do not want to admit to themselves that they ought to go further. You need not rely on authority but only have open eyes, then the striving in spiritual science proves to be a real and necessary one in our time.

On the other hand, you must be aware that some of what is called spiritual science is capable of blocking people's minds to the real spiritual world. This is the case with worldviews that otherwise mean well, for example Eucken's. But they blind people by speaking of spirit in words, words, words, which, however, mean nothing other than what is given by the physical reflection of the soul. There is no need to be unjust about it. You can see it in my book *The Riddles of Philosophy*[73] undertaken in such a way that it cannot be called unjust what is to be said about such people as Eucken. But you also have to know that the view towards a correct spiritual science is obstructed by an incorrect one. It is infinitely more comfortable to speak of the spiritual in Eucken's way than to engage with the real spirit, which can be investigated.

The next chapter:

Difference between sensory science and spiritual science

> In this they differ essentially from the truths that can be obtained by means of the ordinary senses, since here the verification of the facts can be undertaken by innumerable people and the logical concatenation of them is subject to the judgement of each. In the case of occult findings, the most important criterion for the credibility of the communication from an occult researcher is the moral value of their personality.

That is not the important thing, but the important thing is that they stand on the ground of true spiritual striving, that they endeavour to lead people into the spiritual world in the right way. If we see the paths that lead into ordinary science and can thereby conceive of the possibility of how it might be carried forward, then we get documents that do not incur the caveat that we simply believe the spiritual researcher as a decent human being.

> If there are reasons to doubt their truthfulness, their occult communications are naturally of little value.

That would be just the same as if, when someone has achieved something in ordinary science, we made our personal approval of their research dependent on their personality.

> If there is no confidence in their power of judgement in ordinary life, it is highly improbable that they would stand the test under the infinitely difficult circumstances, for example, of investigating the Akasha Chronicle.

It is possible, after all, to investigate whether what has been discovered from the Akasha Chronicle corresponds to life.

> But even with unusual occult gifts, with the highest development of the intellect, with complete lack of bias of the investigator, it is not likely that human beings who are never infallible in earthly matters should be so in transcendental ones.

We should not speak of infallibility at all, but of course only of the fact that it is a matter of the spiritual scientist representing things from a certain point of view. But that basically has nothing to do with the way we relate to the communications of the occult researcher.

> We are therefore compelled to approach the communications of the occult researcher with considerably harsher criticism than is called for in the case of any witness of earthly observations.

So no approach with rejection or criticism. Most of what is done is rejection *without* criticism; if it were rejection *with* criticism, there wouldn't be half as much rejection.

> A more or less reliable sense of their likelihood must guide the inner agreement of the various communications, but above all the trust in the person of the occult researcher.

So we must not get the wrong idea about such trust. In contrast, what comes next is particularly important:

> If their communications from those worlds which are inaccessible to most human beings contradict what has been unmistakably proven by means of sensory perception, no unbiased person will waver as to which communication is to be preferred. If, for example, I really know all the facts which support the idea that the earth revolves freely floating in space, and an occult researcher tells me that they have ascertained from occult perceptions that the earth does not revolve, but that the fixed stars move around the earth, a person with sound senses will not pay any attention to such occult research.

So occult science must agree with external science; and if it does not agree, it must state why and try to harmonize with science.

> Of course, such a contradiction can only refer to facts of the sensory world, that is, not to transcendental questions that lie beyond all sensory experience.

Nevertheless, the transcendental questions can also be considered.

> Thus, to take another example, an astronomer who considers the Kant-Laplace hypothesis of the origin of the solar system probable cannot, as in the former case, tell the occult researcher who informs them of a quite different cosmogony that his assertion is erroneous,

> for every sane person will regard the rotation of the earth as proven, whereas the origin of the solar system from a nebula, according to the Kant-Laplace hypothesis, may well be regarded as probable, but not as proven.

Mr von Wrangell says this quite correctly. I have always pointed out the inadequacy of the Kant-Laplace hypothesis that the world formed out of a primordial nebula, which is already shown to children in school with the well-known experiment. You pour a drop of oil onto water, pierce it with a needle to which a section of card is attached, turn, move this needle and then see how the individual drops split off. You then immediately have the process of the emergence of a system of worlds, if you ignore yourself in the process. But when you do this experiment, it should be so that you point out that the teacher is there, turning the needle, because otherwise you also forget the teacher, the great one who turns the system of worlds.

> So, it is my deepest conviction that in a dispute between really proven facts of the sensory world and results of occult research, victory will always remain on the side of science.

There will be no victory, but when the facts of sensory science are reliably investigated and, on the other hand, the facts of spiritual science are reliably investigated, they will agree.

> When some occultists express the view that there is nothing fixed in earthly science, this is only possible for those who are acquainted with sciences only at second hand, but not with the foundations in question.
>
> However, the leading theosophists of Europe at the present time, Mrs A Besant, Dr R Steiner and others, claim that there is no contradiction between their occult researches and the reliable results of earthly science, and Dr Steiner, in particular, is well qualified to judge this through his extensive and thorough knowledge of the exact sciences in their methods. Whether the occult researcher is mistaken in this may be left open, and in my opinion is not of great importance, for if such a contradiction were proved, it seems to me that the question whether the basic teachings of theosophy correspond to the truth or not would not be touched by it. All these teachings refer to areas that lie beyond sensory experience, so they can neither be confirmed nor refuted by science based exclusively on sensory perceptions.

This is important because it shows that the person who professes to be a scientist comes from his scientific conviction to the view that a spiritual worldview is necessary, and that a person is necessarily led to it if they are a scientific person in our time.

The next chapter is headed:

Theosophy—a religion

> These theosophical teachings claim to give people information about the purpose and goal of the world as a whole and of individual human life, and thus to be a religious worldview.

My dear friends, it is necessary that we are clear that spiritual science proper, our spiritual-scientific movement, really has nothing directly to do with religion, that it does not want to be a religious movement. Let us be clear that in relation to the religious life, spiritual science can also give nothing other than an inner relationship between the human soul and Christ. That is the religious moment, that is the religious element, but that is Christianity. Hegel and especially spiritual science acknowledge that Christianity is the fulfilment of humanity's religious aspirations, that the foundation of new religions will neither take place nor can take place. We should get to know the spiritual facts and spiritual science is a new instrument for this, but it does not want to establish a new religion. It does not want to set itself up as a new movement alongside Christianity but only provides the research, just as Copernicus provided his discovery.

But what was it like at that time? In the fifteenth century Copernicus came along and gave what he had to give, but it was not until 1822 that the Catholic Church allowed people to believe in the Copernican teaching.[74] And Luther said:[75] The new astrologer, Copernicus, wants to prove that the earth moves and not the heavens, the sun and the moon. Now think how long it took for Copernicus to be accepted. Now, if people come and say that it is a fantasy to teach repeated earth lives, that is understandable, but it is not up to us to teach people an opinion as if it were a question of founding a new religion. Christianity is the synthesis, the confluence of the world religions. Through spiritual science we want to learn to understand Christian truths better than they can be understood without spiritual science. But we do not want to leave it in people's minds that in theosophy they are dealing with a new religion, with a new religious worldview. Spiritual science must defend itself against this. It wants to be a science and thereby also deepen religious life. But religious life is also deepened by Copernicanism. Thus the Catholic theologian Müllner, of whom I spoke on the occasion of the recitation of delle Grazie's poems, said of Galileo in the [eighteen] nineties:[76] The person who is really a Christian and understands the religious relationship of the human soul to the divine worlds can only experience a deepening of the religious life by investigating the world more closely, and not a danger.

It must be emphasized time and again that it is a weakness to oppose what is brought by spiritual science in terms of deepening the religious. Imagine if Columbus had been told: Just make sure not to discover America; because there could be other people, other gods there. Imagine what a weakness that would be if we did not stand so firmly on the ground of Christianity as to be able to say: Whatever will be discovered, the ground of Christianity is so strong that it will withstand it! Therefore it is nothing but proof of the lameness of those who say we must reject spiritual science. You have to say to them: This is not Christianity if you believe that your teachings can be overturned by spiritual science. Copernicus did not overturn things either; on the contrary, religious life was deepened by him. It is weak lame-heartedness which, from an external, official, so-called Christian point of view wishes to imposes a fight on what spiritual science intends.

This is the position we must adopt against those who come to us with their dull, lame-hearted objections to theosophy.

> [The chapter 'Theosophy—a religion' is read to the end:] It seems doubtful whether any solution of the riddle of the universe can fully satisfy the critically educated person of the present day with regard to its rational justification. It will always be a question of the extent to which the spirit and mind of the human being are satisfied by the solution to the great, eternal questions presented to them. Since a rational argument for or against is not possible here, the feeling must decide on the greater or lesser probability of one or the other solution.

> We will compare some of the worldviews as they present themselves to the educated person of European culture from this perspective.

In the following chapters Wrangell then compares materialism, agnosticism and occultism with each other and then has a chapter on reincarnation and karma. He then arrives at Lessing's view of reincarnation[77] and a recapitulation of the whole strand of thought. There is not enough time to discuss the final chapters. We will therefore continue tomorrow at seven o'clock, because we still have some important things to say about the final chapters.

Fifth Lecture

DORNACH, 4 OCTOBER 1915

In our discussion of Wrangell's pamphlet we have come to the chapter which begins on page 37 and is entitled 'Materialism'. I will begin by reading this little chapter:

Materialism

> As previously stated, the materialist view recognizes only such findings as can be gained through sensory perceptions and logical conclusions based on them and denies the reality of occult perceptions. The sensory perceptions of most people do not provide direct evidence for the reality of spiritual forces and phenomena which are not bound to material bodies. From this the materialist concludes that the assumption of such forces and beings independent of matter is not justified, and declares the conclusions to be drawn from this to be worthless. According to them, world events are the necessary consequence of the forces and states present in matter from the beginning which permit only one course and which, according to the law of the dissipation of energy, must finally lead to the state of equilibrium, consequently to eternal death. The intellectual task of the human being was to investigate the laws according to which the course of such world evolution proceeds in order to endure as little suffering and waste of energy as possible by adapting to these laws. If the occult proofs for the existence of spiritual entities are rejected on principle, then logically there can be no objection to the materialistic outlook.

We indeed see characterized here in a few concise sentences the essence of the materialistic train of thought. But in order to achieve clarity about the whole significance of the materialistic worldview in our time, we must actually take various things into account.

We must be clear that those who have become honest materialists in our time do indeed find it difficult to arrive at a spiritualistic worldview. And when we speak of 'honest' opponents of spiritualism, we must first and foremost consider the theoretical materialists, for those people who believe from the outset, I would like to say 'professionally', that they must represent this or that worldview need not always be called 'honest' representatives of a worldview. But Ludwig Büchner, for example, was an honest representative of materialism in the second half of the nineteenth century, more honest than many who, from some religious point of view as they think, believe themselves to be opponents of a spiritual worldview in the sense of spiritual science.

Well, I said the materialists have a hard time coming to a spiritual worldview. For materialism as it appears to us today among those who say: Yes, the human being has their senses and perceives the world through the senses; they observe the processes which the senses can follow and cannot, on the basis of what the senses present to them, come to the assumption of a spiritual entity which is independent of the world of the senses—this materialism has emerged with a certain necessity from the development of modern humanity, for it is based on something which had to come in the development of modern humanity.

Anyone who takes the trouble to study the older spiritual life of humankind will find that it came to an end with the fourteenth, fifteenth and sixteenth centuries among the actual civilized peoples. Today we need only really look into what the present can give to the consciousness of the human being and then take a book in our hands which, with regard to its conception, still stands completely within the way in which the world was viewed scientifically in the thirteenth, fourteenth and fifteenth centuries; and we will find that the human being of today, if they take things seriously and with dignity, no longer has, and can no longer have, a correct understanding of what is really said in the older literature up to the turning point I indicated.

Of course it happens, but really only among those who are dilettantes, indeed even among those who have not yet become dilettantes, that they repeatedly dig out all kinds of page-turners from this older literature that deal with natural science and then come to all kinds of judgements about what is supposed to be contained profoundly in them. But anyone who values a true relationship with what they make their own will have to conclude that the human being of today cannot really have true relationships with this older way of looking at nature. It is different with the philosophical views. But the view of nature of more ancient times doesn't really mean a lot to the person of today because all the concepts they can form about nature are only a few centuries old, and we have to approach nature with these today. Our physical concepts basically all go back to the Galilean worldview and nothing earlier. It takes extensive historical academic study to engage with earlier works of natural science, for the precise investigation of the material world, the outer world of the senses in whose current we find ourselves today, has actually only begun in the last few centuries.

You will remember that we have just been talking about measurement in connection with Wrangell's booklet. Measuring also includes weighing, as we have seen. However, introducing weighing as an instrument in scientific methods has only been common since about Lavoisier, so it is not yet older in this way than 150 years, and all the basic ideas of today's chemistry, for example, are based on such weighing.

Again, if we want to develop ideas today, for example, about the action of electrical forces or even just of thermal forces, they must be those that take into account the research from the last half of the nineteenth century. People today can no longer cope with the older conceptions. Similarly we could say the same in relation to biological science. However, anyone who needs to know the evolution of science should also get to know the older literature; but we who want to cultivate spiritual science seriously must get out of the habit of what we so often encounter with so-called theosophists. I have often spoken about how, for example, I got to know a community of theosophists in Vienna in the [eighteen] eighties.[78] It was almost a kind of custom to pick out all kinds of old page-turners and read up on things that really weren't understood very well because basically it takes quite a lot to read a scientific work, for example from the fourteenth century. But people formed judgements. These judgements were always pretty much the same. Namely when someone once again pretended to have read such a book—they only leafed through it—they said 'profoundly deep'. Or some similar verdict. At the end of the eighties, I heard no phrase as often—relatively speaking of course—as the words 'profoundly deep'. Of course, I also often heard the word 'shallow'.

What we must bear in mind is the great significance of the views, concepts and ideas which have been acquired under the influence of the views of the last centuries. When you have experienced the explanations of the basic mechanical concepts, when you consider the abundance of physical, chemical and biological concepts, and also many things that have been collected in order to see how the soul expresses itself in the outer physical body, then we have before us as a result of the last centuries, and especially of the second half of the last century, tremendously extensive research results. And these research results must necessarily be acquired—not only because all external, technical, economic and material life which humanity has had to achieve is based on them but also because a large part of our conception of the world is based on them. And you are actually— even if in a certain respect it does no harm in a limited field, but it is true nevertheless—you are actually wet behind the ears in terms of a worldview such as that of today's science if you don't know anything about physics, biology and so on as they have developed today.

Certainly, it must be emphasized time and again that the research results of spiritual science are obtained on the basis of those perceptual abilities that have often been spoken about. They cannot be obtained in the same way, although with the same certainty, as the scientific-materialistic results. And of course—if you devote yourself to what was indicated yesterday—this spiritual science is a reality. But for our present time, for our present, much more is necessary than just somehow having a spiritual relationship with the results of spiritual science, which can certainly be grasped by common sense. It is much more necessary to familiarize ourselves with the materialistic worldview, at least with an extract of it, than to somehow snatch scraps of the spiritual world if we want to be able to really represent to the outside world today what spiritual science intends. For you cannot stand before the world and truly represent spiritual science if you have no idea of the way the scientist undertakes research today; how they must think and how they must manage research alongside elucidation. And if you always disdain to pick up a scientific book in order to acquaint yourself with the natural sciences of today, you will never be able to avoid committing clumsy acts when advocating the spiritual-scientific worldview in relation to that which is the sediment of the external worldview. Today it is also much less important to listen to the traditional systems of religion than to the honestly obtained respectable results of materialistic research. You just have to be able to relate to these materialistic-research results in the right way.

Just to show what we are dealing with at the present moment, let us pick out a field; let's take the field of human anatomy and physiology. If you pick up any common book today—and I have always recommended such books in the course of many cycles—you will get a picture of how the physiologist of today builds up their ideas about the structure of the human body on the basis of the bone system, the cartilage, tendon, muscle systems, the main nervous, blood, sensory systems, and so on. And a picture will emerge of how people today living in materialistic thoughts imagine the interaction, say, of the heart and the lungs, and again of the heart with the other vascular systems of the body. Then an answer can be found to the question: How does a person today, who has acquired their concepts from materialistic research, actually relate to these things? What conceptions do they actually have living within them? And here it has to be said: significant conceptions have indeed been obtained; conceptions that had to be obtained in such a way as to really refrain from anything spiritual, from bringing spiritual thoughts into research. It was simply necessary to get involved with the material realm as it presents itself to the five senses, as the saying goes, and with the connection that arises with the five senses. It was simply necessary to read the world in this way, and much remains to be done in this field, in all kinds of fields of scientific research.

But now suppose for a moment that you have acquired such a picture of the structure of the human body as the anatomist and physiologist have today, then you will find that the anatomist and the physiologist say: Well, the human being is built up of various organs and organ systems, and these work together in a certain way.

You see, when today the anatomist, the physiologist, speaks and summarizes their conceptions into an overall picture of the human being, then within this picture, underlying the same, sensory observation remains. This gives rise to very specific conceptions that can be taken up. But you have to relate to them in the right way. I can perhaps make this clear by way of a comparison. For example, someone could say: I want to meet Raphael; what do I have to do? I would say to them: If you want to get to know Raphael, then try to immerse yourself in Raphael's paintings; study the *Marriage of the Virgin* from the Milan paintings, then the various paintings up to the *Sistine Madonna*, up to the *Assumption*, and get an idea of how Raphael tried to distribute the figures in space; how he tried to distribute light and shadow, to enliven one place in the picture at the expense of the other, to make one stand out and the other recede, and so on, then you will know something about Raphael. Then you will perhaps be prepared to learn even more about Raphael; then you will gradually get a picture of the configuration of Raphael's soul, of what he wanted, of the sources in his mind from which the creations emerged. Now, you could imagine someone coming and saying: Oh, looking at the paintings, that doesn't suit me. I'm a clairvoyant and I look directly into Raphael's soul, see how Raphael created and then talk about Raphael. I can imagine someone coming and saying: I don't need to see anything by Raphael at all, but immerse myself directly in Raphael's soul. Naturally this would be considered nonsense in Raphael studies, but in the field of spiritual science it is practised a great deal, a great deal, despite the many warnings in all the years that we have been doing spiritual science. You could see how few felt compelled to use the literature that has been mentioned in the course of the lecture-cycles and to use it in such a way as to get a picture of what materialistic research has delivered.

But just as you would go wrong if you stopped at the picture and did not want to progress to the soul element which is expressed through the picture, so the materialist stops. What you could say to the materialist, for example, is this: Yes, you are looking at a picture, but you do not consider that what you are looking at should be seen as the outer revelation of a spiritual inwardness. But it is true that materialistic research has gathered an immense wealth of material. If you consider this as an outer revelation of a spiritual inwardness, you are on the right path. The materialist only makes the mistake of having the material and not wanting to accept that it is the expression of something spiritual. But on the other hand you will always remain in the wrong if you claim something spiritual and the materialist tells you things of which you have no idea. Of course, you can survey the abundant field of research and still have no clue about a great many things; but you have to have an idea of the way things are acquired. And if our School of Spiritual Science will serve to enable a number of people who have studied one or other of these fields to interpret the basic materialistic conditions that are necessary according to the present development, then our School of Spiritual Science will accomplish a great deal.

We could certainly do it today by saying that the material laid down in our cycles could suffice; we could conclude with this and use the time ahead to demonstrate to our friends the basic material preconditions that must be in place. You will then certainly see, if you look at today's physics, chemistry and biology in a corresponding way, that what is in our cycles will result. Then you would have adopted the right attitude towards materialism.

People are on completely the wrong track, my dear friends, when they talk about materialism being wrong. What nonsense! To say that materialism is wrong is just like saying: The *Sistine Madonna* has blue here, red there, surely that's wrong, it's only matter. Materialism is right in its field; and if we take what it has contributed to human knowledge, it is something immense. It is not necessary to fight materialism but only to show in its development how materialism, when it comprehends itself, leads beyond itself, just as I have shown how anatomy and physiology lead beyond themselves and necessarily lead into the spiritual field.

All we can do is ask: Why are there so many people who, instead of accepting materialism as a mere method of research, stop at it as a worldview? The right thing to say would be that today it would indeed be something completely perverse and foolish to do alchemy instead of chemistry; you have to do chemistry today and not alchemy like in the twelfth century. That goes without saying. But it is necessary to ascend from today's research into spiritual life. If our friends would only take the trouble to study the little booklet *Haeckel and His Opponents*,[79] they would find that all its underlying thoughts are dominated by the basic biogenetic law. It is quite telling that we have not yet managed to publish a second edition of this little text *Haeckel and His Opponents*. And yet it is extremely important to keep informed, even if not about the latest research results—you don't necessarily need to know them in detail—but about the way the researcher proceeds and how they follow their research method. This is of exceptional importance.

If someone says: I don't need to study that book; what do I need to do that for?; for me the spiritual world is clear from the beginning; I don't have to clamber up that ladder—if someone says that, they are today an egoist who only thinks of themselves and does not consider what the time demands of us. But we must pay attention to these things if we want to render service to the spirit of the time. It is extremely important that we focus on these things in particular. Certainly a person has a right to say: Why do I need a scientific basis?; for me the spiritual world is clear. That may be true. But if we want to learn something in the field of the spiritual world—we can of course do it in such a way that we interpret what is there—but if we want to learn something, we must familiarize ourselves with what exists in materialistic science.

On the other hand, we must ask: How is it that there are many anatomists, physiologists, physicists, chemists and so on today as natural scientists, and even those who call themselves experimental psychologists, and that they want to hold on to materialism not as a research method but as a worldview? Here we must in all honesty have the courage to answer: In order to do materialistic research, it is only necessary to stare at the world with the five senses and to use the external methods. You only need to surrender passively to the world, then you are firmly in place. Pulling apart a plant, counting the stamens, taking the microscope, staining a cross-section to then study the structure and so on—I could of course list many more things—that's what people are capable of. All you have to do is stand there, just be passive and let nature have its effect on you. You let nature take over.

I called this the dogmatism of experience in the very first writings I published. The dogmatism of experience is what people adhere to. You can read what I say about the dogmatism of experience in my book *Goethe's Theory of Knowledge. An Outline of the Epistemology of His Worldview*.[80] I also subsequently called it 'fact fanaticism'. But in order to enter the spiritual world, it is necessary to work inwardly; inward activity is necessary for this. And that is where people can definitely run out of steam. You can see in our time that the steam has run out. If you make comparisons in the field of anatomy, for example, you will find that you can almost point your finger at the point where the steam has run out.

Take the anatomist Hyrtl, who was replaced as professor by the anatomist Langer. Compare the writings of the two scientifically, and you will see how, in the succession of the two scholars, one is absolutely clear about the fact that there is something spiritual behind the external and the other is no longer concerned about it. Why is that? Because, commendable as materialism is as a method of research, having thereby produced great and mighty things without which people today could not live, people have been too lazy to bring up into active life what they have grasped. Laziness, real inertia of spirit has made people persist in materialism. Because materialism became so dominant and claimed to be reality, that is why people did not ascend into the spiritual. It is laziness and inertia, and we must have the courage to see this reason.

Immerse yourself in the fields of scientific research and you will see that this scientific research is great and worthy of admiration. If you immerse yourself in all that is fabricated by the monists and other associations as 'worldviews', you will see that they are based on a laziness and inertia, on an ossification of thought. This is what must be clearly understood, that we must distinguish—if we stand on the ground of true spiritual science—between the entirely justified materialistic research methods and research results and the so-called materialistic worldview.

Mostly, those who research materialistically cannot think at all, because it is easier to research materialistically than to think spiritually. I will give you an example to illustrate that the materialists simply stumble when they want to advance from the materialistic method of research to a worldview. So let's say I have tried to obtain an atomistic worldview. So I want to say: Bodies consist of atoms. You have to think of these in motion, so that when you have a material object in front of you, it consists—this is how we must think of it—of atoms. There are spaces between the atoms. The atoms are in motion, and through the motion—according to the materialistic worldview—heat is generated. If you were to say: Heat is the result of the movement of atoms, then you would be right; then you would only be affirming something. But you come to the view that it is impossible to speak of the atoms as something that actually exists. The atoms are thought up—and they must be thought up if they are to have any meaning—but what is observed is supposed to be caused in the first place by the atoms. So you can't see an atom. You can see, the so-called atomistic view of the world is composed of nothing visible, of nothing perceptible by the senses.

But now you can reflect and say: The world consists of atoms and these are in motion. People want to investigate the nature of the movement that underlies heat, light, magnetism, electricity and so on, and they come to assume that certain movements of the atoms are the causes of the sensory perception. So you end up with atoms. So you divide up what is given and if you divide over and over again you must eventually arrive at the indivisible, and that is the atom. Divisible atoms are meaningless. The last pieces, that is, the atoms, must be indivisible. Nowadays, however, people also want to explain movement from the atoms—I can only indicate this, but you can pursue it further in the philosophical scientific literature of more recent times—they want to explain movement from the nature of the atoms. But if you think about how one atom has to collide with another so that the movement can result that you have with heat, electricity and so on, then you cannot think of the atoms rigidly, then you have to think of them elastically. It is necessary to think of them as elastic, for rigid atoms would not give the movement in a collision that must result if heat, electricity or magnetism are to result.

So these atoms must be elastic. But what does that mean? It means that the atom can be compressed and then springs back to its former state. So it has to be compressible and spring back again, otherwise you can't conceive of the collision of the atoms at all. Now we have won two things: first, the atom must be indivisible; second, it must be elastic. Modern thinking, which pays homage to atomism, stands behind these two things. The atom must be thought indivisible, otherwise it is no longer an atom, and it must be thought elastic, for it would be a senseless idea to attribute atomic motion to rigid atoms. English thinkers in particular have emphasized these two propositions very keenly: firstly, the atom is indivisible, and secondly, the atom must be thought of as elastic. If I allow a body to be elastic, it is inconceivable other than that the parts are compressed and then spring back into the original position to produce the elastic body. The latter is inconceivable without being divisible, moveable. But the atom must be indivisible on the one hand and divisible on the other, otherwise it cannot be elastic. But what does that mean?

This means that if we want to imagine atoms, we come up with two contradictory basic assumptions. You can't get beyond these. There is tremendously interesting literature on thinking of our image of the world as composed of non-rigid atoms. But then the atom is no longer an atom, because it must be thought of as divisible. That is, you come to the conclusion that the idea of the atom is impossible as long as you assume that the atom is material. In the moment when you think the atom is not material, when you think the atom is not something material but something else, the atom can be thought of as indivisible, just as the human I is also thought of as indivisible. If you assume that the atom is a force, then you can also think of it as being composite. If you don't think materialistically, you don't need to think that there are spaces in between. So the two things are quite compatible if we think of atoms as non-material.

If, taking careful account of what optics, the theory of electricity and so on offer us, we draw the final conclusions as to how the atom must be, then we come to say: The atom cannot be material. This is where of necessity you enter into the spiritual. But you have to take this step. It then makes no difference whether the atom is elastic or rigid. We don't care about that; we don't go along with that. But materialism must not be fought, but understood. The great sum of work and positive achievements must not be scorned by spiritual science.

Let us now move on to the next chapter of Wrangell's text:

Doubts about the materialistic worldview

> But doubt arises in the mind of many a person: should it really be the case that the world as a whole is not based on any rational, any moral thought, and that the concepts of the purposeful, the moral, arise only in the human breast, but have no validity outside it?
>
> We feel within us the striving towards good and the concept of good is inseparable from the concept of freedom, for where there is absolute necessity, there is nothing evil or good. A stone must fall in a certain direction at a certain speed and it would be pointless to call this fall evil or good.
>
> Should that which we feel in our innermost being to be the actual measure of life's value be only deception and delusion, and should this idea of the good, that is, of morality chosen in freedom, not be found in the world as a whole, of which the human being is only a negligible fraction? Should the minor part, the human being, endowed with sublime feelings and thoughts, stand higher in this respect than the whole, which, without consciousness, without a concept of purpose, follows its course like dead clockwork, ending in eternal death? Most people's minds resist such a solution and look for another.

It is good to speak of the mind resisting this, but it is much more important in our time to say that the thinking resists it. If you only want to stand on the ground of materialism, you have to go to the atom and conceive of it as matter. But you can also call it a force, and then you come to the conclusion that where matter is thought to be, that is where the cosmic world of thought is. Then the moral world order has its entire place in it.

Now, however, some have found it more convenient to say: Well, if you think about the world in this way, scruples and doubts arise everywhere for sensory knowledge, and it is not acceptable to allow such sensory knowledge to apply solely and exclusively; but it is simply the case that the human being is predisposed not to be able to penetrate deeper. This results in approximately the following situation: here stands the human being who is perhaps a very good researcher in the field of the outer sensory world and who can produce enduring, beautiful, great things as a materialistic researcher, but they are not inclined to enter further into it. And so they say: There must be all kinds of things behind matter; but we are not capable of penetrating there with the human faculty of cognition. They call themselves agnostic. They do not realize that such words, the human being does not have the ability and so on, are inspired by Ahriman, and they do not hear what good spirits inspire them with; that they don't listen to. In truth, they are just lazy. It's called laziness when you are honest; it's called agnosticism in science.

The next chapter in Wrangell is now called:

Agnosticism

> The answer to the question as to the origin and goal of the world as a whole and as to the destiny of the human being, which offers the least difficulty to the intellect but leaves the demands of the mind completely unsatisfied, is the standpoint of the agnostic ('one who does not know'), when they say: These questions exceed the limits of human cognition, must therefore, by their very nature, remain unanswered, and it is more reasonable to devote one's time and energies to tasks where there is a prospect of managing them.

There is nothing wrong with saying: I want to devote myself to a task that I can manage. That lies in the freedom of the human being. But it is not within the human being's freedom to say: What I do not know, no one else may know. All philosophizing about what the human being cannot know is basically scientific infamy, and what's more, it is unparalleled scientific grandstanding because you set yourself up as the ruler of what may and may not be researched, because you set up what you yourself want to assume as authoritative for everyone else.

What impotence lies in the words: 'There are limits to cognition'! But we should also realize what arrogance and self-regard lie therein. This should not be whispered into ears, but shouted out.

> Without denying the existence of spiritual entities, the agnostic claims that this field is at any rate not accessible to everyone, whereas everything based on sensory experience is within the realm of knowledge of the normal human being and they should be content with that. Those people in whom the critically trained intellect prevails can persist in this point of view without becoming paralyzed in their actions; but for most people this answer is no answer at all. If we place ourselves in the position of a person without personal occult experiences and without knowledge of reports of others about such perceptions which appear credible to them, then, logically judged, they are free to express themselves for or against the existence of spiritual worlds.

Of course, in human interaction everyone is free to speak out against the existence of a spiritual world. But we should be clear that such a statement is worthless. You can also argue against three times three being nine.

> But they are not entitled to deny scholarly status to the opposing view.
>
> The degree of credibility of the reports of others cannot be measured with objective, i.e. universally valid rigour, and the judgement on this is necessarily influenced by subjective motives in each individual case.

Yes, that can be shown.

> If it is a matter of facts that can be checked by any normal person, then in most cases a person does not need to take the trouble to check them personally because with the present organization of scientific research it is assured that an erroneous observation or false report will soon be discovered, and this forces every observer and reporter to be as careful and truthful as possible for the sake of their reputation alone, and in any case an observation error does not remain undiscovered for long.

Basically, that doesn't say much more than if someone were to state the following: With the way scientific work is organized today, if you go to Basel and buy a chemistry book you can already believe what is written in it because it contains chemical results, and it cannot occur to a chemist to lie. But all that does is legitimize the belief in authority. And if people were to admit this to themselves, they would realize how much they accept in good faith today. I have often emphasized that spiritual science is at its beginnings but can be tested. Spiritual science is still young; when it has grown older, then the same will apply with regard to the spiritual scientist as applies today with regard to the chemist: people will then realize that in spiritual science there is no lying.

> With occult perceptions, on the other hand, it is different, and this essential difference has so long caused the men of exact science, who are accustomed to controllable facts, to be not only critical, that is scrutinizing, but sceptical, that is directly defensive, towards occult communications.

The real reason is that they are too lazy.

> Now, however, this no longer seems possible, for the evidence for the immaterial existence of spiritual entities is so weighty that men of undoubted scientific training consider this question proven. Suffice it to recall names like Zöllner, Wallace, du Prel, Crookes, Butlerow, Rochas, Oliver Lodge, Flammarion, Morselli, Schiaparelli, Ochorowicz, James and others.

Here Mr von Wrangell relies on those who draw on atavistic faculties, whereas we assume that every human being can acquire the faculties that enable us to test the spiritual in the same way as we test the scientific.

> Not only do these men find no contradiction between occult facts and established results of exact sensory research, but their very habituation to unprejudiced criticism leads them to reject the scepticism of the materialist and to devote themselves to the study of occult phenomena.

But they do not do it in the right way; they drag everything down to the same laboratory level at which chemistry is located, even those things that can only be attained in free activity of thought. Instead of being inwardly creative, they go around with the yardstick, as it were, and measure.

> These authorities may be mistaken in their judgement, but their standpoint can serve as proof that we are justified in supposing the existence of spiritual entities without exposing ourselves to the reproach of scientific ignorance. Assuming that we have no occult abilities ourselves, we have to rely on the reports of others and test them for their credibility.

It would be better if we tried to engage with what is said in *Knowledge of the Higher Worlds. How is it Achieved?*. It is much easier than many think. Most people just don't acknowledge it; but all kinds of complexities are acknowledged. It would really be relatively very easy to experience in a few years at least as much of the spiritual world as is necessary to recognize it in general. But people say: That's not anything; because they strive for what I have called gut clairvoyance.[81] And if there is no gut clairvoyance, then it all counts for nothing to them.

> The sources of error in occult perceptions lie in both the subject and the object. Even a cursory examination of the perceptual material piled up by spiritualists and other occultists shows us that here, admittedly, the sources of error flow abundantly ...

They truly do not. It is no different from saying: Nature never lies! But it lies all the time. Take a glass of water and put a stick in it, it will appear broken to you; but it isn't. Take the passage of the sun across the celestial vault, compare its size in the morning and its size at noon: all day long, nature is lying to you. The spiritual world lies just as much and just as little. For example, it is exceedingly interesting to visualize the processes in the etheric part of the human being when you have an ailment in the intestines, or to observe what the etheric body does when the digestive processes are occurring. It is just as interesting as when you ordinarily study anatomy or physiology, indeed even more interesting. But what is not justified is to regard something which is nothing other than a process in the etheric body during digestion as a grand process of the cosmic world. So the spiritual world itself does not lie; you just have to interpret it in the right way. Nor is it necessary to despise what goes on in the etheric body during digestion. We just have to avoid misunderstanding it. Nor are the senses deceptive in reality. If you reach into the water, you will find with your sense of touch ... [Gap in the transcript]. Over time, natural science has acquired good rules through study while it is believed in spiritual science that the fewer studies a person has undergone, the better they are suited to it.

So: 'Even a superficial acquaintance with the perceptual material piled up by spiritualists and other occultists shows us that here, admittedly, the sources of error flow abundantly ...'

> for they lie not only, as in the sensory world, in the subject but moreover in the object, in that numerous malignant entities shall make it their task to mislead the inquiring human being. If we could rightly say of ordinary sensory perceptions: nature never lies, only human beings sometimes misunderstand it—it is different in the spiritual world, according to the occult researchers. Thus if the reality of spiritual phenomena independent of matter is conceded, it is a great and difficult task to separate the wheat from the chaff there. This is the task of spiritual science, which, if it is to be pursued seriously, requires all the time and strength of a person, as is the case, incidentally, with every other branch of knowledge, though perhaps to a lesser extent.
>
> For the majority of people, however, such studies are neither possible nor even necessary. Just as a person can be a Christian and find comfort and edification in the teachings of Jesus, see the moral ideal realized in his person without being a theologian, so a person can recognize in the basic teachings of theosophy an interpretation of the actual meaning and purpose of their own life without being familiar with the extensive edifice of occult science.

This is an assertion that cannot be sustained without further qualification, for if people are not chemists by training, if they are not biologists by training, it is nevertheless possible to live today. But the human being will progressively have to know those things that belong to the world to which the human soul itself belongs. It is a kind of unjustified rejection to say that in order to be a theosophist you do not need to be familiar with occult science any more than you need to be a theologian in order to be a Christian.

> That worldview will be most conducive to the human being's actions and sensibilities which most satisfies both their intellect and their feelings.

The next chapter is headed:

Continued existence of the soul after death

> If we assume that the spiritual principle in the human being, that which is described by the word soul, is an entity which continues to exist even after the death of the body, then various ideas are possible concerning its further fate, of which we shall only consider here the Christian conception and the teaching of reincarnation as being the most important for us at present. The teachings of Christ have been a source of comfort and moral strength to millions and are likely to continue to be so. However, it cannot be denied that for the scientifically educated European difficulties of an intellectual nature have accumulated and do not allow the struggle between faith and knowledge to be balanced on the basis of Christian doctrine. The existing contradiction requires a sacrifice, either of the intellect or of the mind. In addition to these intellectual difficulties, some people have grave moral misgivings about the usual understanding of Christianity. All Christian denominations teach that after death the soul of the human being endures a fate that is eternal: eternal salvation or eternal damnation. Every human being probably feels that this belief contradicts the demand for justice. The basis of all morality is justice.

If only people knew a little more! Of course, Wrangell is right when he says that you cannot speak of eternal salvation and eternal damnation in this way, since they contradict justice. Because 'eternal' is an absurdity if you believe that it is something infinite. 'Eternal' is only an age, an aeon, and actually, even in Christianity, we should not speak of 'eternal' in any other way than as an age, and that corresponds roughly to the time between death and a new birth.

> In every human breast there lies deep and unshakable the desire that to each be done as they merit. The view of merit is admittedly changing; also the appreciation of what has been experienced and felt. But there can be no doubt that human beings would be happier, better, more satisfied if they had the conviction that the events of the world as a whole also correspond to the demand for justice in the individual case. We do not see justice prevailing in what we experience in ourselves and others in the course of our physical life, regardless of whether we use soul, spiritual or physical suffering and joy as a measure of the value of what we have experienced. According

to the teachings of the Christian Churches, this apparent injustice of earthly life is to be compensated for in the hereafter; but it is basically made infinitely worse by the everlasting consequences of temporal transgressions or merits.

It goes without saying that Wrangell is speaking only of what the Christian Churches say, which arose after Justinian had closed the Greek philosophical schools. But he overlooks the fact that we have the task of making such blocked wisdom accessible to humanity again. You do have to look for the right reasons. It could also be shown that those who teach Christianity today do not teach true Christianity, but one that has been made to fit.

The next chapter is called:

Reincarnation and Karma

The teaching of reincarnation and karma, on the other hand, offers us the possibility of resolving the visible injustice of a life's destiny by the fact that it was self-inflicted in previous lives and that there is the possibility of rectifying it for subsequent reincarnations.

Such faith, when it becomes inner certainty, gives a person the strength to bear their fate, even the hardest one, without inner rebellion, and spurs them on to improve it for the future by following the voice we call 'conscience'.

The sense of responsibility present in our consciousness is strengthened and the danger of humanity seeking to exploit the short span of temporal life in sensual frenzy and selfishness would be eliminated. The teaching of reincarnation and karma sets the human being free, because it makes them reliant on themselves.

Certainly, the great riddle of the 'wherefore' of the whole remains unresolved, but the purpose and task of the individual life are clear and determined.

The next chapter makes reference to the conclusion of Lessing's *The Education of the Human Race*:

Lessing's view on the teaching of reincarnation

Is this hypothesis [of reincarnation] so ridiculous because it is the oldest? Because the human mind, before it was distracted and weakened

> by sophistry and school, immediately succumbed to it? Why should I not return as often as I am sent to gain new knowledge, new skills? Do I suddenly take away so much that it is not worth the effort to come back?
>
> According to the teaching of reincarnation, it is our lot to live on this earth until we reach our destination: Knowledge of God, which is self-knowledge. Death is not annihilation; the consciousness of our I, our actual being, merely enters another body. Even the suicide does not escape, they only cut the thread of life that must be reattached according to inexorable laws.

So said Lessing. Those were powerful words. But these were also the words of a man who had the education of his time within him and was necessarily led to the teaching of reincarnation by what this and Christianity could give him. We see here the remarkable learning; we see the critic of history. But now people say: Of course Lessing is a great man; he wrote *Nathan* and so on, that's good, but, having grown old, he indulged in such fanciful reveries as the teaching of reincarnation; there is no going along with that. Well, clearly the private tutor is much cleverer than Lessing became in old age. Many people believe, after all, that they are much cleverer than Lessing, although they are prepared to recognize that he might be a great man. We should at least realize the ridiculousness of such recognition; realize that we must strive for what Lessing had worked his way towards in the end. We should realize the ridiculousness of not wanting to follow as far as this most mature fruit of Lessing's thought, let alone refusing to consider what has followed in more recent intellectual life. These people speak without addressing the actual basic core that already underlies modern intellectual life, but which is a closed book for many who interpret it. Well, Wrangell goes on to say:

> We know from what Eckermann and Boisserée said that Goethe also believed in reincarnation. Kant says in his 'Lectures on Psychology': 'The beginning of life is birth, but this is not the beginning of the soul's life but of the human being; birth, life and death are thus only states of the soul ... Therefore the substance remains, although the body passes away, and therefore the substance must also have been there when the body came into being.'

Now the last chapter follows:

Brief summary of the line of reasoning

Let us try to briefly summarize the line of reasoning set out above.

The concept of lawfulness, the necessary concatenation of cause and effect in events, is not an original cognition. On the contrary, immediate consciousness gives us the conception of conditional freedom.

The concept of lawfulness, on which every science is based, probably first appeared to human beings from observation of the chronologically regular course of celestial phenomena. Then this concept was applied with ever increasing success to the inanimate phenomena (physics, chemistry), then to the animate ones, finally also to the spiritual ones.

The concept of lawfulness can only be tested and irrevocably proven in such phenomena that can be quantitatively determined, that can be measured.

The extension of the idea of necessity from the material to the spiritual is an assumption which, by analogy with what happens in the material, can be granted a certain probability, but which cannot be proven because the touchstone of measurability is missing here.

Numerous facts, verified by discerning men of science, do not permit any truth-seeking person to deny the existence of spiritual beings without providing evidence as to why they reject the facts in question and their evidential value.

The basic teachings of theosophy—reincarnation and karma—do not contradict any scientific fact, satisfy the intellect and, better than other teachings, satisfy the basis of all morality—the demand for fairness.

Faith in these basic assumptions must strengthen the human being to endure undesired destinies in life and promote the striving for the good in them.

Now, my dear friends, this pamphlet is placed before us as a document of our time, as the expression of a person who stands firmly in the workings of scientific methods and wants to bear witness to the fact that it is possible to be a good, fully conscious scientist and precisely—not in spite of this, but precisely because of it—to arrive at a worldview that recognizes the spirit.

You will have seen from the last chapters of Mr von Wrangell's pamphlet that he has not yet concerned himself very deeply with spiritual science, that he has not broached the difference between what spiritual science wants and dilettante theosophy. And therefore it is all the more important to see how someone who is scientifically trained asks for what can only really be given through spiritual science, so that we can say: We have come to know through such a pamphlet how an unprejudiced scientist can position himself with regard to a view that acknowledges the spirit.

You can still draw other threads and we will do that occasionally. In this way we shall enter further into the matter, to cultivate spiritual science not only in an egoistic way but really to regard it as a cultural ferment and through it to contribute to the course of development of humanity. That is the extremely important thing, that we get into the habit of really participating in everything.

Sometimes you can experience something particular in our ranks. Don't be cross if I speak of this experience, but it can really be had. For there are certain members in our ranks who say: Public lectures, they are not important for us—and they say this in a way from which one can see how they do not really participate. They say the public lectures, that's not the most important thing; the branch lectures yes, they are for us, but we have progressed beyond what the public lectures give. And yet it is precisely the case that the public lectures are designed for those who have a connection with the outside world. And much more reference is made to contemporary science in the public lectures than in the private lectures which show how very often delicate consideration must be given to the fact that people do not like to take strictly scientific questions as a basis. And this delicate consideration is often interpreted in such a way that people say: The public lectures are not so important.

In truth, something else is the case. In these things, too, there is just a certain kind of egoism that underlies them. I don't want to take up arms for the public lectures; I just want to challenge the baseless opinion that many people have. It may be easier to omit this or that connecting strand in the branch lectures in one place or another; but the public lectures must be structured strand by strand. Many people who in their work are not involved in the entire cultural process of our time don't like that. But it is precisely such engagement in the cultural process of the time, such not closing yourself off, that is important.

It is of course also easier to talk about angels, Lucifer and Ahriman than about electrons, ions and so on. But you see, we also have to be aware that we have to draw the threads towards the present culture. But I would ask you not to take the matter one-sidedly again, as if I were to ask you to buy the entire Göschen scientific collection tomorrow and sit down to cram, as the students would say, the whole of it bit by bit. That is not what I mean at all. I only mean that where we wish to speak authoritatively about the position of spiritual science in our culture, we must also have an awareness of it and should not lapse into the mistake of saying that this external science is sheer invention. You can certainly say as an individual that you don't have time to concern yourself with it; but the whole institution, the whole operation should be given a certain direction by what I have said. And it should come as no surprise that a school of spiritual science wants to pursue individual branches of science in such a way that they will gradually lead towards spiritual science. We need the materialistic culture outside. And those anthroposophists are wrong who say: What do I care about materialistic culture?; it is none of my business, it is for crude materialists; I cultivate that which you experience when you dream, when you are not quite fully conscious; the other stuff is none of my business; I have the teachings of reincarnation and karma and so on. On the other side there is the world out there that says: We have the real science, the serious and worthy methods, and here now come the anthroposophists with their spiritual science; they are the very purest of fools.

It must not remain at this opposing position, and mediation cannot be expected to come from outside. Mediation must come from inside. We must understand and not get lazy and say: If we first have to climb up into the spiritual world through science, that is much too laborious for us.

I wanted to speak about the importance of materialistic culture and draw your attention to it because as I have often emphasized: materialism comes from Ahriman, but we have to know about Ahriman, just as we have to know about Lucifer and reckon with him. And the trinity, which we were able to look at yesterday on the model,[82] is the one with which humanity will have to acquaint itself.

I would like to repeat once again: Do not try to annoy the outside world by talking about a new religion. If we were to speak of the Group as a 'Christ statue', that would be a big mistake. It is sufficient to say: There stands the representative of humanity. Everyone can see what is meant. It is important that we always find the right words, that is, that we consider how we should place ourselves in the whole world of culture and how we wish to arrive at describing the matter with the right words. That is the thing that must be repeated over and over again. Let us not say to others: Only here do we have the representation of the real Christ. We may know that and keep it to ourselves. It is important for us to acknowledge all the blessings of materialistic culture, otherwise we will commit the same mistake as the others who do not examine things.

Let's ask ourselves if we don't do the same with regard to the others. While we need not withhold true judgement, we must understand what is going on outside. Then we will also be able to approach what is outside in the right words. But, my dear friends, we will have much, much to do in this regard, because the laziness of which I have spoken today is very, very widespread and we must find the courage to say to people: You are too lazy to enter into the activity of thinking.

If we understand what is outside, then we may also use strong words, engage in a vigorous fight. But we have to familiarize ourselves with it and draw the threads to outer culture. That is why I also wanted to give an example with Wrangell's very meritorious pamphlet which shows how someone is strong as a scientist but has not concerned himself sufficiently with the spiritual-scientific worldview, yet through the whole direction of his soul is inclined towards spiritual science.

We have often shown how such threads can be drawn, mostly using concrete personalities, and I advise you, where there are branches, to do this also in collaboration. Of course, this cannot be the work of just one person; they would never be able to finish. But there must be someone who, say, takes on a pamphlet on Eucken's worldview and another takes a pamphlet that deals with the blood, muscular and nervous systems and so on and they work through them with others. This can be work done in the branches. This can be arranged in such a way that you work purely on spiritual science on one branch evening and then go through such a subject on the next. If one person did it one day, another person can do it another time. Everyone can use something as a starting point that is of interest to them in some way. And why should someone who has no scientific training at all not also be able to use one or another subject as a starting point? There are questions of life that can also be linked to such things. It is much more useful to use the time for such studies than to extract all sorts of occult complexities and material from dreams and tell people about it. This is not meant to be one-sided either. It is not to say that you can never speak of occult experiences; but it is about drawing the right connecting line. It is not a question of despising the science of the senses but of mastering it. The science of the senses is not to be trampled to death or destroyed but mastered.

Sixth Lecture

DORNACH, 9 OCTOBER 1915

Using Wrangell's pamphlet on *Science and Theosophy*, we have attempted to discuss various thoughts which show how someone who wants to stand completely firmly on the ground of modern science is nevertheless impelled towards the acknowledgement that there can be cognition of the spiritual life. And as you have seen, we did not so much have to object to Wrangell's pamphlet as to supplement it along the lines of spiritual science. In this brochure, therefore, there is what at first appears to be a subjective judgement on the path of the modern scientist towards spiritual science; how, in other words, you can perfectly well be a modern scientist and still find the path to spiritual science.

It is important to consider this line of thought in particular, because it seems to me quite necessary that those who stand on the ground of spiritual science should clearly recognize that the objections of the so-called scientists are not really scientific at all, but come from the fact that today a person can be an excellent scientist who knows how to handle the materialistic scientific methods in a given field of science quite well but can at the same time be a dilettante in all other questions regarding views of the world.

Now today—in continuation, so to speak, of the thoughts developed on the basis of the pamphlet—I would like to go on to develop a number of other thoughts of importance for us. I would like to show how the present development of humanity has reached a point which should suggest to the insightful scientist, to someone who really takes science seriously and knows how to appreciate it, that they should engage in the study of spiritual science and not do it in the way that has been preferred up to now: to regard it as something to be rejected from the outset.

As some of you will remember, I have in some respects sung the praises of the materialistic-scientific method in the reflections that were built on Wrangell's pamphlet. I said that it produced great and significant results in recent times, that we need only adopt a proper point of view towards this materialistic-scientific method and we would appreciate and not underestimate it. We will familiarize ourselves with its results particularly if we intend to draw the connecting threads between it and spiritual science, as needs to be done.

Now I would first like to start from what is to a certain extent a natural scientific line of reasoning, which can show us how the thinking natural scientist—especially when they understand themselves in the right way—should knock on the door of spiritual science. I would like to draw attention to a chapter of modern natural science which is also of great importance in social and ethical terms, but which cannot attain this in a way that is satisfactory for human beings as long as natural science has not found its way to spiritual science. I would like to elaborate a little on some lines of reasoning in what is called criminal anthropology.

One of the great researchers in criminal anthropology is Professor Dr Moriz Benedikt, whom I have already mentioned several times. He was one of the first to examine criminal brains in a very modern systematic way[83] by subsequently dissecting criminals, especially murderers, who had been sentenced to death. The results were indeed so surprising compared to many of the previous views that at first, after the initial investigations, he might have thought he was dealing with a kind of scientific adventure and not at all with anything on the trail of truth. So when he examined criminal brains, they always showed—that is, for those familiar with the configuration, with the plasticity of the normal human brain—very specific internal structures with very specific features that differed from the structure of the brain of a person who was not a criminal. And so that we don't spread ourselves too widely, I want to stick to the main characteristic.

It turned out that a certain part of the human brain called the occipital lobe, which covers the cerebellum, is too small in criminals, so that it only barely covers the cerebellum, or does not cover at all, which it otherwise covers completely.

Now imagine that you dissect a criminal brain and find that this criminal brain differs from a normal brain in such a way that the occipital lobe does not completely cover the cerebellum, then you must come to the conclusion: if someone is born in such a way that it is impossible to develop the occipital lobe to such an extent that it covers the cerebellum, then no matter what they do in life, they simply become a criminal and consequently they can't help it. And if you now examine monkey brains, you will see the same peculiarity: the occipital lobe does not completely cover the cerebellum. So that we have to say: In the various moments of evolution on the way from monkey to human, it must also be noted that the human being has progressed beyond monkey evolution and has become a more perfect being in that their occipital lobe has grown and completely covers the cerebellum. This means that when a person becomes a criminal, they revert to the monkey organization. In the case of the criminal, then, we are dealing with distinct atavism. This means nothing other than that there are individuals walking around among human beings who have atavistically reverted to the monkey image in their brain structure. These atavistic individuals simply become criminals.

Now think of the ethical and social consequences of such a view and then you will know what it means under the conditions of the present materialistic worldview—I do not mean the prevailing natural science—to have to submit to these facts. For the facts exist and only a fool could deny them. Thus the person who is guided by the materialistic worldview is faced with the challenge: just look at the brains of criminals; you can see that the brain structure reverts to monkey-like. So you see clearly how that which reveals itself morally in the human being is simply a consequence of the material organization of the body. You can see it clearly there. The person who had this brain became a criminal precisely because he had this brain. With the same necessity with which the clockwork serves us when it works correctly so that we can catch the train at ten o'clock while a clockwork that goes wrong and perhaps only shows seven o'clock makes us late for the train, with the same necessity a brain that has not managed the full formation of the occipital lobe indicates a criminal person who has remained behind. As you will probably choose not to fantasize a demon into the clock that drives the hands around, you will also choose not to magic the 'soul' demon into the brain.

If we were to resist the proven results of criminal anthropological investigations of criminal brains without further ado, this would mean practising ostrich politics in science; it would simply mean not wanting to reckon with those things that have been fully investigated.

Now, as you know, apart from materialistic science there is also philosophy. But if you look at this philosophy, perhaps especially among those who are often counted among its most important representatives today, you will find that this philosophy is completely powerless in the face of materialistic methods. The concepts that philosophers obtain either amount to saying as I have shown you with Otto Liebmann,[84] who is a very perceptive man and who says that one cannot get beyond certain points, that one cannot go beyond certain limits. I gave you the example of the hen's egg. Or if you take the philosophy of Rudolf Eucken in Jena, you can see how they bandy words around and fudge them beautifully, but how the concepts that are developed there cannot come close to the materialistic methods. These are like the actions of a man who stands here on one bank of the river and makes all kinds of efforts to cross over to the other bank but cannot get across.* On the other side is the materialistic scientific method, but he cannot get across; so philosophizing remains just waffle.

What is actually going on there? Well, let us go back to something we have known for a long time; let us go back to the division of the human being into physical body, etheric body, astral body and I. Let us take this crudest division to begin with as it has presented itself to us in the course of our spiritual-scientific investigations and ask ourselves: What happens when we look at something outwardly sensory—and a criminal brain is by all means also something outwardly

---

* Here there was obviously drawing on the blackboard; the drawing, however, has not been preserved.

sensory—what happens there? The outwardly sensory acts on our sense organs. They are in the physical body. That is where sensory perception arises. No one denies that. We would be fools to deny it as spiritual scientists. It would be obtuse if we did not deal with such results as I have cited from criminal anthropology. We must not deny their force either, because they certainly prove that the criminal walks around with a monkey brain and the normal human being no longer has this monkey brain. So when we philosophize, as today's philosophers do, what are we doing? In which regions of the human being do we then move? Then we move in the sphere of the I. That is where all the philosophical concepts are today. And precisely among those who philosophize most astutely today, you will be able to see everywhere that they are, as it were, just bobbing around in the region of the I. You can find scholarly proof of this in the introductory chapter of my *Riddles of Philosophy*, where I have shown how in our time philosophy tends essentially to be a bobbing about in the I. But between natural science and philosophy there is a wide gap, that is the river over which philosophy cannot cross; that is to say that we have the philosophical concepts on the one side—inwardly in the human being—and all external sensory perceptions on the other side.

I once symptomatically, but only symptomatically my dear friends, quite vividly had this abyss between philosophizing and natural-scientific perception before me—but please note that this is only meant symptomatically—at the sixtieth birthday celebration for Ernst Haeckel. That's when I took part in the celebration in Jena. All kinds of people spoke there, followers of Haeckel and so on. Now it was interesting for me to learn what would emerge when Haeckel's philosophical colleagues, among whom was also Dr Rudolf Eucken, gave a so-called toast during the lunch as is so customary. For then it would have been possible to see in some way how the representatives of philosophy at a university relate to the representatives of natural science and sensory perception. The toast—it was given by Eucken—had approximately the following content; I only give the main thought. Eucken said something like: At a birthday celebration like today's, it is customary to have to say what particularly characterizes the birthday child. Now I tried to think what might particularly characterize our birthday child, but I found nothing in particular in my own thinking. I asked our celebrant's daughter and she told me that it was one of our celebrant's characteristic peculiarities that he couldn't get to grips with his tie, for example, when he wanted to put it on. The toast continued in this vein.

Well, as I said, I was symptomatically confronted with what the representatives of philosophy at a university had to say about the representatives of sensory, scientific perceptions. It is really symptomatic because there is no real bridge between contemporary philosophy and natural science because the concepts of the philosophers are quite meagre and the sensory facts that natural science brings to light are beyond its shore. You can't get across with the philosophical concepts.

Now I have already drawn to your attention that there is a way of bringing the facts of natural science into flux, properly into flux. This possibility consists in really engaging with the spirit of Goethe's scientific reflections. Remember that I have explained to you how Goethe came to regard the bones of the skull as transformed dorsal vertebrae, even though their outer form is quite different from that of the vertebrae. I drew your attention to this theory of transformation when I told you[85] that our boiler house is only a transformation of our main building in that it is partly enlarged and partly atrophied. I also in another lecture[86] drew to your attention that when you ascend from ordinary concepts to spiritual-scientific concepts, you have to set the concepts in motion. I recommended in this respect reading Goethe's poems on the metamorphosis of plants and animals. There you will see how mobile the concepts are and how he has shaped it all.

If you take what I have said on these various occasions together with what we must be directed towards today, then you will say to yourself: If I take the sensory perceptions as such, they are more limited, but if I go over to the Goethean worldview, then such a dorsal vertebra appears to me in such a way that it is more elastic, softer, so that gradually it turns into a part of the skull. I look into creative nature in this way. I see, for example, how in fish the individual bones of the skull are very similar to the dorsal vertebrae, and how then the development towards the human being occurs in that the dorsal vertebrae develop into the bones of the skull...

However, you can only follow this spiritually; you can't look at that with the senses. If you wanted to look at it with the senses, you would have to observe for thousands, millions of years how one transforms into the other. So you have to spiritualize the observation, the sensory perception.

You see, Goethe instinctively got this spiritualization of sensory perception right. I have often drawn attention to that meaningful conversation between him and Schiller[87] when on one occasion they were leaving the Natural History Society in Jena together after a lecture by the botanist Batsch. Schiller said he had found everything in Batsch just so unconnected. Goethe then drew his archetypal plant, which is what you get when you transition from one plant form to another. Then Schiller said: But that is not an observation, that is an idea—and Goethe replied: Then I have my ideas in front of my eyes. He was aware that he was not only seeing the individual transformations but that he saw a plant in all parts of the plant. Underlying this is that Goethe instinctively observed everything in the way that you cannot just observe with the physical senses but when you immediately capture the physical perception in the observation of the etheric body. That is to say, Goethe includes the metamorphosing perception—and this is a perpetually fluid perception—in his view of nature. This sets the whole sensory world in motion for him. The individual part is then only a specific expression of something very general, but not so general as the abstract philosophers make it, but of something general that winds its way through the individual sensory perceptions. There you see sensory perception raised up into the imaginative sphere which arises in the human being when we do not disdain to add our etheric body to sensory perception.

You cannot understand what Goethe wrote about animals and plants if you do not consider that he included the etheric body. Now you have already raised it a bit higher. We would now have accomplished something if we had still moved the philosophical concepts over here so that they could come close [to the perceptions] [...*].

Now take what we have often considered over the years—this belongs to the first stage of what it says in *Knowledge of the Higher Worlds. How is it Achieved?*—that it is possible to raise physical, concrete perception to a higher level, to imaginative perception. But remember the characteristic I have stated over and over again—it is found in innumerable passages in our cycles—of which this imaginative perception consists. It consists of working back through the I into the etheric body. As long as we only form concrete concepts, as the philosopher does as well—that they work in the spirit is merely a delusion of grandeur—we will not get any further. We must pass from concrete to imaginative cognition, that is to say, as soon as life enters into the concepts we return from the I on its own back into the etheric body. We work on the astral body to become the spirit self; that is to say, we can say that philosophical concepts become imaginative concepts or conceptions, if we can still use the word 'concept' here.

But now things have become unified: the imaginative concepts are no longer separated from the metamorphosing perceptions by a gulf but are immediately adjoining.

We shall now see that while philosophy and sense perception are separated by a gulf and cannot come together because physical perception has its process in the physical body and the philosopher has their process in the I, here however [evidently something was drawn again] the imaginative concepts and the perceptions come together because the concrete concept is in the physical body and the metamorphosed concepts are in the etheric body. So it is a deepening in both directions. On the one hand we must approach the world with the whole person, and on the other hand we must deepen the concepts by bringing them to life, by turning them into imaginations.

That is what the philosophers want to avoid. They cannot engage with the concept of imagination, and the natural scientists

---

* A few incomplete lines still follow here in the original shorthand note which do not convey any coherent meaning.

cannot engage with a grasp of metamorphosing perception. But this is brought about by spiritual science. Our whole spiritual science is actually an answer to the question: How does the rational human being living in their astral body perceive the perceptions living and metamorphosing in their etheric body? How do they think them? That is what is so important, that we really know that we are bringing the outer world closer to the inner world, that they are coming closer together, that we are bringing them together.

Only now can we gain some perspective on what something like the reality of criminal anthropology is all about. Of course, a person who is born in such a way that their growth is such that the occipital lobe does not properly cover the cerebellum will walk around all their life with such a monkey-like occipital lobe. But where does such a monkey-like occipital lobe come from? The latter in terms of spiritual science is the consequence of the preceding life, for what the human being was in the past works from within on the development of their body. This is how they create the structure of their body and brain, and thus also of their occipital lobe. So we can say: If a person walks around with a stunted occipital lobe, they have not acquired enough strength in their previous life to form the occipital lobe normally. This is no consolation because there is always the possibility that such a person will become a criminal, because the occipital lobe cannot, after all, be enlarged. We could now say: People are then divided into two groups: into those who have too small an occipital lobe and are born criminals, and into those who have a fully developed occipital lobe and do not become criminals. For the materialistic worldview there is little to argue here. That is the conclusion it will reach. For spiritual science there is theoretically no other answer either, but since it knows that the physical body is not the only body but also carries an etheric body within itself, the situation changes for it. Because if a person is born with a stunted occipital lobe, that is, with an unfavourable disposition, then we can still educate that person properly. We can structure education in such a way that we teach them appropriate moral and ethical concepts. This means that although the physical body cannot be changed in the present incarnation, the etheric part of the occipital lobe can. It can be enlarged by what is taught to the human being through the right education. It is therefore possible by means of suitable education to help a human being who has too short an occipital lobe as a result of the previous incarnation. By educating such a person properly, we make the etheric part of the occipital lobe larger and the person in question can thereby be saved from criminality.

But now, given the fact that we find an occipital lobe that is too short in those who have become criminals, we would also have to do the opposite experiment. We would have to dissect normal people and prove that they all had normally developed occipital lobes; and in doing so, we might discover that even in normally developed people it happens that they have an occipital lobe that is too small but they nevertheless have not become criminals because the etheric occipital lobe has become larger through appropriate education.

Ethical education, then, adds to the etheric, not the physical constitution. However, education must be organized in such a way that it conforms with spiritual laws. If you take what has been developed as a principle of education in the small publication *Educating Children Today*,[88] you will find that the principles of development from [one] seven [years] to [the next] seven years were followed. When you start to take these laws and translate them into appropriate action, you are intervening more deeply than with the purely rationalistic educational methods that have been commonplace for a long time. Nor do we get any further with what has emerged as Froebelism.[89] With all the educational methods that are used today, you only approach the I. And for as long as you only approach the I, you can't do anything—the occipital lobe remains too small. But if you eavesdrop on the secrets of spiritual existence and turn them into educational measures, you will enter the etheric body. Then you really make the etheric body normal, that is, you gain powerful concepts with spiritual science, concepts that really have a power over the human being, that can change them. If you take the concepts that can be obtained today—be it on the one hand from the observation of the sensory world of perception, be it on the other hand from the abstract talk that comes only from the I—you get no educational principles and also no principles for social life that really impinge on the human being. The concepts remain powerless. You can search through whole libraries—and there is plenty written about education—but all of that represents a desire to regulate out of the I, no matter whether you think you are educating more theoretically or otherwise. For as long as nothing is learned from the mystery of human nature and the spiritual principles of education, and thereby made effective into the etheric body, the concepts remain powerless against what grows up in the human being. But if we do so, we also approach with such concepts, as they grow more powerful, what develops and grows in the world, so that we practically incorporate nothing theoretical. If we go from philosophical to imaginative concepts, as spiritual science does, and if we go from sensory perception to metamorphosing perception, we will make our principles more closely related to the spiritual, and then we will obtain corresponding measures and principles from spiritual science.

From what I have said you can see how right, how necessary it is in our time—after the world has been reduced by centuries of development to just sensory perception and has thus been pushed back to just comprehension in the I—how necessary it is to bring outer perception and inner soul life closer together again, both for reflection and for practical life. With spiritual science we gain powerful concepts that intervene in life, concepts that really have something to do with life. Such concepts as those of Eucken's philosophy never intervene in real life. With spiritual science we grasp what is real; we grasp it where it is more real than sensory perception.

When we approach what is real with our ordinary concepts, with ordinary sensory perception, we look at what is on the surface, we look with our sensory tools. We look for example at the mountain with its flora. And now there are these two kinds of people: some look at the mountain with its plant world and forget themselves (Haeckel), others don't look at the outside world at all but only ramble on in concepts and stare into the void; thus philosophy becomes empty (Eucken's philosophy). Spiritual science approaches what is real with metamorphosing perception and thereby looks at something that does not express itself on the surface but something that lies beneath. But also, when it looks at the human being, it proceeds from simple sensory perception of the physical sense organs back to metamorphosing perception (etheric body) and from the mere philosophical concept to imaginative conception, and as a result has something like a subterranean channel between simple sensory perception (physical sense organs) and the simple philosophical concept (I). Now you will also understand that a bleak worldview must come about if spiritual science does not spread, for philosophy will of course become quite impotent with its concepts in relation to the human being; it will not be believed, something that is already happening. After all, there is no denying sensory perception; it will be less and less possible to deny it. So it is natural that the materialistic worldview will say: How can you help becoming a criminal? How can you help having an occipital lobe that is too short? Just think what this means for the concept of responsibility and for legal concepts! We have to look at this perspective. It is cowardly not to look at it.

There is, however, a possibility of going beyond this if the etheric body is worked on from within through appropriately good education, so that the etheric occipital lobe is developed as a result. Such education, however, must be an education of the heart and of love, as has been shown in *Educating Children Today*. When you realize this, then you say to yourself: Certainly, such a person with an occipital lobe that is too short will walk around all their life with the occipital lobe shortened and will experience temptation. But through the development of the etheric occipital lobe they will always be able to find the necessary balance. In this way spiritual science will become a major factor when those who only know the achievements of the materialistic worldview knock at the door of spiritual science.

Secondly, I would like to show you another thing that can be taken from the soul life. Especially in our time today, we have the opportunity to see that feelings can spread through entire national communities, for example feelings of hatred. Now someone who still holds a naïve worldview, when asked: Why do you hate?—naturally they don't know exactly why something is hateful, because they still have the naive worldview—they will perhaps say: I hate because I find it hateful.

Now today there is a psychological worldview that has gone beyond such naivety, that knows something more than that you hate something because it is hateful, just as the criminal anthropologist knows more than the person who believes that someone became a criminal because he was a bad fellow and didn't get any better; because the criminal anthropologist knows that the subject has an occipital lobe that is too small. And so that is also a naïve judgement when you say: I hate this or that because it is hateful.

Well, here too some people have already come to a correct judgement. Anyone who takes a closer look at human nature sees how the feelings that are developed in the soul belong to the tools, to the conditions of life of the soul. And if we do not look at the world of the soul naively, but with real observation of the facts today, we arrive at the conclusion that there is latently stored up in the human being, without it becoming visible, a certain quantum of the need to hate. They must hate. And when so much hatred has accumulated that the barrel overflows, so to speak, they seek an object for their power of hatred.

Now consider the way in which a person arrives at a worldview. We endeavour to show how we should arrive at a spiritual-scientific worldview in an objective way. But this is not always how people arrive at a spiritual-scientific worldview, nor at a materialistic worldview, but it happens because they are emotionally predestined to do so. What logically speaks in favour of a worldview only takes second or even third place. Go, for example, to the meetings of communists or materialists and examine what they put forward to logically substantiate their worldview, then you can notice that not their logic but their feeling is predestined for it. And so it is also with the spiritual-scientific worldview. Perhaps you have the mystical worldview out of your feelings because it is more comfortable for you than a materialistic worldview. The emotional, the affective factor plays an enormous role here. It is the same with hatred towards the outside world. When a person hates something, the psychologist will not ask: What is the object like? but they will ask: What is the person like? The need to hate is within them and the object then arises of its own accord. They must hate, as they must eat at certain times. This is an insight that contemporary psychology has already reached.

I have in my hand an issue of the journal *Die Zukunft*[90] (The Future) from 25 September 1915, in which there is an essay by Franz Blei entitled 'Wahrheiten' (Truths). Something along the lines of what I have just said is set out there. Then it explains what Avenarius—Franz Blei is a student of Avenarius—established with his empirical critical philosophy. This is summarized in individual sentences, and in these sentences you will find very nicely expressed what today can already be understood as psychological research results: 'Pure feelings are to be theoretically assumed as pre-existent to feelings freighted with ideational components and cannot be experienced. In practice, we do not know any feeling that does not have an ideational component.' This sentence does not exactly relate to what we need, so let us not dwell on this sentence. It is not necessary for us to dissect it, otherwise we would have to examine the concepts that have been used. But another sentence may well be more important for us, namely that: 'Pure ideas must be theoretically assumed as pre-existent to humanly conceived ideas and cannot be purely experienced. In practice, we know of no idea (thought, image) that has not already served as a component for a feeling.'

So, when an idea arises in us, we have to ask ourselves: What feeling has prompted this idea in us? In one person the idea arises: The world is separable into atoms. What feeling prompted them? In another person, the idea arises: The world has a hierarchy, a stepladder. What feeling prompted them? So the component of feeling is in all of it. And if someone is filled with hate, what is the feeling that prompts them? Blei says: 'It is not ideas that call forth feelings, but pure feelings seize upon ideas that can satisfy these feelings.' For example: the social democrat hates the bourgeois person. They hate them because a quantum of hatred is necessary for them, and they direct it towards the bourgeois person. Or the anti-Semite needs hatred and the Jews present themselves for this purpose. Franz Blei says in point 8: 'It is not the truth of an idea in itself that determines its acceptance by people, but its affective content.'

So you see, he already knows that too! You do not become a materialistic monist because you see the truth but because you are predestined for it by your feeling, and you do not become a spiritualist because it is true but because you are predestined for it by your feeling.

This essay goes on to say: 'Ideas are accepted whose probability is zero, others again together with and at the same time as those that are the opposite of the former. Consider the manifold nature of "Thou shalt not kill!". Here only the believer is permitted an objection to which Hegel once gave the expression of the "deviousness of the idea" which makes use of our passion for its realization in that people think they are working for themselves while in reality they are doing it for the "world spirit". The Christian believer speaks of the inscrutability of God's ways.'

So the whole essay is about it not being the ideas, the so-called truths, that take hold of people, but the emotional content.

Anyone who looks at the world today as it has gradually developed will find this quite correct, and it is very significant that a school of philosophers like that of Avenarius has come to realize that the social democrat does not hate the bourgeois because they find them hateful, but because they themselves need a certain quantum of hate. So Avenarius' school of philosophy has already arrived at that today.

But let us consider what in turn the social consequence of this is. If you put yourself in the position—and we might say that this position, if you still have any real feeling at all, must turn into the most bitter pill for the soul—of taking these things seriously as truths, you will have to say to yourself: Truth no longer decides anything, but the affects decide. I am indeed led into a worldview but only because I do not know the truth. This then leads into absolute desolation. There is no escape. Just as in criminal anthropology there is no escape from admitting that an occipital lobe that is too short makes a criminal, so in external psychology there is no escape from the fact that people are driven by their affects to what they call truth.

Friedrich Nietzsche most clearly, most significantly and most plausibly tried to present this in a great many variants in his worldview. This underlies the whole of Nietzscheanism. I have cited the passage myself[91] in my book *Friedrich Nietzsche, ein Kämpfer gegen seine Zeit*. It is about the question: What is truth? And because Nietzsche did not accept the correctness of this proposition because of the truth, but rejected it because of the whole preparation of human subjectivity, that is why Nietzsche wanted to put an end to the fantasy [of the will to truth], that is, also to Christianity. That is why he wrote the *Antichrist*, the next was to be *The Immoralists* and the whole was then to be *The Will to Power*.

Desolation, absolute nihilism is what precisely such schools of philosophy lead to with their realization that whoever is predisposed to believe that they can best come into a relationship with the world by adhering to matter becomes a materialist; and anyone who believes that they live by dependence on the spiritual world becomes a spiritualist out of their affect.

Well, my dear friends, you need only take one thing to counter this: you need only open the last chapter of *Theosophy*[92] where the path to knowledge is described and take the fact from which it starts. For the start is not made by assuming that you should ruminate logically in order to arrive at these truths, but by assuming that it is necessary to form and shape the whole affective world of the human being, the direction of feeling, in a certain way. It deals with what lies at the heart of the search for truth. It tackles what psychology points to but doesn't know what to do with. Why do we not refute materialism with logical reasons; why do we not justify spiritualism with logical reasons? Because none of this means anything. On the contrary, something else needs to be shown. It needs to be shown: You have to do this and this with your affects, so that you are no longer guided by the subjective, but ... [Gap].

Take this chapter of *Theosophy* and you will see that everything depends on objectifying the affective life and then you can see how this intervenes in the dead end of the modern worldview ... [The final sentences are no longer decipherable in the shorthand note].

III

EPISODIC OBSERVATIONS ABOUT SPACE, TIME, MOVEMENT

Episodic Observations About Space, Time, Movement

DORNACH, 20 AUGUST 1915

I THOUGHT that at most a dozen people would be here today and I wanted to say something, as will indeed happen, that is quite episodic, something that does not belong at all to our other reflections but which can be important for some, who can live their way into the matter a little, in order to assess some of the things that play a role in relation to certain notions of space and time and movement in time.

There are theoretical physicists[93] today who are of the opinion that a profound revolution is taking place with regard to the simplest concepts of the world. Among these simple concepts of the world that underlie theoretical physics we want to look a little bit today at something that relates to time, space and movement. This will provide the basis for more extensive observations to be made in the near future,[94] which can lead us deeper into what is aimed for in fundamental physical observations at the present time in particular.

You will certainly all have heard that what is called the theory of relativity in modern physics is now gaining ground. The theory of relativity—there are also various nuances—is advocated today by countless theoretical physicists. It is hoped that it will bring about a complete change in all the concepts that physicists have hitherto accepted as correct when they have made fundamental theoretical observations and which essentially go back to Newton. Now the more recent theoretical physicists of today believe that all these Newtonian concepts, which were still accepted as quite incontrovertible in our student days, must undergo a revolution, indeed that, to a certain extent, the whole theoretical basis of physics, as it has been believed and is still believed, is actually wrong. Now why I have to relate the observations I am about to make to this newly emerging theory of relativity—that will become clear later.

So that what I have to say does not remain completely incomprehensible, I would like to start from very simple, elementary concepts in order to demonstrate to you through them what kind of idea we can associate with the concept of time. Let's start, as I said, from very elementary things. Let us assume that some object that I will call a, a rolling ball or the like, is moving in a direction that I want to indicate by this line; so a moves along the straight line in the direction of b:

$$a \longrightarrow b$$

Now you all know that the distance, the length of the path, which such a moving object covers in one second is called the velocity. So let's assume that a gets here, to a_1, in one second, then in physics this distance from a to a_1 would be called the velocity and labelled c. And if we further assume that the moving object continues to move through the following seconds, then if it were to perform a uniform movement—and this is the only movement we want to talk about—it would be at a_2 at the end of the second second, where $aa_1 = a_1a_2$, that is to say, with the same velocity c the moving object goes from a_1 to a_2 in the second second, from a_2 to a_3 in the third second, from a_3 to a_4 in the fourth second, and so on. Let us now assume that we observe this movement over a certain period of time and that our moving object travels a certain distance, let us assume to a_5,

$$a \quad a_1 \quad a_2 \quad a_3 \quad a_4 \quad a_5$$

then, if this moving object has rolled from a to a_5, the section of space—which we consider here in its one dimension—is called the distance; so that a to a_5 is the distance it has travelled; c is the velocity; the distance is referred to as *s*; and we say: the moving object *a* has travelled distance *s* at velocity *c* in a certain time—in this case five seconds. This elapsed time is referred to as *t*.

Now there is a certain relationship between distance, time and velocity. The simplest relationship that has been found is that we would say here: *s*—the distance—is five times from *a* to a_1, that is, once the distance *a* to a_1 times 5, that is 5 seconds, so that is the time; so we have to multiply what we called the velocity—this section aa_1—by 5, then we get the distance $s = c \cdot t$ (distance = velocity · time). So there are three concepts in this formula: *s*, *c*, *t*.

Now you know that an infinite amount has been written about time by a number of philosophers, mathematicians and also theoretical mechanics. People believe they have an idea, a concept of time, but if they had to explain and think about what they understand by time, everyone would very soon realize that they have no real idea of this concept of time, which is one of the most common concepts used in mechanics. In order to be able to study something about the concept of time, let us stick to this formula, which at first places the concept of time in a uniform, rectilinear movement. But even though this formula can be found in every physics book, in physics it is surrounded by a whole lot of, I don't want to say ambiguities, but by a lack of clarity, by little will to go deeper into the matter. And this stems in particular from the fact that in our schools the teaching of something that we all learn does not teach us certain distinctions, which are however important if we want to arrive at more precise concepts in a certain direction. In our schools we learn to talk about four types of calculation: addition, subtraction, multiplication and division. But with division, I don't think we are often made aware that there are actually two totally different things in the ordinary calculating operation. Let me show you this in a very simple way.

Let us assume we have an ordinary apple and divide it. We can divide it into five parts, into ten parts and so on; then, when we have divided it, we get a certain part of the apple. If we want to share out the pieces, then what we share out is a piece of the apple. We are indeed performing a division here. I shall write it as a fraction, because that is the same as a division. I can say: An apple is divided, let's say into ten parts, then we get a tenth of an apple as a result. Now take a look at what I have written on the blackboard:

$$\frac{1 \text{ apple (tangible)}}{10 \text{ (number)}} = \frac{1}{10} \text{ apple (tangible)}$$

In the numerator or dividend we have a quality, something tangible; in the divisor or denominator we have nothing tangible but a mere number; 10 is just a number here; and in the quotient we again have something tangible: a tenth of an apple.

This situation does not change if we share twenty apples instead of one. Let's say we divide 20 apples by 10, so instead of a tenth of an apple we get 2 apples:

$$\frac{20 \text{ apples}}{10} = 2 \text{ apples}$$

The 20 apples are again something tangible; below is just the number and as a quotient we again get something tangible. That is a division.

But dividing can still have a completely different meaning. I can have 20 apples at the top in the dividend but at the bottom as the denominator or divisor, say, 2 apples; then I have something tangible above and below. What do I get as a result? Then I don't get something tangible as a result, but I find out how often 2 apples are contained in 20 apples, I get 10, that is, I get a number:

$$\frac{20 \text{ apples (tangible)}}{2 \text{ apples (tangible)}} = 10 \text{ (number)}$$

Again, I am dealing with a division but this one now has a completely different meaning from the division in the first case. In the first case, I divide something tangible and get something else tangible; in the second case, I don't divide at all but set myself the task of investigating how often something tangible is contained in something else tangible and that gives me a number.

So we can say: Division is not always dividing, but there are two types of division that are strictly different from each other. So, when teaching, we should always explain that there are two types of

Episodic Observations About Space, Time, Movement ✳ 209

division. In the first case, my task is to explore what results when we divide something; in the second, the task is to find out how often something tangible is contained in something tangible of the same kind—they have to be of the same kind, because of course you cannot ask how often 2 apples are contained in 20 pears—and then we get a number.

This must be taken into account when studying the formula $s = c \cdot t$.

Now this formula can also be written differently. I don't always need to search for s, I can also search for c or t, then the formula changes. If I look for c, I get it by dividing s by t. By dividing the whole space by t, I get the space that has been traversed in 5 seconds divided by 5, that is, the velocity c:

$$c = \frac{s}{t}$$

But equally you can get t: the time. Suppose you divide s by c. If you ask: How often is the path of one second contained in the whole path?; it is contained five times. That's where you get the time:

$$t = \frac{s}{c}$$

Let us take a closer look at these formulas. Let's take the second one first and compare: s, that's the distance here, the length a to a_5 that's what we have in the numerator; here in the denominator we have c. What is c? Well, that's the distance in a second. These are distances: s is a distance, c is a distance. What form of division does this resemble? Well, that resembles this form (20 apples : 2 apples = 10). Here (in the numerator) you have apples and here (in the denominator) you have apples; here (in the numerator of $\frac{s}{c}$) you have distance and here (in the denominator) you have distance. What then has to be there in front? Just a number. That is, t results in our physics considerations as nothing other than a number. For if I regard s and c as distances, that is, as something tangible—both are distances or a part of a distance—then, by nature of the division, time t can only figure as a number. Just as the number 10 (20 apples : 2 apples = 10) is a number and nothing less or more, so in this division t, time, cannot be anything other than a number.[95]

You can also take the form of division (1 apple : $10 = \frac{1}{10}$ apple), then this resembles the formula $c = \frac{s}{t}$. If, on the other hand, something tangible is divided by something tangible, what must result? A number like here ($t = \frac{s}{c}$), where we are dealing with a mere number with t. That is, both formulas indicate that—insofar as we stop at physics—we get nothing but a number for time depending on the nature of the division. Namely, here (20 apples : 2 apples = 10) is a number that refers to apples and shows how often 2 apples are contained in 20 apples, and here with time ($\frac{s}{c} = t$) is a number that shows how often speed is contained in space.

Now probably none of you will see something tangible in the number as such. If you give any boy or girl not 3 apples, but only the number 3, they will not be full. So in the number we cannot see something tangible but rather a mere abstraction, something that merely indicates relationships in the outer world, as it were.

From this observation we can see that time itself slips out of our hands through physical observation; it shrinks down to a mere number for us. We can no more philosophize about time than we can philosophize about number; that is, it has been reduced to the conception of a number. That is also why we cannot find time in things, no matter how long we keep searching, because it only appears as a number. What is this related to? Well, I don't think a boy or a girl needs to be very old to give an answer that comes from a healthy feeling when you ask: What interests you, the apples or the number? Certainly someone could use sophistry and say: I am interested in the number, because I prefer 8 apples to 6; but that is only because 8 apples are more than 6. So the number is not what this is about at all; it is about the apples, the tangible thing.

But it follows from this that we must stick to the tangible in the first place and not to the number when we speak of time, space and velocity. And if we now consider the tangible, then time is discounted from the outset, that is, it is a number and not tangible. So you will be able to say to yourself: We have s, the space, the section of space that our moving object passes through.

If it continues to roll, it can pass through much, much more space. After all, space is something tangible outside. But that's not what matters in the first instance, because you can think of space as going on and on. But something else has a lot to do with what matters to us, which is *c*. Because how *a* passes through space depends entirely on whether it passes along, say, 20 or 25 or 50 cm and so on in a second, and again, how much it passes along depends on how fast it runs. But how fast it runs, that's within it, that's intrinsic to it. And the whole process in general depends on that which is intrinsic to the moving object. So it is the velocity of the moving object that matters; it belongs to the moving object as such, it is an inner quality of the moving object. And when we look at the world, in so far as we look at it in terms of mechanical processes, then when we speak of reality, we must speak of the inner velocity of bodies or atoms or molecules. And the whole process forces us to speak of the inner velocity as belonging to things, just as the red colour belongs to the rose.

So the fundamental concept is velocity; this is what matters. It follows that we must not adhere to the formula which has *c* here ($c = \frac{s}{t}$), and must not believe that with space and time we have anything particularly real, but what is real in objects is velocity, not time. Time, in turn, is only abstracted from the concept of velocity because things have different velocities. If we look at the different velocities and want to reduce them to a common factor, we get the concept of time. This is an abstraction, just as the generic term 'apple' is an abstraction and only the particular, the concrete apple is real. So if we address the mechanically real nature of things, we must address velocity and not think that we can put the concept of time to the fore. This is the great mistake that is made everywhere in physics, that no attention is paid to the fact that we must start from the velocity that is intrinsic to things, that belongs to them as life belongs to living bodies.

So keep this in mind, my dear friends: not time, but velocity is what must underlie mechanics. You might now say that these are quibbles, making these distinctions. But they are not quibbles but these things are fundamentally important for the understanding of certain conditions of reality, and I want to point out something to you right away that shows how fundamentally important they are.

In the various discussions about the theory of relativity, people were concerned precisely with coming to terms with the concept of time and the concept of velocity. Now I will use two speculations to show you the way certain people think, how they formulate their thinking when they talk about time and velocity. Here I must introduce you to a curious personality, Mr Lumen, who plays a certain role in the theory of relativity. What kind of a curious gentleman is he? Well, you see, this is a, I would like to say, 'imaginary acquaintance' that Flammarion has made.[96] This Mr Lumen has a very strange ability, which we can make clear to ourselves in something like the following way.

You all know from your physics lessons that light has a certain speed; it travels 300,000 km per second c, that is, everything that is an intrinsic mechanical part of light according to our understanding is a speed of 300,000 km per second. Let us assume, for example, that this is the earth and that from the objects and occurrences that happen on earth a ray of light travels out into space [was indicated diagrammatically on the blackboard], and people say, after all, because the light travels out, we see the things. Let us now assume the following. We have here this somewhat abstract mathematics and physics lesson, and, let's say, from three to four o'clock there was a eurythmy lesson. From all of this, light travels out into space and you can observe from outside what is happening here. And since light travels at a speed of 300,000 km per second, what happened here this afternoon between three and four o'clock also travelled out into space at a speed of 300,000 km per second, so that if you imagine an observer who is 300,000 km away, they will only see what is happening here on earth after one second.

Now Flammarion assumes that this Mr Lumen is hurtling out into space even faster than light, namely at a speed of 400,000 km per second. What will be the consequence of this? He will continually overtake the light because after the light has travelled a second, he is already 100,000 km further away and he must, as he hurtles out and looks back, arrive at the disclosures of the light where he sees what has happened here now and between three and four o'clock. But since he not only catches up with the light but overtakes it, it must follow that he does not first perceive the eurythmy session and then our session, but everything the other way round, first the end and then that which came earlier. It is a strange spectacle that this Mr Lumen experiences. He sees everything in such a way that he first sees the end and then the beginning, because he is overtaking the light.

Such ideas have, as I said, played a certain role precisely in the discussions about the theory of relativity. I would like to present another conception to you, which also played a certain role and which was developed by the naturalist Baer.[97] He said to himself: We could imagine that a person lives through their life not in about 70 or 80 years, but in 70 or 80 seconds. Their pulse would simply have to beat so much faster that a year would be contained in one second. This could cause the human being to be not even like a one-day mayfly but like a 70-second creature, if only their pulse beat at a correspondingly fast rate. What would be the consequence? Such a person would go through incredible things in 70 seconds. If, for example, they looked at a plant that has remained true to its species, they would never come to the conclusion that a plant grows out of the earth but they would come to the conclusion that plants are eternal entities. So such a person would relate to the world quite differently, simply in that the speed of their life should be thought to be magnified to the same degree as the speed of their pulse beat in comparison to the rest of us human beings. Or, says Baer, let us imagine that humans don't live for 80 seconds or 80 years, but for 80,000 years, and that the pulse beat goes that much slower, then the whole world would be different again. For example, the sun, while going at a certain speed for us, would then race across the sky like a fiery wind; it would not be the individual sun that would be distinguished but it would race around like a reddish wheel. Plants would shoot up quickly and perish again at breakneck speed, and so on.

Baer put this forward as a possible idea to show how the worldview depends on the subjective constitution of the organism. As you can see, everything, everything becomes shaky.

When considering the kind of thinking that underlies such a notion as Flammarion's Mr Lumen or Baer's, one thing is important to note. Let us take Mr Lumen once more. It is assumed that Mr Lumen would be able to fly 400,000 km per second, thus overtaking light and catching up with the later light images. But now take that which you can take as real when you go deeper into our spiritual-scientific concepts. We can even disregard the coarser physical body altogether and go straight to the etheric body. Well, when we look at the etheric body, what is it? It is ether, light ether; it is itself weaving light. Keep that in mind, because what follows from that? It follows, after all, that if we move in space, we can in the ultimate case move with the speed inherent to light. So when someone says that a human being like Mr Lumen moves at a speed of 400,000 km per second, we have to ask—I will even omit the physical body and just assume that an etheric body could travel out—how fast could it possibly move? Well, at most at a speed of 300,000 km per second, the speed of light. It cannot be said of the etheric body that it overtakes light, for it is itself moving light. So Mr Lumen cannot be woven from anything that exists in space; in other words, he is an unreal conception, he is purely a figment of the imagination. For the speed of the tangible or substantial in the world is immanent or inherent to it. It is intrinsic. It is its characteristic. We cannot rip it out. We cannot say: We separate the speed from the thing, but it is a property of the thing. We cannot speak of a characteristic that lies separately outside the thing. So we must also say with regard to Baer's conceptions: The moment we understand that the speed of the pulse is part of what makes human beings human, we also understand that we cannot have any other speed than that of our pulse. We are human by having a certain speed of the pulse and we cannot think of it as being arbitrary because we would cease to be human if the pulse were, for example, a thousand times faster than it is in reality. The speed belongs to our inherent nature.

It is important to see how spiritual science leads to the essence of things and what that thinking leads to which has developed up to and into our time without engaging with spiritual science. It leads to the formation of conceptions such as that of Mr Lumen or that of the pulse beating a thousand times faster, which are utterly impossible or unreal. We calculate with fanciful concepts if we do not realize that time is a mere number. Thus so-called rational mechanics has led to quite unreal concepts. Spiritual science leads us to say: What indeed is such a Mr Lumen, who speeds along at 400,000 km, whereas 300,000 is the most he ... [Gap in the transcript] ... He is nothing other than the famous gentleman who pulls himself up by his own bootstraps.

Spiritual science, then, from this point of view exists to bring the thinking of the human being, which has fallen into the realm of fantasy, back to reality, not to lead it away from reality. You see, while spiritual science is accused of being fanciful, it is actually there to bring the fanciful ideas and concepts of physics back to reality. And it will be extremely important for healthy thinking that in the future the minds of children are really taught something like the two kinds of division, so that they do not calculate with all kinds of ambiguities, but with definite concepts. We cannot arrive at conceptions and concepts that have a meaning for reality in any other way than by really confronting reality, that is, by thinking with spiritual science, because that is where we arrive at real, not fanciful concepts.

Before the theory of relativity, physics had Newton's conception that space is a void, a vessel, as it were—infinite or not, we will not examine that now—and that time flows along like a uniform stream; objects are in space and processes take place in time, and depending on the time it takes an object to travel through a given space, a certain velocity is attributed to it. This conception is untrue because it does not look at the essence of space and time and thus separates velocity, which is actually an intrinsic property, into the two unreal concepts: space and time. Velocity is really the original thing, whereas physics always sees velocity as a function of space and time. But what belongs to things is their essence, and spiritual science shows that we must take certain paths in order not to arrive at fantasies about space and time—such as that of infinite space or that of time as a flowing stream—but to arrive at the genuine reality of velocity. The whole of mechanics which we absorbed in our youth as something tremendously certain, as the most certain thing there is in science after mathematics, operates with quite vague concepts because it does not know what the nature of velocity is and does not know how to regard it as fundamental.

Now the impulse for the theory of relativity from Minkowski, Einstein, Planck, Poincaré, the late mathematician and physicist, and so on, came precisely because they could no longer come to terms with this childish Newtonian idea of empty space and regularly flowing time and things moving at a certain velocity. Certain experiments gave rise to concepts[98] that did not coincide with what had been regarded as being of the utmost certainty.

Now I set out a concept for you here recently purely in connection with spiritual science which may have come as a surprise to some. I set out the concept that it is not at all true to believe that the most important thing in the head is substance, matter, because precisely where we assume matter to be it is hollow, and from the spiritual-scientific point of view we are all empty-headed. I used the comparison of the air bubbles in a bottle of sparkling water. There it is also the case that where we believe we perceive something real, actual, there is nothing. The spiritual reality is all around and there are holes in it everywhere; you can see them, just as with sparkling water you can only see the bubbles, which are air, you can't see the water. And if people think that there is something where I bump into the table, that is not true either, because there is actually nothing there. I bump into the cavity and because there is nothing there, I can't go any further.

We have arrived at this quite systematically on the basis of spiritual-scientific premises. By another route, certain insightful and knowledgeable physicists have been driven to a similar view because certain processes in nature are simply not compatible with the concepts of Newtonian mechanics, which are regarded as so certain. And these things include, for example, the processes connected with cathode rays with which you are well acquainted and which, as you know, can be observed in certain evacuated glass tubes. There you are dealing with something that has velocity as a moving thing, with electrons, metaphorically speaking with flowing electricity. And through observation, through the experiment that physicists arrived at by observing cathode rays in the tube, which are flowing electricity, they have arrived at very curious ideas. And I would like to read to you one such conception. It is found in a lecture by Poincaré on 'The New Mechanics'.[99] He starts out from the conceptions that arise from the cathode ray experiment, because this does not correspond with Newton's concept of velocity in particular. And then, after a rather confused train of thought, he feels compelled to make the following concession:..... [Gap in the transcript] ..., and here the physicist feels moved to say the following:

'Matter has now become completely passive. The property of resisting the forces that seek to change its movement no longer attaches to it in the true sense of the word. When a cannonball moves at a great speed and thereby becomes the bearer of a living force, of a mighty energy which scatters death and destruction, it is no longer the iron molecules which form the seat of this energy, but this seat is to be sought in the ether which surrounds the molecules. It can almost be said that there is no more matter, there are only holes in the ether.' Well, what more do you want, my dear friends? 'And to the extent that these holes seem to play an active role, it consists in that these holes cannot change their location without affecting the surrounding ether, which exerts a reaction against such changes.'

Matter is holes in the ether! So physics, according to its present experience, is compelled to admit this. And following on from such experience, another physicist, Planck, spoke words[100] that are most remarkable, namely the words stating: We experienced in the forties of the nineteenth century that Helmholtz approached a certain problem—it was not Helmholtz but Julius Robert Mayer, but we do not want to get involved in this important question of priority now—in the way someone does who now doesn't put the cart before the horse, but rather puts the horse before the cart. People had always said previously that the distribution of forces in space must be studied in a certain way.

Helmholtz reversed the matter; he said that the universe must be studied in such a way that only the whole universe can be a perpetual motion machine, while the individual process in the universe can never be a perpetual motion machine. The people before had namely tried to explain the worldview entirely without perpetual motion.

Now, however, Planck says that a similar process must occur with regard to the ether. There are countless theories about the ether, ranging from the conception that people had in the past, when they imagined the ether as diluted matter, to the conception of Lord Kelvin or JJ Thompson who imagined the ether as a rigid liquid—it should not be thought of as a liquid like water, of course—all intermediate stages are represented. And now Planck, as a physicist, says: Physics will only become healthy when we start from the following major premise: no conception of the ether gives a tenable physics which attributes material properties to the ether. These are the words spoken by one of the most important physicists of our time. This means, then, that if the ether is to be a tenable basis of physics, only spiritual properties may be ascribed to it. And so it follows that today's physicists are urged to think of matter as holes and all around them the ether which, however, must be imagined as having no material but only spiritual properties. So: holes surrounded by spiritual ether, that is what must be taken as a basis in order to arrive at a tenable physics. The ground is being prepared for that today; that exists.

Now the question may be raised: Well, so what has then happened to the possibility of justifying a materialistic view of the world if physicists say that matter consists of holes and that the ether can only have spiritual properties? So you almost have to say: There is no more matter, there are only holes in the spiritual ether and matter cannot change its place without exerting an influence on the surrounding ether, a reaction in the spiritual ether. That is where physics has arrived.

We will, however, need a keen logic, will not have to shy away from tackling such questions as to how the concept of velocity is really to be grasped if it is not to contradict what comes to expression in the experiment.

Take these things as something that ought to be said to prove that spiritual science, so reviled as unscientific, is infinitely more scientific in its foundations than that which is considered science today, for it goes to the heart of things, I might say, with the keenest logic. And this is what we must seek above all: a keen grasp of concepts, a precise grasp of what otherwise confronts us as vagueness in the world.

NOTES

Textual sources: The four lectures of Part I were officially taken down in shorthand by Franz Seiler, unofficially by Helene Finckh and Elisabeth Vreede. The first edition (Basel 1958) was published on the basis of the plain text transcription by Finckh and Vreede. For the present edition, this text was compared with the original shorthand notes by Seiler and Finckh, which made it possible to correct numerous transcription errors that had been included in the first edition. Analogous amendments by the editors have been placed in square brackets.

Only one transcript is available for the six lectures of Part II: by Franz Seiler. Its plain text transcription was also checked against the original shorthand note. Deficiencies or gaps, especially in lecture 6, as far as they were identifiable from the shorthand note, were marked. The insertions in round brackets appear thus in the shorthand note; the insertions in square brackets, on the other hand, are by the editors.

For the episodic reflection on space, time and movement included as Part III, two transcripts are available: by Elisabeth Vreede and Johanna Arnold. The plain text transcription by Elisabeth Vreede (original shorthand note not available) was compared with the original shorthand note by Johanna Arnold. Both transcripts have certain deficiencies, which is why the text had to be slightly edited for printing.

The drawings: All drawings in the text were made by Leonore Uhlig from sketches in the audience transcripts. Not all the drawings that were drawn on the blackboard have been preserved by the note takers. The three drawings in the lecture of 2 October 1915 have been reproduced in accordance with those inserted by Rudolf Steiner himself in the transcript. For illustration 7 (page 132), see the note 59.

The title of this volume and the table of contents are by the editors.

Works by Rudolf Steiner which are part of the Complete Works (CW—Gesamtausgabe GA) are indicated in the notes with their bibliography number. See also the overview at the end of the volume.

1. See *Zufall, Notwendigkeit und Vorsehung. Imaginative Erkenntnis und Vorgänge nach dem Tode*, GA 163.
2. Cf. in this regard and with regard to the quote from Leibniz a little further on also Rudolf Steiner's account in *Von Seelenrätseln* (1917) GA 21, 1976, page 103f. and the note referring to p. 175. Aristotle's words can be found analogously in *De anima*, Book 3, Chapter 8; Leibniz's in *New Essays on Human Understanding*, Book II, Chapter 1. Rudolf Steiner, however, clearly took the wording from Vincenz Knauer's work *Die Hauptprobleme der Philosophie in ihrer Entwicklung und teilweisen Lösung von Thales bis Hamerling* (1892), where it says in lecture 21: 'But all cognition takes its beginning with that which is given through the senses, for *nihil est in intellectu, quod non prius fuerit in sensu.*'
3. In the lectures of 30 August and 4 September 1915 in *Zufall, Notwendigkeit und Vorsehung*, GA 163.
4. For example the lectures of 26 November 1914 and 15 January 1915 in *Aus schicksaltragender Zeit*, GA 64.
5. In the lecture of 16 September 1915 (not yet published).
6. *Knowledge of the Higher Worlds. How it is Achieved?* (1904/05), CW 10.
7. Psychoanalysis had been variously mentioned in the previous lectures (not yet published) of 12–16 September 1915.
8. In *The Guardian of the Threshold* (Scene 6), CW 14.
9. *The Spiritual Guidance of the Individual and Humanity. Some Results of Spiritual-Scientific Research into Human History and Development* (1911). CW 15.
10. In his *Phenomenology of Spirit* (1807).
11. In the lecture in Dornach on 27 August 1915 in *Zufall, Notwendigkeit und Vorsehung*, GA 163.
12. GA 1.
13. Rudolf Steiner's Introduction to the first volume of Goethe's scientific writings begins by quoting this sentence: 'On 18 August 1787, Goethe

wrote to Knebel from Italy: "From what I have seen of plants and fish near Naples and in Sicily, I would, if I were ten years younger, be very tempted to make a trip to India, not in order to discover something new, but to look in my own way at what has already been discovered."'

14 See Haeckel's *Die Welträtsel*, Bonn 1899 (Chapter 5, Section 'Transformismus').

15 The sentence written by Rudolf Steiner on the blackboard comes from Saint-Martin's work *Le Nouvel Homme*, Paris n.y. (Chapter 28).

16 See for example the lecture in Dornach of 27 March 1915 in *Artistic Sensitivity as a Spiritual Approach to Knowing Life and the World*, CW 161.

17 See *The Guardian of the Threshold* (People, Figures and Events) in CW 14.

18 Prof. Dr med hc Alfred Gysi. 1864–1957. Professor and director at the Dental Institute of the University of Zurich, of which he was one of the founders. However, the suggestion of writing an embryological work did not get beyond certain beginning stages. See also a corresponding statement by Rudolf Steiner in the lecture of 23 February 1924 in *Natur und Mensch in geisteswissenschaftlicher Betrachtung*, GA 352.

19 See lecture in Dornach on 30 January 1915 in *Artistic Sensitivity as a Spiritual Approach to Knowing Life and the World*, CW 161.

20 Christian Morgenstern, 'The aesthetic weasel' (cf. page 61 in this volume).

21 *The Guardian of the Threshold* (Scene 1), GA 14.

22 *Christianity as Mystical Fact* (1902), CW 8.

23 See *The Effects of Esoteric Development*, CW 145.

24 *The Riddles of Philosophy* (1914), CW 18.

25 In a number of lectures in September 1915 (not yet printed.)

26 Cf. *The Genius of Language*, CW 299, as well as the lectures in Dornach of 17 and 18 July 1915 in *Artistic Sensitivity as a Spiritual Approach to Knowing Life and the World*, CW 161.

27 Cf. *Anthroposophy in the Light of Goethe's Faust*, CW 272, and *Goethe's Faust in the Light of Anthropsophy*, CW 273.

28 Baron Ferdinand von Wrangell (also Wrangel) from the Baltic region, retired Russian state councillor, was a specialist for oceanography and meteorology, including five years (1873-78) leading the physical exploration of the Black Sea, and editor of the Russian Annals of Hydrography from 1901–06. From 1907 onwards he lived in Ascona, Switzerland.

He was also a well-known pacifist and as such was among those who signed Rudolf Steiner's 'Appeal to the German People and to the Cultural World!' (1919). Since he dedicated a copy of his pamphlet *Science and Theosophy* to Adolf Arenson, a leading anthroposophist in Stuttgart 'with gratitude for lessons given', it can be assumed that he had a loose connection with members of the Anthroposophical Society.

29 For example the lecture in Dornach on 31 December 1918 in *How Can Mankind Find the Christ Again? The Threefold Shadow-Existence of Our Time and the New Light of Christ.* CW 187.

30 'Über die Grenzen des Naturerkennens'. *Vortrag gehalten auf der 2. Sitzung der 45. Versammlung deutscher Naturforscher und Ärzte, Leipzig 14. August 1872.* 1st Edition Leipzig 1872. The passage marked by Rudolf Steiner reads verbatim:

If we think of all changes in the physical world as being dissolved into the movements of atoms, which are caused by their constant central forces, then the universe would be scientifically understood. The state of the world during a time differential would appear as the direct effect of its state during the previous one and as the direct cause of its state during the following time differential. Laws and chance would only be other names for mechanical necessity. Indeed, it is possible to imagine a stage of knowledge of nature at which the whole process of the world would be represented by a mathematical formula, by an immeasurable system of simultaneous differential equations, from which the location, direction of movement and speed of every atom in the universe would be derived at any time. 'A mind,' says Laplace, 'that knew for any given moment all the forces at work in nature and the reciprocal position of the entities of which it is composed, if besides it were comprehensive enough to subject this information to analysis, would comprehend in the same formula the motions of the largest cosmic bodies and of the lightest atom: nothing would be uncertain to it and future as well as past would be to present its gaze. The human intellect, in the perfection which it has known how to give to astronomy, presents a feeble image of such a mind.'

31 Heinrich Schramm. Head of the upper secondary school in Wiener-Neustadt. The essay appeared in 1873 in the eighth annual report of the school under the title 'Die Anziehungskraft betrachtet als Wirkung

der Bewegung' (The force of attraction considered as an effect of motion). Cf. Rudolf Steiner, *Autobiography. Chapters in the Course of My Life, 1861–1907* (Chapter 2), CW 28.

32 The lecture to which this remark refers could not be determined; it could possibly be the lecture in Dornach on 20 August 1915 (in this volume).

33 The two main groups of 'explainers of Faust who have explained themselves to death' were called '*Stoffhuber*' (collectors of matter) and '*Sinnhuber*' (collectors of meaning) by Vischer. The *Stoffhuber* are the ones 'who are now searching the Frankfurt church records to see if Mrs Marthe Schwertlein is in them; and the Sinnhuber, who suspect an allegory in everything, for whom everything is allegory'. Cf. Friedrich Theodor Vischer, *Ausgewählte Werke in acht Teilen*, edited and introduced by Theodor Kappstein. Part Four: Faust. Der Tragödie dritter Teil. Pro Domo, Hesse & Becker Verlag, Leipzig n.y.

34 Founder of the energetic worldview; took over the leadership of the German Monist League around 1912 at Haeckel's instigation. His lecture referred to, 'The Overcoming of Scientific Materialism', was given at the third general meeting of the assembly of the Society of German Naturalists and Physicians in Lübeck on 20 September 1895 and printed in the same year. The passage freely reproduced by Rudolf Steiner reads verbatim: '... Imagine getting hit with a stick! What do you feel then, the stick or its energy? There can only be one answer: energy. For the stick is the most harmless thing in the world as long as it is not swung. But we can also bump into a stick at rest! Quite right: what we feel are, as already emphasized, differences of energy states against our sensory apparatuses, and therefore it is immaterial whether the stick moves against us or we move against the stick.'

35 Berlin, 10 April 1913 in *Results of Spiritual Research*, CW 62.

36 'A dirty vortex is existence': freely rendered line from the fourth part of the poems 'At midnight'.

37 For example in the lecture in Stuttgart, 13 November 1909 in *Deeper Secrets of Human Evolution in the Light of the Gospels*, CW 117; cf. also *Autobiography*, CW 28.

38 Four lectures about anthroposophy in Berlin. 23–27 October 1909 in *A Psychology of Body, Soul, and Spirit*, CW 115.

39 This was the name of the journal that Rudolf Steiner published from 1903 to 1908. His essays published in it are collected in the volume *Lucifer-Gnosis*, GA 34.
40 Marie Eugenie delle Grazie was educated by Professor Laurenz Müllner. Cf. *Autobiography*. CW 28.
41 *Gedichte*, Leipzig 1882; '*Hermann*', *ein deutsches Heldengedicht in zwölf Gesängen*, Wien 1883; '*Saul*', *Tragödie in 5 Akten*, 1885; '*Die Zigeunerin*', *Erzählung*, Vienna 1885. Cf. also *Autobiography*, CW 28.
42 By delle Grazie, Vienna 1894.
43 In Colmar on 19 November 1905, of which, however, no transcript exists.
44 Cf. *Anthroposophy in the Light of Goethe's Faust*, CW 272 and *Goethe's Faust in the Light of Anthroposophy*, CW 273.
45 See *Goethes Naturwissenschaftliche Schriften*, edited and elucidated by Rudolf Steiner, 5 volumes 1883-1897, reproduction Dornach 1975, GA 1a-e.
46 Cf. Note 45.
47 Cf. *Autobiography*, CW 28.
48 *Truth and Knowledge* (1892), CW 3.
49 Dornach, 20 August 1915 (in this volume).
50 The name is not known.
51 In the discussions that took place alongside these lectures about internal society matters.
52 *Human and Cosmic Thought*, CW 151.
53 Recent measurements have shown that the earth's rotation is not exactly uniform.
54 In the treatise 'Bemerkungen über die Kräfte in der unbelebten Natur', Liebigs Annalen, Volume 42, 1842. Mayer found the value 1 kcal = 365 mkg instead of 427 mkg for the equivalent of heat. This was not due to incorrect thinking but to insufficiently accurate measurements, which he took from the literature. Until then no one had suspected such a fundamental law behind these measurements, such as behind the difference between the specific heat CP and CV.
55 In 1847 wrote 'Über die Erhaltung der Kraft' and also 'Robert Mayers Priorität' in 'Über die Wechselwirkung der Naturkräfte' in *Vorträge und Reden von Hermann von Helmholtz*, Volume 1 (5th Edition Brunswick 1903).

56 Cf. the lecture in Stuttgart on 13 January 1921 in *Interdisciplinary Astronomy* (lecture 13). CW 323.
57 The six-volume main work of Copernicus, *De revolutionibus orbium coelestium libri VI*, published in 1543, was put on the Index in 1615 and was not removed until 1822 when the Sanctum Officium declared that the publication of works dealing with the movement of the earth and the sun standing still was not prohibited.
58 The story goes that Newton discovered the law of gravity in 1666 by an apple falling from a tree.
59 The diagram was drawn by Rudolf Steiner himself in the margin of the typewritten copy of the lecture transcript. It is unusual. The common diagram has AB parallel to the contact radius of the tangent. Thus it actually holds only for an infinitesimal movement and we draw something contradictory if, as is unavoidable, we draw a finite diagram inside the circle. The present diagram applies in the finite. It is the generalization of the drawing for the horizontal projection where we also consider the total displacement AB which is caused by the force of attraction, when the body would have reached A by the initial momentum alone. The only difference is that in the projection AB remains parallel to itself, whereas here it rotates, albeit more slowly than the radius of point B, namely according to the formula tan v = (û—sin u) : (1—cos u), u = angle of rotation of B, v = rotation that AB performs, û = radian of u. In Rudolf Steiner's illustration u = 37.8°, v = 26.1°, whereas the calculated value for v would only be 12.6°. AB becoming tilted is clearly emphasized, without anything else being said.
60 Cf. Note 31.
61 Schelling, for example. Cf. in *The Riddles of Philosophy*, CW 18 and *The Light Course. First Course in Natural Science*, CW 320.
62 Cf. Note 31.
63 It could be the treatise 'Über die Lebenskraft'. Cf. *Reden von Emil Du Bois-Reymond in zwei Bänden*, Volume 1, Leipzig 1912.
64 Cf. Note 34.
65 Today, only the indestructibility of energy applies, while mass can disappear and come into being.
66 Cf. 'Questions of life. Speech given on 22 September 1886 at the 2nd general session of the 59th Meeting of German Natural Scientists and Physicians', Berlin 1887.

67 Austrian botanist, co-founder of the science of plant raw materials.
68 In the texts *Die Gesetze des Energieverbrauchs bei der Ernährung*, Leipzig and Vienna 1902; *Kraft und Stoff im Haushalte der Natur*, Leipzig 1909.
69 In *Über die Grenzen des Naturerkennens* (cf. Note 30) it says verbatim: 'Where the material conditions for spiritual activity in the form of a nervous system are lacking, as in plants, the naturalist cannot admit a soul life, and only rarely does he meet with contradiction in this. But what would be the answer if, before he consented to accept a world soul, he demanded to be shown somewhere in the world, bedded in neuroglia and fed with warm arterial blood under proper pressure, a convolute of ganglion cells and nerve fibres corresponding in extent to the mental faculty of such a soul?'
70 CW 153.
71 The first Goetheanum, which had been under construction since 1913 and was destroyed by fire on New Year's Eve 1922/23.
72 Schloss Elmau in Upper Bavaria was founded by Johannes Müller as a 'sanctuary for personal life'.
73 *The Riddles of Philosophy* (1914), CW 18.
74 Cf. Note 57.
75 In *Tischreden*, Volume 4, No. 4638 of the complete critical edition, Weimar 1916.
76 In the inaugural speech, Vienna, 8 November 1894, 'Die Bedeutung Galileis für die Philosophie', printed in the journal *Die Drei*, Volume 16, 1933/34.
77 In *Die Erziehung des Menschengeschlechts*, published in 1780.
78 Cf. *Autobiography*, CW 28.
79 Published in 1900. In the complete works in *Methodische Grundlagen der Anthroposophie*, GA 30.
80 *Goethe's Theory of Knowledge. An Outline of the Epistemology of His Worldview* (1886). CW 2 (Chapter 14).
81 Cf. lecture on 27 March and 1 May 1915 in *Artistic Sensitivity as a Spiritual Approach to Knowing Life and the World*. CW 161.
82 Refers to the first larger complete model of the wooden sculpture 'The Representative of Humanity between Lucifer and Ahriman', which was created at that time.

83 See *Anatomische Studien an Verbrecher-Gehirnen. Für Anthropologen, Mediciner, Juristen und Psychologen bearbeitet*, by Moriz Benedikt, Vienna 1879.
84 Lecture in Dornach, 1 May 1915 in *Artistic Sensitivity as a Spiritual Approach to Knowing Life and the World*, CW 161.
85 Lecture in Dornach, 4 January 1915 in *Art as Seen in the Light of Mystery Wisdom*, CW 275.
86 Dornach, 18 September 1915 (in this volume).
87 Goethe reports the conversation from June 1794 in his *Naturwissenschaftliche Schriften*, see Volume 1 (*Bildung und Umbildung organischer Naturen*, the essay 'Glückliches Ereignis'), GA 1a, p. 8ff.
88 Single pamphlet. Within the complete edition in the volume *Luzifer-Gnosis*, GA 34. On the importance of education in the case of an occipital lobe that is too short, see also the lecture in Berlin on 7 March 1916 in *The Human Spirit Past and Present*, CW 167.
89 An educational approach founded by Friedrich Froebel (1782-1852) and modelled on Pestalozzi which emphasizes the all-round promotion of all human faculties, e.g. through 'activity games' for children. Main work *The Education of Man*, 1826. Fröbel founded the first kindergarten and a seminar for kindergarten teachers in 1837.
90 Edited by Maximilian Harden, Vol. XXIII, No. 52, Berlin 25 September 1915.
91 In *Friedrich Nietzsche, ein Kämpfer gegen seine Zeit* (1897), Chapter 1, GA 5.
92 *Theosophy* (1904), CW 9.
93 First and foremost Max Planck, who in 1911 at the meeting of natural scientists in Königsberg 'pointed out without encountering any opposition that with the establishment of the principle of relativity and through the results of recent research into the constitution of matter, for example, a change in our physical worldview was being prepared and a movement of such a radical and revolutionary nature had begun as we have probably only experienced once before in the history of physics, namely 300 years ago when the fiercest scientific battles were fought with the cry: Here the Copernican, here the Ptolemaic world system'. Quoted from F. Himstedt's lecture on 'Neuere Anschauungen über Zeit, Raum und Materie' at the first festive meeting of the Freiburg Scientific Society on 26 October 1912, Freiburg i. Br. and Leipzig 1913 (in Rudolf Steiner's library).

228 * The Value of Thinking

94 Presumably this refers to the lectures on F. von Wrangell's pamphlet *Science and Theosophy* (in this volume).

95 This and the whole of the foregoing is opposed by the dimensional calculus of physics in which every physicist and engineer is trained. However, this training should not obscure the fact that the relationship velocity = distance : time is not a real equation. What it says on the right-hand side is not an executable operation and only has the form, not the content, of a division. The right side is therefore not explained by itself. That is what is implied in these remarks. Now the task is not to examine the meaning of the dimensional calculus in greater detail. It has, of course, proved itself in its way, even though no person is really able to carry out operations like distance : time. On the other hand, practical life shows how little this calculation requires thought, for example in the calculation of interest. Here no one thinks of taking time other than as a pure number, for example in the formula interest = capital $\cdot \frac{P}{100} \cdot$ t. $\frac{P}{100}$ is, as the interest factor q = 1 + $\frac{P}{100}$ shows, a pure number, and as far as interest is concerned, no one has any difficulty in principle in capitalizing it, which leaves for t only dimensionless time.

96 In this account, Rudolf Steiner did not base himself directly on Flammarion's work *Lumen*, although it is in his library, but on the account given by Henri Poincaré in his small work *Die neue Mechanik*, Leipzig and Berlin 1913 (2nd edition, p. 8/9).

97 Professor of anatomy in Königsberg (present-day Kaliningrad) und Petersburg. Considered the founder of modern evolutionary history. His conception, cited by Rudolf Steiner, is found in the speech from the year 1860 'Welche Auffassung der lebenden Natur ist die richtige?' ('Which conception of living nature is the correct one?'). Republished in Karl Baer, *Entwicklung und Zielstrebigkeit in der Natur. Schriften des frühen Goetheanismus*, Stuttgart 1983.

98 This probably refers to Michelson's experiment which proved the speed of light to be independent of the motional state of the system in which it is done.

99 Cf. Note 96. The quotation cited can be found on page 18/19.

100 They are found in Planck's lecture, delivered on 23 September 1910 at the 82nd Assembly of German Natural Scientists and Physicians in Königsberg (present-day Kaliningrad): 'In his Königs-

berg lecture, which I mentioned at the beginning, Helmholtz stressed with particular emphasis that the first step towards the discovery of the principle of energy had been taken when the question first arose: What relationships must exist between the forces of nature if it is said to be impossible to build a perpetual motion machine? Similarly, it can certainly be rightly said that the first step towards the discovery of the principle of relativity coincides with the question: What relationships must exist between the forces of nature if it is said to be impossible to demonstrate any material properties in the light ether? That is, if the light waves propagate through space without adhering to a material carrier at all? Then, of course, the speed of a moving body in relation to the light ether would not be definable at all, let alone measurable.

I need not emphasize that the mechanical view of nature is utterly incompatible with this view.' ('Die Stellung der neueren Physik zur mechanischen Naturanschauung', Physikal. Zeitschr. 11, p. 922-932, 1910; Max Planck: *Physikalische Abhandlungen und Vorträge*, Brunswick 1958, Vol. 3, p. 30-46).

Rudolf Steiner's Collected Works

The German Edition of Rudolf Steiner's Collected Works (the *Gesamtausgabe* [GA] published by Rudolf Steiner Verlag, Dornach, Switzerland) presently runs to 354 titles, organized either by type of work (written or spoken), chronology, audience (public or other), or subject (education, art, etc.). For ease of comparison, the Collected Works in English [CW] follows the German organization exactly. A complete listing of the CWs follows with literal translations of the German titles. Other than in the case of the books published in his lifetime, titles were rarely given by Rudolf Steiner himself, and were often provided by the editors of the German editions. The titles in English are not necessarily the same as the German; and, indeed, over the past 75 years have frequently been different, with the same book sometimes appearing under different titles.

For ease of identification and to avoid confusion, we suggest that readers looking for a title should do so by CW number. Because the work of creating the Collected Works of Rudolf Steiner is an ongoing process, with new titles being published every year, we have not indicated in this listing which books are presently available. To find out what titles in the Collected Works are currently in print, please check our website at www.rudolfsteinerpress.com (or www.steinerbooks.org for US readers).

Written Work

CW 1   Goethe: Natural-Scientific Writings, Introduction, with Footnotes and Explanations in the text by Rudolf Steiner

CW 2   Outlines of an Epistemology of the Goethean World View, with Special Consideration of Schiller

CW 3   Truth and Science

CW 4   The Philosophy of Freedom

CW 4a   Documents to 'The Philosophy of Freedom'

CW 5   Friedrich Nietzsche, A Fighter against His Time

CW 6   Goethe's Worldview
CW 6a Now in CW 30
CW 7   Mysticism at the Dawn of Modern Spiritual Life and Its Relationship with Modern Worldviews
CW 8   Christianity as Mystical Fact and the Mysteries of Antiquity
CW 9   Theosophy: An Introduction into Supersensible World Knowledge and Human Purpose
CW 10 How Does One Attain Knowledge of Higher Worlds?
CW 11 From the Akasha-Chronicle
CW 12 Levels of Higher Knowledge
CW 13 Occult Science in Outline
CW 14 Four Mystery Dramas
CW 15 The Spiritual Guidance of the Individual and Humanity
CW 16 A Way to Human Self-Knowledge: Eight Meditations
CW 17 The Threshold of the Spiritual World. Aphoristic Comments
CW 18 The Riddles of Philosophy in Their History, Presented as an Outline
CW 19 Contained in CW 24
CW 20 The Riddles of the Human Being: Articulated and Unarticulated in the Thinking, Views and Opinions of a Series of German and Austrian Personalities
CW 21 The Riddles of the Soul
CW 22 Goethe's Spiritual Nature and its Revelation in 'Faust' and through the 'Fairy Tale of the Snake and the Lily'
CW 23 The Central Points of the Social Question in the Necessities of Life in the Present and the Future
CW 24 Essays Concerning the Threefold Division of the Social Organism and the Period 1915-1921
CW 25 Cosmology, Religion and Philosophy
CW 26 Anthroposophical Leading Thoughts
CW 27 Fundamentals for Expansion of the Art of Healing according to Spiritual-Scientific Insights
CW 28 The Course of My Life
CW 29 Collected Essays on Dramaturgy, 1889-1900
CW 30 Methodical Foundations of Anthroposophy: Collected Essays on Philosophy, Natural Science, Aesthetics and Psychology, 1884-1901
CW 31 Collected Essays on Culture and Current Events, 1887-1901
CW 32 Collected Essays on Literature, 1884-1902
CW 33 Biographies and Biographical Sketches, 1894-1905
CW 34 Lucifer-Gnosis: Foundational Essays on Anthroposophy and Reports from the Periodicals 'Lucifer' and 'Lucifer-Gnosis,' 1903-1908
CW 35 Philosophy and Anthroposophy: Collected Essays, 1904-1923
CW 36 The Goetheanum-Idea in the Middle of the Cultural Crisis of the Present: Collected Essays from the Periodical 'Das Goetheanum,' 1921-1925

CW 37   Now in CWs 260a and 251
CW 38   Letters, Vol. 1: 1881-1890
CW 39   Letters, Vol. 2: 1890-1925
CW 40   Truth-Wrought Words
CW 40a Sayings, Poems and Mantras; Supplementary Volume
CW 42   Now in CWs 264-266
CW 43   Stage Adaptations
CW 44   On the Four Mystery Dramas. Sketches, Fragments and Paralipomena on the Four Mystery Dramas
CW 45   Anthroposophy: A Fragment from the Year 1910

Public Lectures
CW 51   On Philosophy, History and Literature
CW 52   Spiritual Teachings Concerning the Soul and Observation of the World
CW 53   The Origin and Goal of the Human Being
CW 54   The Riddles of the World and Anthroposophy
CW 55   Knowledge of the Supersensible in Our Times and Its Meaning for Life Today
CW 56   Knowledge of the Soul and of the Spirit
CW 57   Where and How Does One Find the Spirit?
CW 58   The Metamorphoses of the Soul Life. Paths of Soul Experiences: Part One
CW 59   The Metamorphoses of the Soul Life. Paths of Soul Experiences: Part Two
CW 60   The Answers of Spiritual Science to the Biggest Questions of Existence
CW 61   Human History in the Light of Spiritual Research
CW 62   Results of Spiritual Research
CW 63   Spiritual Science as a Treasure for Life
CW 64   Out of Destiny-Burdened Times
CW 65   Out of Central European Spiritual Life
CW 66   Spirit and Matter, Life and Death
CW 67   The Eternal in the Human Soul. Immortality and Freedom
CW 68   Public lectures in various cities, 1906-1918
CW 69   Public lectures in various cities, 1906-1918
CW 70   Public lectures in various cities, 1906-1918
CW 71   Public lectures in various cities, 1906-1918
CW 72   Freedom—Immortality—Social Life
CW 73   The Supplementing of the Modern Sciences through Anthroposophy
CW 73a Specialized Fields of Knowledge and Anthroposophy
CW 74   The Philosophy of Thomas Aquinas
CW 75   Public lectures in various cities, 1906-1918
CW 76   The Fructifying Effect of Anthroposophy on Specialized Fields
CW 77a The Task of Anthroposophy in Relation to Science and Life: The Darmstadt College Course
CW 77b Art and Anthroposophy. The Goetheanum-Impulse

CW 78	Anthroposophy, Its Roots of Knowledge and Fruits for Life
CW 79	The Reality of the Higher Worlds
CW 80	Public lectures in various cities, 1922
CW 81	Renewal-Impulses for Culture and Science—Berlin College Course
CW 82	So that the Human Being Can Become a Complete Human Being
CW 83	Western and Eastern World-Contrast. Paths to Understanding It through Anthroposophy
CW 84	What Did the Goetheanum Intend and What Should Anthroposophy Do?

Lectures to the Members of the Anthroposophical Society

CW 88	Concerning the Astral World and Devachan
CW 89	Consciousness—Life—Form. Fundamental Principles of a Spiritual-Scientific Cosmology
CW 90	Participant Notes from the Lectures during the Years 1903-1905
CW 91	Participant Notes from the Lectures during the Years 1903-1905
CW 92	The Occult Truths of Ancient Myths and Sagas
CW 93	The Temple Legend and the Golden Legend
CW 93a	Fundamentals of Esotericism
CW 94	Cosmogony. Popular Occultism. The Gospel of John. The Theosophy in the Gospel of John
CW 95	At the Gates of Theosophy
CW 96	Origin-Impulses of Spiritual Science. Christian Esotericism in the Light of New Spirit-Knowledge
CW 97	The Christian Mystery
CW 98	Nature Beings and Spirit Beings—Their Effects in Our Visible World
CW 99	The Theosophy of the Rosicrucians
CW 100	Human Development and Christ-Knowledge
CW 101	Myths and Legends. Occult Signs and Symbols
CW 102	The Working into Human Beings by Spiritual Beings
CW 103	The Gospel of John
CW 104	The Apocalypse of John
CW 104a	From the Picture-Script of the Apocalypse of John
CW 105	Universe, Earth, the Human Being: Their Being and Development, as well as Their Reflection in the Connection between Egyptian Mythology and Modern Culture
CW 106	Egyptian Myths and Mysteries in Relation to the Active Spiritual Forces of the Present
CW 107	Spiritual-Scientific Knowledge of the Human Being
CW 108	Answering the Questions of Life and the World through Anthroposophy
CW 109	The Principle of Spiritual Economy in Connection with the Question of Reincarnation. An Aspect of the Spiritual Guidance of Humanity
CW 110	The Spiritual Hierarchies and Their Reflection in the Physical World. Zodiac, Planets and Cosmos

CW 111	Contained in CW 109
CW 112	The Gospel of John in Relation to the Three Other Gospels, Especially the Gospel of Luke
CW 113	The Orient in the Light of the Occident. The Children of Lucifer and the Brothers of Christ
CW 114	The Gospel of Luke
CW 115	Anthroposophy—Psychosophy—Pneumatosophy
CW 116	The Christ-Impulse and the Development of I-Consciousness
CW 117	The Deeper Secrets of the Development of Humanity in Light of the Gospels
CW 118	The Event of the Christ-Appearance in the Etheric World
CW 119	Macrocosm and Microcosm. The Large World and the Small World. Soul-Questions, Life-Questions, Spirit-Questions
CW 120	The Revelation of Karma
CW 121	The Mission of Individual Folk-Souls in Connection with Germanic-Nordic Mythology
CW 122	The Secrets of the Biblical Creation-Story. The Six-Day Work in the First Book of Moses
CW 123	The Gospel of Matthew
CW 124	Excursus in the Area of the Gospel of Mark
CW 125	Paths and Goals of the Spiritual Human Being. Life Questions in the Light of Spiritual Science
CW 126	Occult History. Esoteric Observations of the Karmic Relationships of Personalities and Events of World History
CW 127	The Mission of the New Spiritual Revelation. The Christ-Event as the Middle-Point of Earth Evolution
CW 128	An Occult Physiology
CW 129	Wonders of the World, Trials of the Soul, and Revelations of the Spirit
CW 130	Esoteric Christianity and the Spiritual Guidance of Humanity
CW 131	From Jesus to Christ
CW 132	Evolution from the View Point of the Truth
CW 133	The Earthly and the Cosmic Human Being
CW 134	The World of the Senses and the World of the Spirit
CW 135	Reincarnation and Karma and their Meaning for the Culture of the Present
CW 136	The Spiritual Beings in Celestial Bodies and the Realms of Nature
CW 137	The Human Being in the Light of Occultism, Theosophy and Philosophy
CW 138	On Initiation. On Eternity and the Passing Moment. On the Light of the Spirit and the Darkness of Life
CW 139	The Gospel of Mark
CW 140	Occult Investigation into the Life between Death and New Birth. The Living Interaction between Life and Death
CW 141	Life between Death and New Birth in Relationship to Cosmic Facts

CW 142	The Bhagavad Gita and the Letters of Paul
CW 143	Experiences of the Supersensible. Three Paths of the Soul to Christ
CW 144	The Mysteries of the East and of Christianity
CW 145	What Significance Does Occult Development of the Human Being Have for the Sheaths—Physical Body, Etheric Body, Astral Body, and Self?
CW 146	The Occult Foundations of the Bhagavad Gita
CW 147	The Secrets of the Threshold
CW 148	Out of Research in the Akasha: The Fifth Gospel
CW 149	Christ and the Spiritual World. Concerning the Search for the Holy Grail
CW 150	The World of the Spirit and Its Extension into Physical Existence; The Influence of the Dead in the World of the Living
CW 151	Human Thought and Cosmic Thought
CW 152	Preliminary Stages to the Mystery of Golgotha
CW 153	The Inner Being of the Human Being and Life Between Death and New Birth
CW 154	How Does One Gain an Understanding of the Spiritual World? The Flowing in of Spiritual Impulses from out of the World of the Deceased
CW 155	Christ and the Human Soul. Concerning the Meaning of Life. Theosophical Morality. Anthroposophy and Christianity
CW 156	Occult Reading and Occult Hearing
CW 157	Human Destinies and the Destiny of Peoples
CW 157a	The Formation of Destiny and the Life after Death
CW 158	The Connection Between the Human Being and the Elemental World. Kalevala—Olaf Åsteson—The Russian People—The World as the Result of the Influences of Equilibrium
CW 159	The Mystery of Death. The Nature and Significance of Middle Europe and the European Folk Spirits
CW 160	In CW 159
CW 161	Paths of Spiritual Knowledge and the Renewal of the Artistic Worldview
CW 162	Questions of Art and Life in Light of Spiritual Science
CW 163	Coincidence, Necessity and Providence. Imaginative Knowledge and the Processes after Death
CW 164	The Value of Thinking for a Knowledge That Satisfies the Human Being. The Relationship of Spiritual Science to Natural Science
CW 165	The Spiritual Unification of Humanity through the Christ-Impulse
CW 166	Necessity and Freedom in the Events of the World and in Human Action
CW 167	The Present and the Past in the Human Spirit
CW 168	The Connection between the Living and the Dead
CW 169	World-being and Selfhood
CW 170	The Riddle of the Human Being. The Spiritual Background of Human History. Cosmic and Human History, Vol. 1

CW 171	Inner Development-Impulses of Humanity. Goethe and the Crisis of the 19th Century. Cosmic and Human History, Vol. 2
CW 172	The Karma of the Vocation of the Human Being in Connection with Goethe's Life. Cosmic and Human History, Vol. 3
CW 173	Contemporary-Historical Considerations: The Karma of Untruthfulness, Part One. Cosmic and Human History, Vol. 4
CW 174	Contemporary-Historical Considerations: The Karma of Untruthfulness, Part Two. Cosmic and Human History, Vol. 5
CW 174a	Middle Europe between East and West. Cosmic and Human History, Vol. 6
CW 174b	The Spiritual Background of the First World War. Cosmic and Human History, Vol. 7
CW 175	Building Stones for an Understanding of the Mystery of Golgotha. Cosmic and Human Metamorphoses
CW 176	Truths of Evolution of the Individual and Humanity. The Karma of Materialism
CW 177	The Spiritual Background of the Outer World. The Fall of the Spirits of Darkness. Spiritual Beings and Their Effects, Vol. 1
CW 178	Individual Spiritual Beings and their Influence in the Soul of the Human Being. Spiritual Beings and their Effects, Vol. 2
CW 179	Spiritual Beings and Their Effects. Historical Necessity and Freedom. The Influences on Destiny from out of the World of the Dead. Spiritual Beings and Their Effects, Vol. 3
CW 180	Mystery Truths and Christmas Impulses. Ancient Myths and their Meaning. Spiritual Beings and Their Effects, Vol. 4
CW 181	Earthly Death and Cosmic Life. Anthroposophical Gifts for Life. Necessities of Consciousness for the Present and the Future.
CW 182	Death as Transformation of Life
CW 183	The Science of the Development of the Human Being
CW 184	The Polarity of Duration and Development in Human Life. The Cosmic Pre-History of Humanity
CW 185	Historical Symptomology
CW 185a	Historical-Developmental Foundations for Forming a Social Judgement
CW 186	The Fundamental Social Demands of Our Time—In Changed Situations
CW 187	How Can Humanity Find the Christ Again? The Threefold Shadow-Existence of our Time and the New Christ-Light
CW 188	Goetheanism, a Transformation-Impulse and Resurrection-Thought. Science of the Human Being and Science of Sociology
CW 189	The Social Question as a Question of Consciousness. The Spiritual Background of the Social Question, Vol. 1
CW 190	Impulses of the Past and the Future in Social Occurrences. The Spiritual Background of the Social Question, Vol. 2

CW 191	Social Understanding from Spiritual-Scientific Cognition. The Spiritual Background of the Social Question, Vol. 3
CW 192	Spiritual-Scientific Treatment of Social and Pedagogical Questions
CW 193	The Inner Aspect of the Social Riddle. Luciferic Past and Ahrimanic Future
CW 194	The Mission of Michael. The Revelation of the Actual Mysteries of the Human Being
CW 195	Cosmic New Year and the New Year Idea
CW 196	Spiritual and Social Transformations in the Development of Humanity
CW 197	Polarities in the Development of Humanity: West and East Materialism and Mysticism Knowledge and Belief
CW 198	Healing Factors for the Social Organism
CW 199	Spiritual Science as Knowledge of the Foundational Impulses of Social Formation
CW 200	The New Spirituality and the Christ-Experience of the 20th Century
CW 201	The Correspondences Between Microcosm and Macrocosm. The Human Being—A Hieroglyph of the Universe. The Human Being in Relationship with the Cosmos: 1
CW 202	The Bridge between the World-Spirituality and the Physical Aspect of the Human Being. The Search for the New Isis, the Divine Sophia. The Human Being in Relationship with the Cosmos: 2
CW 203	The Responsibility of Human Beings for the Development of the World through their Spiritual Connection with the Planet Earth and the World of the Stars. The Human Being in Relationship with the Cosmos: 3
CW 204	Perspectives of the Development of Humanity. The Materialistic Knowledge-Impulse and the Task of Anthroposophy. The Human Being in Relationship with the Cosmos: 4
CW 205	Human Development, World-Soul, and World-Spirit. Part One: The Human Being as a Being of Body and Soul in Relationship to the World. The Human Being in Relationship with the Cosmos: 5
CW 206	Human Development, World-Soul, and World-Spirit. Part Two: The Human Being as a Spiritual Being in the Process of Historical Development. The Human Being in Relationship with the Cosmos: 6
CW 207	Anthroposophy as Cosmosophy. Part One: Characteristic Features of the Human Being in the Earthly and the Cosmic Realms. The Human Being in Relationship with the Cosmos: 7
CW 208	Anthroposophy as Cosmosophy. Part Two: The Forming of the Human Being as the Result of Cosmic Influence. The Human Being in Relationship with the Cosmos: 8
CW 209	Nordic and Central European Spiritual Impulses. The Festival of the Appearance of Christ. The Human Being in Relationship with the Cosmos: 9

CW 210	Old and New Methods of Initiation. Drama and Poetry in the Change of Consciousness in the Modern Age
CW 211	The Sun Mystery and the Mystery of Death and Resurrection. Exoteric and Esoteric Christianity
CW 212	Human Soul Life and Spiritual Striving in Connection with World and Earth Development
CW 213	Human Questions and World Answers
CW 214	The Mystery of the Trinity: The Human Being in Relationship with the Spiritual World in the Course of Time
CW 215	Philosophy, Cosmology, and Religion in Anthroposophy
CW 216	The Fundamental Impulses of the World-Historical Development of Humanity
CW 217	Spiritually Active Forces in the Coexistence of the Older and Younger Generations. Pedagogical Course for Youth
CW 217a	Youth's Cognitive Task
CW 218	Spiritual Connections in the Forming of the Human Organism
CW 219	The Relationship of the World of the Stars to the Human Being, and of the Human Being to the World of the Stars. The Spiritual Communion of Humanity
CW 220	Living Knowledge of Nature. Intellectual Fall and Spiritual Redemption
CW 221	Earth-Knowing and Heaven-Insight
CW 222	The Imparting of Impulses to World-Historical Events through Spiritual Powers
CW 223	The Cycle of the Year as Breathing Process of the Earth and the Four Great Festival-Seasons. Anthroposophy and the Human Heart (*Gemüt*)
CW 224	The Human Soul and its Connection with Divine-Spiritual Individualities. The Internalization of the Festivals of the Year
CW 225	Three Perspectives of Anthroposophy. Cultural Phenomena observed from a Spiritual-Scientific Perspective
CW 226	Human Being, Human Destiny, and World Development
CW 227	Initiation-Knowledge
CW 228	Science of Initiation and Knowledge of the Stars. The Human Being in the Past, the Present, and the Future from the Viewpoint of the Development of Consciousness
CW 229	The Experiencing of the Course of the Year in Four Cosmic Imaginations
CW 230	The Human Being as Harmony of the Creative, Building, and Formative World-Word
CW 231	The Supersensible Human Being, Understood Anthroposophically
CW 232	The Forming of the Mysteries
CW 233	World History Illuminated by Anthroposophy and as the Foundation for Knowledge of the Human Spirit

CW 233a   Mystery Sites of the Middle Ages: Rosicrucianism and the Modern Initiation-Principle. The Festival of Easter as Part of the History of the Mysteries of Humanity
CW 234   Anthroposophy. A Summary after 21 Years
CW 235   Esoteric Observations of Karmic Relationships in 6 Volumes, Vol. 1
CW 236   Esoteric Observations of Karmic Relationships in 6 Volumes, Vol. 2
CW 237   Esoteric Observations of Karmic Relationships in 6 Volumes, Vol. 3: The Karmic Relationships of the Anthroposophical Movement
CW 238   Esoteric Observations of Karmic Relationships in 6 Volumes, Vol. 4: The Spiritual Life of the Present in Relationship to the Anthroposophical Movement
CW 239   Esoteric Observations of Karmic Relationships in 6 Volumes, Vol. 5
CW 240   Esoteric Observations of Karmic Relationships in 6 Volumes, Vol. 6
CW 243   The Consciousness of the Initiate
CW 245   Instructions for an Esoteric Schooling
CW 250   The Building-Up of the Anthroposophical Society. From the Beginning to the Outbreak of the First World War
CW 251   The History of the Goetheanum Building-Association
CW 252   Life in the Anthroposophical Society from the First World War to the Burning of the First Goetheanum
CW 253   The Problems of Living Together in the Anthroposophical Society. On the Dornach Crisis of 1915. With Highlights on Swedenborg's Clairvoyance, the Views of Freudian Psychoanalysts, and the Concept of Love in Relation to Mysticism
CW 254   The Occult Movement in the 19th Century and Its Relationship to World Culture. Significant Points from the Exoteric Cultural Life around the Middle of the 19th Century
CW 255   Rudolf Steiner during the First World War
CW 255a   Anthroposophy and the Reformation of Society. On the History of the Threefold Movement
CW 255b   Anthroposophy and Its Opponents, 1919–1921
CW 256   How Can the Anthroposophical Movement Be Financed?
CW 256a   Futurum, Inc. / International Laboratories, Inc.
CW 256b   The Coming Day, Inc.
CW 257   Anthroposophical Community-Building
CW 258   The History of and Conditions for the Anthroposophical Movement in Relationship to the Anthroposophical Society. A Stimulus to Self-Contemplation
CW 259   The Year of Destiny 1923 in the History of the Anthroposophical Society. From the Burning of the Goetheanum to the Christmas Conference
CW 260   The Christmas Conference for the Founding of the General Anthroposophical Society

Rudolf Steiner's Collected Works * 241

CW 260a	The Constitution of the General Anthroposophical Society and the School for Spiritual Science. The Rebuilding of the Goetheanum
CW 261	Our Dead. Addresses, Words of Remembrance, and Meditative Verses, 1906-1924
CW 262	Rudolf Steiner and Marie Steiner-von Sivers: Correspondence and Documents, 1901-1925
CW 263/1	Rudolf Steiner and Edith Maryon: Correspondence: Letters, Verses, Sketches, 1912-1924
CW 264	On the History and the Contents of the First Section of the Esoteric School from 1904 to 1914. Letters, Newsletters, Documents, Lectures
CW 265	On the History and from the Contents of the Ritual-Knowledge Section of the Esoteric School from 1904 to 1914. Documents, and Lectures from the Years 1906 to 1914, as well as on New Approaches to Ritual-Knowledge Work in the Years 1921–1924
CW 266/1	From the Contents of the Esoteric Lessons. Volume 1: 1904–1909. Notes from Memory of Participants. Meditation texts from the notes of Rudolf Steiner
CW 266/2	From the Contents of the Esoteric Lessons. Volume 2: 1910–1912. Notes from Memory of Participants
CW 266/3	From the Contents of the Esoteric Lessons. Volume 3: 1913, 1914 and 1920–1923. Notes from Memory of Participants. Meditation texts from the notes of Rudolf Steiner
CW 267	Soul-Exercises: Vol. 1: Exercises with Word and Image Meditations for the Methodological Development of Higher Powers of Knowledge, 1904–1924
CW 268	Soul-Exercises: Vol. 2: Mantric Verses, 1903–1925
CW 269	Ritual Texts for the Celebration of the Free Christian Religious Instruction. The Collected Verses for Teachers and Students of the Waldorf School
CW 270	Esoteric Instructions for the First Class of the School for Spiritual Science at the Goetheanum 1924, 4 Volumes
CW 271	Art and Knowledge of Art. Foundations of a New Aesthetic
CW 272	Spiritual-Scientific Commentary on Goethe's 'Faust' in Two Volumes. Vol. 1: Faust, the Striving Human Being
CW 273	Spiritual-Scientific Commentary on Goethe's 'Faust' in Two Volumes. Vol. 2: The Faust-Problem
CW 274	Addresses for the Christmas Plays from the Old Folk Traditions
CW 275	Art in the Light of Mystery-Wisdom
CW 276	The Artistic in Its Mission in the World. The Genius of Language. The World of Self-Revealing Radiant Appearances—Anthroposophy and Art. Anthroposophy and Poetry
CW 277	Eurythmy. The Revelation of the Speaking Soul
CW 277a	The Origin and Development of Eurythmy

CW 278	Eurythmy as Visible Song
CW 279	Eurythmy as Visible Speech
CW 280	The Method and Nature of Speech Formation
CW 281	The Art of Recitation and Declamation
CW 282	Speech Formation and Dramatic Art
CW 283	The Nature of Things Musical and the Experience of Tone in the Human Being
CW 284/285	Images of Occult Seals and Pillars. The Munich Congress of Whitsun 1907 and Its Consequences
CW 286	Paths to a New Style of Architecture. 'And the Building Becomes Human'
CW 287	The Building at Dornach as a Symbol of Historical Becoming and an Artistic Transformation Impulse
CW 288	Style-Forms in the Living Organic
CW 289	The Building-Idea of the Goetheanum: Lectures with Slides from the Years 1920–1921
CW 290	The Building-Idea of the Goetheanum: Lectures with Slides from the Years 1920–1921
CW 291	The Nature of Colours
CW 291a	Knowledge of Colours. Supplementary Volume to 'The Nature of Colours'
CW 292	Art History as Image of Inner Spiritual Impulses
CW 293	General Knowledge of the Human Being as the Foundation of Pedagogy
CW 294	The Art of Education, Methodology and Didactics
CW 295	The Art of Education: Seminar Discussions and Lectures on Lesson Planning
CW 296	The Question of Education as a Social Question
CW 297	The Idea and Practice of the Waldorf School
CW 297a	Education for Life: Self-Education and the Practice of Pedagogy
CW 298	Rudolf Steiner in the Waldorf School
CW 299	Spiritual-Scientific Observations on Speech
CW 300a	Conferences with the Teachers of the Free Waldorf School in Stuttgart, 1919 to 1924, in 3 Volumes, Vol. 1
CW 300b	Conferences with the Teachers of the Free Waldorf School in Stuttgart, 1919 to 1924, in 3 Volumes, Vol. 2
CW 300c	Conferences with the Teachers of the Free Waldorf School in Stuttgart, 1919 to 1924, in 3 Volumes, Vol. 3
CW 301	The Renewal of Pedagogical-Didactical Art through Spiritual Science
CW 302	Knowledge of the Human Being and the Forming of Class Lessons
CW 302a	Education and Teaching from a Knowledge of the Human Being
CW 303	The Healthy Development of the Human Being
CW 304	Methods of Education and Teaching Based on Anthroposophy
CW 304a	Anthroposophical Knowledge of the Human Being and Pedagogy

CW 305	The Soul-Spiritual Foundational Forces of the Art of Education. Spiritual Values in Education and Social Life
CW 306	Pedagogical Praxis from the Viewpoint of a Spiritual-Scientific Knowledge of the Human Being. The Education of the Child and Young Human Beings
CW 307	The Spiritual Life of the Present and Education
CW 308	The Method of Teaching and the Life-Requirements for Teaching
CW 309	Anthroposophical Pedagogy and Its Prerequisites
CW 310	The Pedagogical Value of a Knowledge of the Human Being and the Cultural Value of Pedagogy
CW 311	The Art of Education from an Understanding of the Being of Humanity
CW 312	Spiritual Science and Medicine
CW 313	Spiritual-Scientific Viewpoints on Therapy
CW 314	Physiology and Therapy Based on Spiritual Science
CW 315	Curative Eurythmy
CW 316	Meditative Observations and Instructions for a Deepening of the Art of Healing
CW 317	The Curative Education Course
CW 318	The Working Together of Doctors and Pastors
CW 319	Anthroposophical Knowledge of the Human Being and Medicine
CW 320	Spiritual-Scientific Impulses for the Development of Physics 1: The First Natural-Scientific Course: Light, Colour, Tone, Mass, Electricity, Magnetism
CW 321	Spiritual-Scientific Impulses for the Development of Physics 2: The Second Natural-Scientific Course: Warmth at the Border of Positive and Negative Materiality
CW 322	The Borders of the Knowledge of Nature
CW 323	The Relationship of the various Natural-Scientific Fields to Astronomy
CW 324	Nature Observation, Mathematics, and Scientific Experimentation and Results from the Viewpoint of Anthroposophy
CW 324a	The Fourth Dimension in Mathematics and Reality
CW 325	Natural Science and the World-Historical Development of Humanity since Ancient Times
CW 326	The Moment of the Coming Into Being of Natural Science in World History and Its Development Since Then
CW 327	Spiritual-Scientific Foundations for Success in Farming. The Agricultural Course
CW 328	The Social Question
CW 329	The Liberation of the Human Being as the Foundation for a New Social Form
CW 330	The Renewal of the Social Organism
CW 331	Work-Council and Socialization
CW 332	The Alliance for Threefolding and the Total Reform of Society. The Council on Culture and the Liberation of the Spiritual Life

CW 332a	The Social Future
CW 333	Freedom of Thought and Social Forces
CW 334	From the Unified State to the Threefold Social Organism
CW 335	The Crisis of the Present and the Path to Healthy Thinking
CW 336	The Great Questions of the Times and Anthroposophical Spiritual Knowledge
CW 337a	Social Ideas, Social Reality, Social Practice, Vol. 1: Question-and-Answer Evenings and Study Evenings of the Alliance for the Threefold Social Organism in Stuttgart, 1919-1920
CW 337b	Social Ideas, Social Realities, Social Practice, Vol. 2: Discussion Evenings of the Swiss Alliance for the Threefold Social Organism
CW 338	How Does One Work on Behalf of the Impulse for the Threefold Social Organism?
CW 339	Anthroposophy, Threefold Social Organism, and the Art of Public Speaking
CW 340	The National-Economics Course. The Tasks of a New Science of Economics, Volume 1
CW 341	The National-Economics Seminar. The Tasks of a New Science of Economics, Volume 2
CW 342	Lectures and Courses on Christian Religious Work, Vol. 1: Anthroposophical Foundations for a Renewed Christian Religious Working
CW 343	Lectures and Courses on Christian Religious Work, Vol. 2: Spiritual Knowledge—Religious Feeling—Cultic Doing
CW 344	Lectures and Courses on Christian Religious Work, Vol. 3: Lectures at the Founding of the Christian Community
CW 345	Lectures and Courses on Christian Religious Work, Vol. 4: Concerning the Nature of the Working Word
CW 346	Lectures and Courses on Christian Religious Work, Vol. 5: The Apocalypse and the Work of the Priest
CW 347	The Knowledge of the Nature of the Human Being According to Body, Soul and Spirit. On Earlier Conditions of the Earth
CW 348	On Health and Illness. Foundations of a Spiritual-Scientific Doctrine of the Senses
CW 349	On the Life of the Human Being and of the Earth. On the Nature of Christianity
CW 350	Rhythms in the Cosmos and in the Human Being. How Does One Come To See the Spiritual World?
CW 351	The Human Being and the World. The Influence of the Spirit in Nature. On the Nature of Bees
CW 352	Nature and the Human Being Observed Spiritual-Scientifically
CW 353	The History of Humanity and the World-Views of the Folk Cultures
CW 354	The Creation of the World and the Human Being. Life on Earth and the Influence of the Stars

SIGNIFICANT EVENTS IN THE LIFE OF
Rudolf Steiner

1829: June 23: birth of Johann Steiner (1829–1910)—Rudolf Steiner's father—in Geras, Lower Austria.

1834: May 8: birth of Franciska Blie (1834–1918)—Rudolf Steiner's mother—in Horn, Lower Austria. 'My father and mother were both children of the glorious Lower Austrian forest district north of the Danube.'

1860: May 16: marriage of Johann Steiner and Franciska Blie.

1861: February 25: birth of *Rudolf Joseph Lorenz Steiner* in Kraljevec, Croatia, near the border with Hungary, where Johann Steiner works as a telegrapher for the South Austria Railroad. Rudolf Steiner is baptized two days later, February 27, the date usually given as his birthday.

1862: Summer: the family moves to Modling, Lower Austria.

1863: The family moves to Pottschach, Lower Austria, near the Styrian border, where Johann Steiner becomes stationmaster. 'The view stretched to the mountains . . . majestic peaks in the distance and the sweet charm of nature in the immediate surroundings.'

1864: November 15: birth of Rudolf Steiner's sister, Leopoldine (d. November 1, 1927). She will become a seamstress and live with her parents for the rest of her life.

1866: July 28: birth of Rudolf Steiner's deaf-mute brother, Gustav (d. May 1, 1941).

1867: Rudolf Steiner enters the village school. Following a disagreement between his father and the schoolmaster, whose wife falsely accused the boy of causing a commotion, Rudolf Steiner is taken out of school and taught at home.

1868: A critical experience. Unknown to the family, an aunt dies in a distant town. Sitting in the station waiting room, Rudolf Steiner sees her 'form', which speaks to him, asking for help. 'Beginning with this experience, a new soul life began in the boy, one in which not only the outer trees and mountains spoke to him, but also the worlds that lay behind them. From this moment on, the boy began to live with the spirits of nature...'

1869: The family moves to the peaceful, rural village of Neudorfl, near Wiener Neustadt in present-day Austria. Rudolf Steiner attends the village school. Because of the 'unorthodoxy' of his writing and spelling, he has to do 'extra lessons'.

1870: Through a book lent to him by his tutor, he discovers geometry: 'To grasp something purely in the spirit brought me inner happiness. I know that I first learned happiness through geometry.' The same tutor allows him to draw, while other students still struggle with their reading and writing. 'An artistic element' thus enters his education.

1871: Though his parents are not religious, Rudolf Steiner becomes a 'church child', a favourite of the priest, who was 'an exceptional character'. 'Up to the age of ten or eleven, among those I came to know, he was far and away the most significant.' Among other things, he introduces Steiner to Copernican, heliocentric cosmology. As an altar boy, Rudolf Steiner serves at Masses, funerals, and Corpus Christi processions. At year's end, after an incident in which he escapes a thrashing, his father forbids him to go to church.

1872: Rudolf Steiner transfers to grammar school in Wiener-Neustadt, a five-mile walk from home, which must be done in all weathers.

1873–75: Through his teachers and on his own, Rudolf Steiner has many wonderful experiences with science and mathematics. Outside school, he teaches himself analytic geometry, trigonometry, differential equations, and calculus.

1876: Rudolf Steiner begins tutoring other students. He learns bookbinding from his father. He also teaches himself stenography.

1877: Rudolf Steiner discovers Kant's *Critique of Pure Reason*, which he reads and rereads. He also discovers and reads von Rotteck's *World History*.

1878: He studies extensively in contemporary psychology and philosophy.

1879: Rudolf Steiner graduates from high school with honours. His father is transferred to Inzersdorf, near Vienna. He uses his first visit to Vienna 'to purchase a great number of philosophy books'—Kant, Fichte, Schelling, and Hegel, as well as numerous histories of philosophy. His aim: to find a path from the 'I' to nature.

October 1879–1883: Rudolf Steiner attends the Technical College in Vienna—to study mathematics, chemistry, physics, mineralogy, botany, zoology, biology, geology, and mechanics—with a scholarship. He also attends lectures in history and literature, while avidly reading philosophy on his own. His two favourite professors are Karl Julius Schröer (German language and literature) and Edmund Reitlinger (physics). He also audits lectures by Robert Zimmermann on aesthetics and Franz Brentano on philosophy. During this year he begins his friendship with Moritz Zitter (1861–1921), who will help support him financially when he is in Berlin.

1880: Rudolf Steiner attends lectures on Schiller and Goethe by Karl Julius Schröer, who becomes his mentor. Also 'through a remarkable combination of circumstances', he meets Felix Koguzki, a 'herb gatherer' and healer, who could 'see deeply into the secrets of nature'. Rudolf Steiner will meet and study with this 'emissary of the Master' throughout his time in Vienna.

1881: January: '... I didn't sleep a wink. I was busy with philosophical problems until about 12:30 a.m. Then, finally, I threw myself down on my couch. All my striving during the previous year had been to research whether the following statement by Schelling was true or not: *Within everyone dwells a secret, marvellous capacity to draw back from the stream of time—out of the self clothed in all that comes to us from outside—into our innermost being and there, in the immutable form of the Eternal, to look into ourselves.* I believe, and I am still quite certain of it, that I discovered this capacity in myself; I had long had an inkling of it. Now the whole of idealist philosophy stood before me in modified form. What's a sleepless night compared to that!'

Rudolf Steiner begins communicating with leading thinkers of the day, who send him books in return, which he reads eagerly.

July: 'I am not one of those who dives into the day like an animal in human form. I pursue a quite specific goal, an idealistic aim—knowledge of the truth! This cannot be done offhandedly. It requires the greatest striving in the world, free of all egotism, and equally of all resignation.'

August: Steiner puts down on paper for the first time thoughts for a 'Philosophy of Freedom'. 'The striving for the absolute: this human yearning is freedom.' He also seeks to outline a 'peasant philosophy', describing what the worldview of a 'peasant'—one who lives close to the earth and the old ways—really is.

1881–1882: Felix Koguzki, the herb gatherer, reveals himself to be the envoy of another, higher initiatory personality, who instructs Rudolf Steiner to penetrate Fichte's philosophy and to master modern scientific thinking as a preparation for right entry into the spirit. This 'Master' also teaches him the double (evolutionary and involutionary) nature of time.

1882: Through the offices of Karl Julius Schröer, Rudolf Steiner is asked by Joseph Kürschner to edit Goethe's scientific works for the *Deutschen National-Literatur* edition. He writes 'A Possible Critique of Atomistic Concepts' and sends it to Friedrich Theodor Vischer.

1883: Rudolf Steiner completes his college studies and begins work on the Goethe project.

1884: First volume of Goethe's *Scientific Writings* (CW 1) appears (March). He lectures on Goethe and Lessing, and Goethe's approach to science. In July, he enters the household of Ladislaus and Pauline Specht as tutor to the four Specht boys. He will live there until 1890. At this time, he meets Josef Breuer (1842–1925), the co-author with Sigmund Freud of *Studies in Hysteria*, who is the Specht family doctor.

1885: While continuing to edit Goethe's writings, Rudolf Steiner reads deeply in contemporary philosophy (Eduard von Hartmann, Johannes Volkelt, and Richard Wahle, among others).

1886: May: Rudolf Steiner sends Kürschner the manuscript of *Outlines of Goethe's Theory of Knowledge* (CW 2), which appears in October, and which he sends out widely. He also meets the poet Marie Eugenie Delle Grazie and writes 'Nature and Our Ideals' for her. He attends her salon, where he meets many priests, theologians, and philosophers, who will become his friends. Meanwhile, the director of the Goethe Archive in Weimar requests his collaboration with the *Sophien* edition of Goethe's works, particularly the writings on colour.

1887: At the beginning of the year, Rudolf Steiner is very sick. As the year progresses and his health improves, he becomes increasingly 'a man of letters', lecturing, writing essays, and taking part in Austrian cultural life. In August–September, the second volume of Goethe's *Scientific Writings* appears.

1888: January–July: Rudolf Steiner assumes editorship of the 'German Weekly' *(Deutsche Wochenschrift)*. He begins lecturing more intensively, giving, for example, a lecture titled 'Goethe as Father of a New Aesthetics'. He meets and becomes soul friends with Friedrich Eckstein (1861–1939), a vegetarian, philosopher of symbolism, alchemist, and musician, who will introduce him to various spiritual currents (including Theosophy) and with whom he will meditate and interpret esoteric and alchemical texts.

1889: Rudolf Steiner first reads Nietzsche *(Beyond Good and Evil)*. He encounters Theosophy again and learns of Madame Blavatsky in the theosophical circle around Marie Lang (1858–1934). Here he also meets well-known figures of Austrian life, as well as esoteric figures like the occultist Franz Hartmann and Karl Leiningen-Billigen (translator of C.G. Harrison's *The Transcendental Universe*). During this period, Steiner first reads A.P. Sinnett's *Esoteric Buddhism* and Mabel Collins's *Light on the Path*. He also begins travelling, visiting Budapest, Weimar, and Berlin (where he meets philosopher Eduard von Hartmann).

1890: Rudolf Steiner finishes Volume 3 of Goethe's scientific writings. He begins his doctoral dissertation, which will become *Truth and Science* (CW 3). He also meets the poet and feminist Rosa Mayreder (1858–1938), with whom he can exchange his most intimate thoughts. In September, Rudolf Steiner moves to Weimar to work in the Goethe-Schiller Archive.

1891: Volume 3 of the Kürschner edition of Goethe appears. Meanwhile, Rudolf Steiner edits Goethe's studies in mineralogy and scientific writings for the *Sophien* edition. He meets Ludwig Laistner of the Cotta Publishing Company, who asks for a book on the basic question of metaphysics. From this will result, ultimately, *The Philosophy of Freedom* (CW 4), which will be published not by Cotta but by Emil Felber. In October, Rudolf Steiner takes the oral exam for a doctorate in philosophy, mathematics, and mechanics at Rostock University, receiving his doctorate on the twenty-sixth. In November, he gives his first lecture on Goethe's 'Fairy Tale' in Vienna.

1892: Rudolf Steiner continues work at the Goethe-Schiller Archive and on his *Philosophy of Freedom*. *Truth and Science,* his doctoral dissertation, is published. Steiner undertakes to write Introductions to books on Schopenhauer and Jean Paul for Cotta. At year's end, he finds lodging with Anna Eunike, née Schulz (1853–1911), a widow with four daughters and a son. He also develops a friendship with Otto Erich Hartleben (1864–1905) with whom he shares literary interests.

1893: Rudolf Steiner begins his habit of producing many reviews and articles. In March, he gives a lecture titled 'Hypnotism, with Reference to Spiritism'. In September, volume 4 of the Kürschner edition is completed. In November, *The Philosophy of Freedom* appears. This year, too, he meets John Henry Mackay (1864–1933), the anarchist, and Max Stirner, a scholar and biographer.

1894: Rudolf Steiner meets Elisabeth Fürster Nietzsche, the philosopher's sister, and begins to read Nietzsche in earnest, beginning with the as yet unpublished *Antichrist*. He also meets Ernst Haeckel (1834–1919). In the fall, he begins to write *Nietzsche, A Fighter against His Time* (CW 5).

1895: May, *Nietzsche, A Fighter against His Time* appears.

1896: January 22: Rudolf Steiner sees Friedrich Nietzsche for the first and only time. Moves between the Nietzsche and the Goethe-Schiller

	Archives, where he completes his work before year's end. He falls out with Elisabeth Förster Nietzsche, thus ending his association with the Nietzsche Archive.
1897:	Rudolf Steiner finishes the manuscript of *Goethe's Worldview* (CW 6). He moves to Berlin with Anna Eunike and begins editorship of the *Magazin für Literatur*. From now on, Steiner will write countless reviews, literary and philosophical articles, and so on. He begins lecturing at the 'Free Literary Society.' In September, he attends the Zionist Congress in Basel. He sides with Dreyfus in the Dreyfus affair.
1898:	Rudolf Steiner is very active as an editor in the political, artistic, and theatrical life of Berlin. He becomes friendly with John Henry Mackay and poet Ludwig Jacobowski (1868–1900). He joins Jacobowski's circle of writers, artists, and scientists—'The Coming Ones' (*Die Kommenden*)—and contributes lectures to the group until 1903. He also lectures at the 'League for College Pedagogy'. He writes an article for Goethe's sesquicentennial, 'Goethe's Secret Revelation', on the 'Fairy Tale of the Green Snake and the Beautiful Lily'.
1898–99:	'This was a trying time for my soul as I looked at Christianity. ... I was able to progress only by contemplating, by means of spiritual perception, the evolution of Christianity.... Conscious knowledge of real Christianity began to dawn in me around the turn of the century. This seed continued to develop. My soul trial occurred shortly before the beginning of the twentieth century. It was decisive for my soul's development that I stood spiritually before the Mystery of Golgotha in a deep and solemn celebration of knowledge.'
1899:	Rudolf Steiner begins teaching and giving lectures and lecture cycles at the Workers' College, founded by Wilhelm Liebknecht (1826–1900). He will continue to do so until 1904. Writes: *Literature and Spiritual Life in the Nineteenth Century; Individualism in Philosophy; Haeckel and His Opponents; Poetry in the Present;* and begins what will become (fifteen years later) *The Riddles of Philosophy* (CW 18). He also meets many artists and writers, including Käthe Kollwitz, Stefan Zweig, and Rainer Maria Rilke. On October 31, he marries Anna Eunike.
1900:	'I thought that the turn of the century must bring humanity a new light. It seemed to me that the separation of human thinking and willing from the spirit had peaked. A turn or reversal of direction in human evolution seemed to me a necessity.' Rudolf Steiner finishes *World and Life Views in the Nineteenth Century* (the second part of what will become *The Riddles of Philosophy*) and dedicates it to

Ernst Haeckel. It is published in March. He continues lecturing at *Die Kommenden*, whose leadership he assumes after the death of Jacobowski. Also, he gives the Gutenberg Jubilee lecture before 7,000 typesetters and printers. In September, Rudolf Steiner is invited by Count and Countess Brockdorff to lecture in the Theosophical Library. His first lecture is on Nietzsche. His second lecture is titled 'Goethe's Secret Revelation'. October 6, he begins a lecture cycle on the mystics that will become *Mystics after Modernism* (CW 7). November–December: 'Marie von Sivers appears in the audience. . . .' Also in November, Steiner gives his first lecture at the Giordano Bruno Bund (where he will continue to lecture until May, 1905). He speaks on Bruno and modern Rome, focusing on the importance of the philosophy of Thomas Aquinas as monism.

1901: In continual financial straits, Rudolf Steiner's early friends Moritz Zitter and Rosa Mayreder help support him. In October, he begins the lecture cycle *Christianity as Mystical Fact* (CW 8) at the Theosophical Library. In November, he gives his first 'theosophical lecture' on Goethe's 'Fairy Tale' in Hamburg at the invitation of Wilhelm Hubbe-Schleiden. He also attends a gathering to celebrate the founding of the Theosophical Society at Count and Countess Brockdorff's. He gives a lecture cycle, 'From Buddha to Christ', for the circle of the *Kommenden*. November 17, Marie von Sivers asks Rudolf Steiner if Theosophy needs a Western–Christian spiritual movement (to complement Theosophy's Eastern emphasis). 'The question was posed. Now, following spiritual laws, I could begin to give an answer. . . .' In December, Rudolf Steiner writes his first article for a theosophical publication. At year's end, the Brockdorffs and possibly Wilhelm Hubbe-Schleiden ask Rudolf Steiner to join the Theosophical Society and undertake the leadership of the German section. Rudolf Steiner agrees, on the condition that Marie von Sivers (then in Italy) work with him.

1902: Beginning in January, Rudolf Steiner attends the opening of the Workers' School in Spandau with Rosa Luxemberg (1870–1919). January 17, Rudolf Steiner joins the Theosophical Society. In April, he is asked to become general secretary of the German Section of the theosophical Society, and works on preparations for its founding. In July, he visits London for a theosophical congress. He meets Bertram Keightly, G.R.S. Mead, A.P. Sinnett, and Annie Besant, among others. In September, *Christianity as Mystical Fact* appears. In October, Rudolf Steiner gives his first public lecture on Theosophy ('Monism and Theosophy') to about three hundred people at the Giordano Bruno Bund. On October 19–21, the

German Section of the Theosophical Society has its first meeting; Rudolf Steiner is the general secretary, and Annie Besant attends. Steiner lectures on practical karma studies. On October 23, Annie Besant inducts Rudolf Steiner into the Esoteric School of the Theosophical Society. On October 25, Steiner begins a weekly series of lectures: 'The Field of Theosophy.' During this year, Rudolf Steiner also first meets Ita Wegman (1876–1943), who will become his close collaborator in his final years.

1903: Rudolf Steiner holds about 300 lectures and seminars. In May, the first issue of the periodical *Luzifer* appears. In June, Rudolf Steiner visits London for the first meeting of the Federation of the European Sections of the Theosophical Society, where he meets Colonel Olcott. He begins to write *Theosophy* (CW 9).

1904: Rudolf Steiner continues lecturing at the Workers' College and elsewhere (about 90 lectures), while lecturing intensively all over Germany among theosophists (about 140 lectures). In February, he meets Carl Unger (1878–1929), who will become a member of the board of the Anthroposophical Society (1913). In March, he meets Michael Bauer (1871–1929), a Christian mystic, who will also be on the board. In May, *Theosophy* appears, with the dedication: 'To the spirit of Giordano Bruno'. Rudolf Steiner and Marie von Sivers visit London for meetings with Annie Besant. June: Rudolf Steiner and Marie von Sivers attend the meeting of the Federation of European Sections of the Theosophical Society in Amsterdam. In July, Steiner begins the articles in *Luzifer-Gnosis* that will become *How to Know Higher Worlds* (CW 10) and *Cosmic Memory* (CW 11). In September, Annie Besant visits Germany. In December, Steiner lectures on Freemasonry. He mentions the High Grade Masonry derived from John Yarker and represented by Theodore Reuss and Karl Kellner as a blank slate 'into which a good image could be placed'.

1905: This year, Steiner ends his non-theosophical lecturing activity. Supported by Marie von Sivers, his theosophical lecturing—both in public and in the Theosophical Society—increases significantly: 'The German Theosophical Movement is of exceptional importance.' Steiner recommends reading, among others, Fichte, Jacob Boehme, and Angelus Silesius. He begins to introduce Christian themes into Theosophy. He also begins to work with doctors (Felix Peipers and Ludwig Noll). In July, he is in London for the Federation of European Sections, where he attends a lecture by Annie Besant: 'I have seldom seen Mrs Besant speak in so inward and heartfelt a manner... Through Mrs Besant I have found the way to H.P. Blavatsky.' September to October, he gives a course of 31 lectures for a small group of esoteric students. In October, the annual meeting of the German Section of the Theosophical Society, which still remains very small, takes place. Rudolf Steiner reports membership has risen from 121 to 377 members. In November, seeking to establish esoteric 'continuity', Rudolf Steiner and Marie von Sivers participate in a 'Memphis-Misraim' Masonic ceremony. They pay 45 marks for membership. 'Yesterday, you saw how little remains of former esoteric institutions.' 'We are dealing only with a "framework" ... for the present, nothing lies behind it. The occult powers have completely withdrawn.'

1906: Expansion of theosophical work. Rudolf Steiner gives about 245 lectures, only 44 of which take place in Berlin. Cycles are given in Paris, Leipzig, Stuttgart, and Munich. Esoteric work also intensifies. Rudolf Steiner begins writing *An Outline of Esoteric Science* (CW 13). In January, Rudolf Steiner receives permission (a patent) from the Great Orient of the Scottish A & A Thirty-Three Degree Rite of the Order of the Ancient Freemasons of the Memphis-Misraim Rite to direct a chapter under the name 'Mystica Aeterna.' This will become the 'Cognitive-Ritual Section' (also called 'Misraim Service') of the Esoteric School. (See: *Freemasonry and Ritual Work: The Misraim Service*, CW 265.) During this time, Steiner also meets Albert Schweitzer. In May, he is in Paris, where he visits Édouard Schuré. Many Russians attend his lectures (including Konstantin Balmont, Dimitri Mereszkovski, Zinaida Hippius, and Maximilian Woloshin). He attends the General Meeting of the European Federation of the Theosophical Society, at which Col Olcott is present for the last time. He spends the year's end in Venice and Rome, where he writes and works on his translation of H.P. Blavatsky's *Key to Theosophy*.

1907: Further expansion of the German Theosophical Movement according to the Rosicrucian directive to 'introduce spirit into the world'—in education, in social questions, in art, and in science. In February, Col Olcott dies in Adyar. Before he dies, Olcott indicates that 'the Masters' wish Annie Besant to succeed him: much politicking ensues. Rudolf Steiner supports Besant's candidacy. April–May: preparations for the Congress of the Federation of European Sections of the Theosophical Society—the great, watershed Whitsun 'Munich Congress,' attended by Annie Besant and others. Steiner decides to separate Eastern and Western (Christian–Rosicrucian) esoteric schools. He takes his esoteric school out of the Theosophical Society (Besant and Rudolf Steiner are 'in harmony' on this). Steiner makes his first lecture tours to Austria and

Hungary. That summer, he is in Italy. In September, he visits Édouard Schuré, who will write the Introduction to the French edition of *Christianity as Mystical Fact* in Barr, Alsace. Rudolf Steiner writes the autobiographical statement known as the 'Barr Document.' In *Luzifer-Gnosis*, 'The Education of the Child' appears.

1908: The movement grows (membership: 1,150). Lecturing expands. Steiner makes his first extended lecture tour to Holland and Scandinavia, as well as visits to Naples and Sicily. Themes: St John's Gospel, the Apocalypse, Egypt, science, philosophy, and logic. *Luzifer-Gnosis* ceases publication. In Berlin, Marie von Sivers (with Johanna Mücke (1864–1949) forms the *Philosophisch-Theosophisch* (after 1915 *Philosophisch-Anthroposophisch) Verlag* to publish Steiner's work. Steiner gives lecture cycles titled *The Gospel of St John* (CW 103) and *The Apocalypse* (104).

1909: *An Outline of Esoteric Science* appears. Lecturing and travel continues. Rudolf Steiner's spiritual research expands to include the polarity of Lucifer and Ahriman; the work of great individualities in history; the Maitreya Buddha and the Bodhisattvas; spiritual economy (CW 109); the work of the spiritual hierarchies in heaven and on earth (CW 110). He also deepens and intensifies his research into the Gospels, giving lectures on the Gospel of St Luke (CW 114) with the first mention of two Jesus children. Meets and becomes friends with Christian Morgenstern (1871–1914). In April, he lays the foundation stone for the Malsch model—the building that will lead to the first Goetheanum. In May, the International Congress of the Federation of European Sections of the Theosophical Society takes place in Budapest. Rudolf Steiner receives the Subba Row medal for *How to Know Higher Worlds*. During this time, Charles W. Leadbeater discovers Jiddu Krishnamurti (1895–1986) and proclaims him the future 'world teacher,' the bearer of the Maitreya Buddha and the 'reappearing Christ.' In October, Steiner delivers seminal lectures on 'anthroposophy,' which he will try, unsuccessfully, to rework over the next years into the unfinished work, *Anthroposophy (A Fragment)* (CW 45).

1910: New themes: *The Reappearance of Christ in the Etheric* (CW 118); *The Fifth Gospel; The Mission of Folk Souls* (CW 121); *Occult History* (CW 126); the evolving development of etheric cognitive capacities. Rudolf Steiner continues his Gospel research with *The Gospel of St Matthew* (CW 123). In January, his father dies. In April, he takes a month-long trip to Italy, including Rome, Monte Cassino, and Sicily. He also visits Scandinavia again. July–August, he writes the first Mystery Drama, *The Portal of Initiation* (CW 14). In November, he gives 'psychosophy' lectures. In December, he submits 'On the

1911: Psychological Foundations and Epistemological Framework of Theosophy' to the International Philosophical Congress in Bologna. The crisis in the Theosophical Society deepens. In January, 'The Order of the Rising Sun,' which will soon become 'The Order of the Star in the East,' is founded for the coming world teacher, Krishnamurti. At the same time, Marie von Sivers, Rudolf Steiner's co-worker, falls ill. Fewer lectures are given, but important new ground is broken. In Prague, in March, Steiner meets Franz Kafka (1883–1924) and Hugo Bergmann (1883–1975). In April, he delivers his paper to the Philosophical Congress. He writes the second Mystery Drama, *The Soul's Probation* (CW 14). Also, while Marie von Sivers is convalescing, Rudolf Steiner begins work on *Calendar 1912/1913*, which will contain the 'Calendar of the Soul' meditations. On March 19, Anna (Eunike) Steiner dies. In September, Rudolf Steiner visits Einsiedeln, birthplace of Paracelsus. In December, Friedrich Rittelmeyer, future founder of the Christian Community, meets Rudolf Steiner. The *Johannes-Bauverein*, the 'building committee,' which would lead to the first Goetheanum (first planned for Munich), is also founded, and a preliminary committee for the founding of an independent association is created that, in the following year, will become the Anthroposophical Society. Important lecture cycles include *Occult Physiology* (CW 128); *Wonders of the World* (CW 129); *From Jesus to Christ* (CW 131). Other themes: esoteric Christianity; Christian Rosenkreutz; the spiritual guidance of humanity; the sense world and the world of the spirit.

1912: Despite the ongoing, now increasing crisis in the Theosophical Society, much is accomplished: *Calendar 1912/1913* is published; eurythmy is created; both the third Mystery Drama, *The Guardian of the Threshold* (CW 14) and *A Way of Self-Knowledge* (CW 16) are written. New (or renewed) themes included life between death and rebirth and karma and reincarnation. Other lecture cycles: *Spiritual Beings in the Heavenly Bodies and in the Kingdoms of Nature* (CW 136); *The Human Being in the Light of Occultism, Theosophy, and Philosophy* (CW 137); *The Gospel of St Mark* (CW 139); and *The Bhagavad Gita and the Epistles of Paul* (CW 142). On May 8, Rudolf Steiner celebrates White Lotus Day, H.P. Blavatsky's death day, which he had faithfully observed for the past decade, for the last time. In August, Rudolf Steiner suggests the 'independent association' be called the 'Anthroposophical Society.' In September, the first eurythmy course takes place. In October, Rudolf Steiner declines recognition of a Theosophical Society lodge dedicated to the Star of the East and decides to expel all Theosophical Society members belonging to the order.

Also, with Marie von Sivers, he first visits Dornach, near Basel, Switzerland, and they stand on the hill where the Goetheanum will be built. In November, a Theosophical Society lodge is opened by direct mandate from Adyar (Annie Besant). In December, a meeting of the German section occurs at which it is decided that belonging to the Order of the Star of the East is incompatible with membership in the Theosophical Society. December 28: informal founding of the Anthroposophical Society in Berlin.

1913: Expulsion of the German section from the Theosophical Society. February 2–3: Foundation meeting of the Anthroposophical Society. Board members include: Marie von Sivers, Michael Bauer, and Carl Unger. September 20: Laying of the foundation stone for the *Johannes Bau* (Goetheanum) in Dornach. Building begins immediately. The fourth Mystery Drama, *The Soul's Awakening* (CW 14), is completed. Also: *The Threshold of the Spiritual World* (CW 147). Lecture cycles include: *The Bhagavad Gita and the Epistles of Paul* and *The Esoteric Meaning of the Bhagavad Gita* (CW 146), which the Russian philosopher Nikolai Berdyaev attends; *The Mysteries of the East and of Christianity* (CW 144); *The Effects of Esoteric Development* (CW 145); and *The Fifth Gospel* (CW 148). In May, Rudolf Steiner is in London and Paris, where anthroposophical work continues.

1914: Building continues on the *Johannes Bau* (Goetheanum) in Dornach, with artists and co-workers from seventeen nations. The general assembly of the Anthroposophical Society takes place. In May, Rudolf Steiner visits Paris, as well as Chartres Cathedral. June 28: assassination in Sarajevo ('Now the catastrophe has happened!'). August 1: War is declared. Rudolf Steiner returns to Germany from Dornach—he will travel back and forth. He writes the last chapter of *The Riddles of Philosophy*. Lecture cycles include: *Human and Cosmic Thought* (CW 151); *Inner Being of Humanity between Death and a New Birth* (CW 153); *Occult Reading and Occult Hearing* (CW 156). December 24: marriage of Rudolf Steiner and Marie von Sivers.

1915: Building continues. Life after death becomes a major theme, also art. Writes: *Thoughts during a Time of War* (CW 24). Lectures include: *The Secret of Death* (CW 159); *The Uniting of Humanity through the Christ Impulse* (CW 165).

1916: Rudolf Steiner begins work with Edith Maryon (1872–1924) on the sculpture 'The Representative of Humanity' ('The Group'— Christ, Lucifer, and Ahriman). He also works with the alchemist Alexander von Bernus on the quarterly *Das Reich*. He writes *The Riddle of Humanity* (CW 20). Lectures include: *Necessity and Freedom in World History and Human Action* (CW 166); *Past and Present in the*

Significant Events In The Life Of Rudolf Steiner * 257

Human Spirit (CW 167); *The Karma of Vocation* (CW 172); *The Karma of Untruthfulness* (CW 173).

1917: Russian Revolution. The U.S. enters the war. Building continues. Rudolf Steiner delineates the idea of the 'threefold nature of the human being' (in a public lecture March 15) and the 'threefold nature of the social organism' (hammered out in May–June with the help of Otto von Lerchenfeld and Ludwig Polzer-Hoditz in the form of two documents titled *Memoranda*, which were distributed in high places). August–September: Rudolf Steiner writes *The Riddles of the Soul* (CW 20). Also: commentary on 'The Chymical Wedding of Christian Rosenkreutz' for Alexander Bernus (Das Reich). Lectures include: *The Karma of Materialism* (CW 176); *The Spiritual Background of the Outer World: The Fall of the Spirits of Darkness* (CW 177).

1918: March 18: peace treaty of Brest-Litovsk—'Now everything will truly enter chaos! What is needed is cultural renewal.' June: Rudolf Steiner visits Karlstein (Grail) Castle outside Prague. Lecture cycle: *From Symptom to Reality in Modern History* (CW 185). In mid-November, Emil Molt, of the Waldorf-Astoria Cigarette Company, has the idea of founding a school for his workers' children.

1919: Focus on the threefold social organism: tireless travel, countless lectures, meetings, and publications. At the same time, a new public stage of Anthroposophy emerges as cultural renewal begins. The coming years will see initiatives in pedagogy, medicine, pharmacology, and agriculture. January 27: threefold meeting: 'We must first of all, with the money we have, found free schools that can bring people what they need.' February: first public eurythmy performance in Zurich. Also: 'Appeal to the German People' (CW 24), circulated March 6 as a newspaper insert. In April, *Towards Social Renewal* (CW 23) appears—'perhaps the most widely read of all books on politics appearing since the war'. Rudolf Steiner is asked to undertake the 'direction and leadership' of the school founded by the Waldorf-Astoria Company. Rudolf Steiner begins to talk about the 'renewal' of education. May 30: a building is selected and purchased for the future Waldorf School. August–September, Rudolf Steiner gives a lecture course for Waldorf teachers, *The Foundations of Human Experience (Study of Man)* (CW 293). September 7: Opening of the first Waldorf School. December (into January): first science course, the *Light Course* (CW 320).

1920: The Waldorf School flourishes. New threefold initiatives. Founding of limited companies *Der Kommende Tag* and *Futurum A.G.* to infuse spiritual values into the economic realm. Rudolf Steiner also focuses on the sciences. Lectures: *Introducing Anthroposophical*

Medicine (CW 312); *The Warmth Course* (CW 321); *The Boundaries of Natural Science* (CW 322); *The Redemption of Thinking* (CW 74). February: Johannes Werner Klein—later a co-founder of The Christian Community—asks Rudolf Steiner about the possibility of a 'religious renewal,' a 'Johannine church.' In March, Rudolf Steiner gives the first course for doctors and medical students. In April, a divinity student asks Rudolf Steiner a second time about the possibility of religious renewal. September 27–October 16: anthroposophical 'university course.' December: lectures titled *The Search for the New Isis* (CW 202).

1921: Rudolf Steiner continues his intensive work on cultural renewal, including the uphill battle for the threefold social order. 'University' arts, scientific, theological, and medical courses include: *The Astronomy Course* (CW 323); *Observation, Mathematics, and Scientific Experiment* (CW 324); the *Second Medical Course* (CW 313); *Colour*. In June and September–October, Rudolf Steiner also gives the first two 'priests' courses' (CW 342 and 343). The 'youth movement' gains momentum. Magazines are founded: *Die Drei* (January), and—under the editorship of Albert Steffen (1884–1963)—the weekly, *Das Goetheanum* (August). In February–March, Rudolf Steiner takes his first trip outside Germany since the war (Holland). On April 7, Steiner receives a letter regarding 'religious renewal,' and May 22–23, he agrees to address the question in a practical way. In June, the Klinical-Therapeutic Institute opens in Arlesheim under the direction of Dr Ita Wegman. In August, the Chemical-Pharmaceutical Laboratory opens in Arlesheim (Oskar Schmiedel and Ita Wegman are directors). The Clinical Therapeutic Institute is inaugurated in Stuttgart (Dr Ludwig Noll is director); also the Research Laboratory in Dornach (Ehrenfried Pfeiffer and Gunther Wachsmuth are directors). In November–December, Rudolf Steiner visits Norway.

1922: The first half of the year involves very active public lecturing (thousands attend); in the second half, Rudolf Steiner begins to withdraw and turn toward the Society—'The Society is asleep.' It is 'too weak' to do what is asked of it. The businesses—*Der Kommende Tag* and *Futurum A.G.*—fail. In January, with the help of an agent, Steiner undertakes a twelve-city German lecture tour, accompanied by eurythmy performances. In two weeks he speaks to more than 2,000 people. In April, he gives a 'university course' in The Hague. He also visits England. In June, he is in Vienna for the East–West Congress. In August–September, he is back in England for the Oxford Conference on Education. Returning to Dornach, he gives the lectures *Philosophy, Cosmology, and*

Religion (CW 215), and gives the third priests' course (CW 344). On September 16, The Christian Community is founded. In October–November, Steiner is in Holland and England. He also speaks to the youth: *The Youth Course* (CW 217). In December, Steiner gives lectures titled *The Origins of Natural Science* (CW 326), and *Humanity and the World of Stars: The Spiritual Communion of Humanity* (CW 219). December 31: Fire at the Goetheanum, which is destroyed.

1923: Despite the fire, Rudolf Steiner continues his work unabated. A very hard year. Internal dispersion, dissension, and apathy abound. There is conflict—between old and new visions—within the Society. A wake-up call is needed, and Rudolf Steiner responds with renewed lecturing vitality. His focus: the spiritual context of human life; initiation science; the course of the year; and community building. As a foundation for an artistic school, he creates a series of pastel sketches. Lecture cycles: *The Anthroposophical Movement; Initiation Science* (CW 227) (in Wales at the Penmaenmawr Summer School); *The Four Seasons and the Archangels* (CW 229); *Harmony of the Creative Word* (CW 230); *The Supersensible Human* (CW 231), given in Holland for the founding of the Dutch Society. On November 10, in response to the failed Hitler-Ludendorff putsch in Munich, Steiner closes his Berlin residence and moves the *Philosophisch-Anthroposophisch Verlag* (Press) to Dornach. On December 9, Steiner begins the serialization of his *Autobiography: The Course of My Life* (CW 28) in *Das Goetheanum*. It will continue to appear weekly, without a break, until his death. Late December–early January: Rudolf Steiner re-founds the Anthroposophical Society (about 12,000 members internationally) and takes over its leadership. The new board members are: Marie Steiner, Ita Wegman, Albert Steffen, Elisabeth Vreede, and Gunther Wachsmuth. (See *The Christmas Meeting for the Founding of the General Anthroposophical Society*, CW 260.) Accompanying lectures: *Mystery Knowledge and Mystery Centres* (CW 232); *World History in the Light of Anthroposophy* (CW 233). December 25: the Foundation Stone is laid (in the hearts of members) in the form of the 'Foundation Stone Meditation.'

1924: January 1: having founded the Anthroposophical Society and taken over its leadership, Rudolf Steiner has the task of 'reforming' it. The process begins with a weekly newssheet ('What's Happening in the Anthroposophical Society') in which Rudolf Steiner's 'Letters to Members' and 'Anthroposophical Leading Thoughts' appear (CW 26). The next step is the creation of a new esoteric class, the 'first class' of the 'University of Spiritual Science' (which was to have been followed, had Rudolf Steiner lived longer, by two more advanced classes). Then comes a new language for

Anthroposophy—practical, phenomenological, and direct; and Rudolf Steiner creates the model for the second Goetheanum. He begins the series of extensive 'karma' lectures (CW 235–40); and finally, responding to needs, he creates two new initiatives: biodynamic agriculture and curative education. After the middle of the year, rumours begin to circulate regarding Steiner's health. Lectures: January–February, *Anthroposophy* (CW 234); February: *Tone Eurythmy* (CW 278); June: *The Agriculture Course* (CW 327); June–July: *Speech Eurythmy* (CW 279); *Curative Education* (CW 317); August: (England, 'Second International Summer School'), *Initiation Consciousness: True and False Paths in Spiritual Investigation* (CW 243); September: *Pastoral Medicine* (CW 318). On September 26, for the first time, Rudolf Steiner cancels a lecture. On September 28, he gives his last lecture. On September 29, he withdraws to his studio in the carpenter's shop; now he is definitively ill. Cared for by Ita Wegman, he continues working, however, and writing the weekly installments of his *Autobiography* and *Letters to the Members/Leading Thoughts* (CW 26).

1925: Rudolf Steiner, while continuing to work, continues to weaken. He finishes *Extending Practical Medicine* (CW 27) with Ita Wegman. On March 30, around ten in the morning, Rudolf Steiner dies.

INDEX

A
Akasha Chronicle, 146, 148, 153, 155
anthroposophy, x–xii, 88
Aristotle, 5–8
Astronomy, 110
atoms, 76, 81, 126, 172, 199, 211
    collision of, 171
    divisible, 170
    jumbled, 99
    movement of, 77, 106, 170
    non-rigid, 171
    present state of, 78
    product of, 82
    rigid, 171
    swirling, 99
    whole hypothesis of, 125

B
Battle of Salamis, 78
Bible, 51
Blavatsky, HP, 143, 145, 150
Böhme, Jakob, 41, 43
Büchner, Ludwig, 79, 162

C
Catholic Church, 158
Christ, 52, 56, 100, 143–144, 151, 158, 178
    statue, 184
Christianity/Christian, 99, 142–144, 158–159, 177–180, 201
    believer, 200
    communities, 144
    essence of, 143–144
    point of view, 159
    true, 179
    truths, 158–159
clairvoyance
    dreamlike, 45
    gut, 176
    imaginative, 45
    old, 45, 85
    visionary, 39–40
cognition, 8, 55, 58–59, 75, 120, 123, 180, 186
    conscious, 38, 53
    dead, 51
    external material, 41
    higher, 51, 53
    human, 52, 173
    imaginative, 14, 20–21, 25, 30, 32–33, 36–38, 40, 43, 47, 53, 193
    intuitive, 47
    Moon, 39, 53
    ordinary physical, 32, 35, 41
    physical earthly, 51
    spiritual-scientific, 13, 38, 62

thrust of higher, 29
value of thinking for, 4
Cohn, Ferdinand, 136
consciousness, 11–13, 16, 21, 38, 54, 59, 90, 116–117, 137, 162
   dead in, 15
   depths of, 36
   direct, 88
   dream, 30
   extension of, 19
   human, 53
   imaginative form of, 14
   Moon, 44
   normal, 14
   ordinary earth, 32
   ordinary normal, 37
   ordinary physical, 20
   spiritual-scientific, 74
   threshold of, 22–24, 36, 53
Copernicus, 129, 158–159
cosmic world, 172, 176
cultural world
   European, 70, 140, 143, 145
   western, 150
culture
   European, 71, 145, 150, 160
   materialistic, 183–184
   Moon, 49
   western, 151

D

Du Bois-Reymond, Paul, 75–78, 106, 116, 133–134, 139

E

earth, 37–39, 43, 48, 53, 82, 124–125, 129–132, 145, 147–149, 157, 212–213
   aura, 52

Christ being on, 143
evolution, 49, 51
existence on, 45, 47
human being on, 39, 46, 60
egoism, 60–61, 168, 182
elemental world, 25–26, 35, 42, 62, 148
epistemological language, 89
etheric body, 7, 37, 61, 146, 176, 189, 193–197, 214
   activity of, 8
   observation of, 192
   physical and, 16, 137

F

feeling, 5, 9, 23–24, 27, 58, 65, 81, 119, 148, 197–198, 200
   direction of, 201
   healthy, 210
   human, 3, 92
   inner, 25
   moral, 72
   possibility of, 97
   pure, 199
   sentiments and, 72
freedom, 82, 87, 149, 173
   of human being, 81
   and morality, 83
   and responsibility, 117

G

Goethe, 30, 32, 34, 41, 58, 62, 109, 192
   judgement, 55
   Kürschner's Deutsche National-Literatur, 106
   scientific findings of, 31
   spirit of, 191
   thought, 26
   view of life/nature, 50, 106

way of thinking, 33
Wilhelm Meister, 47
work, 35
worldview, 106–107, 191
Grazie, Marie Eugenie delle, 84, 92, 97–99, 159

H
Haeckel, Ernst, 31–32, 72, 79, 92, 190
Hartmann, Eduard von, 138
Hegel, 29, 158, 200
Helmholtz, 76, 127, 217
human being, 7–8, 10–12, 14, 17, 19, 21, 30, 33, 35–36, 41–42, 45, 48–49, 52–54, 56, 60, 63–66, 70, 85–86, 88–90, 99, 118, 139, 141–143, 155, 163, 175–181, 187–189, 192, 195–198, 213–215
   consciousness of, 59, 162
   earthly, 38–40, 43–44, 51
   ethical development of, 34
   freedom of, 81, 173
   immortal 'I' of, 146–147, 149
   judgement of, 55
   language of, 61
   life of, 37
   material nature of, 46
   modern, 117
   Moon, 39
   moral life of, 72
   natural, 3
   normal, 39, 190
   overall picture of, 166
   rational, 194
   regression of, 44
   relationship of, 4
   senses of, 140
   separation of, 55
   soul of, 144, 146
   subjective, 111
   true, 47
   whole affective world of, 201
humanity, 41, 51, 71, 73, 164, 179, 184
   development of, 33, 52, 72, 182, 186
   fulfilment of, 158
   historical development of, 72
   modern, 145, 162
   progress of, 28
   spiritual asset of, 66
Hume, David, 109

I
imaginative world, 24–25, 38, 44–45
impulse, 57, 81, 88, 148, 150, 216
   forces and, 63
   of initiation, 5–6
   of inspired world, 54
   of mind, 48
   will, 108
inspiration, 46, 49, 54–55, 59, 63, 65
   artistic, 47, 53
   field of, 54
   of prophets, 51
   unconscious, 17

J
Jesus of Nazareth, 144
Joule, 76

K
Kant, 70, 103
knowledge, x, 10, 58, 141
   astronomical, 117
   dead, 52
   faith and, 144
   of higher worlds, 59
   human, 6–7, 167
   imaginative, 19–20, 23, 35
   mechanical, 51

of nature, 75
object, 19
original, 86
path to, 201
physical, 19–20, 52–53
sensory, 173
Knowledge of the Higher Worlds. How is it Achieved?, 19, 22, 25–27, 30, 61, 140–142, 147–148, 176, 193

L

Laplacean mind, 75, 77–78, 80–81, 86, 92, 116–117
Leibniz, 5, 7

M

materialist/materialism/materialistic, 7, 31, 63, 79, 88, 139, 160, 169, 172, 201
age, 3, 6, 41
consciousness, 14
critical of, xii
culture, 183–184
essence of, 161
diehard, 86
honest, 162
master of, 27
mechanical science, 118
mechanical worldview, 74–75, 81–84, 92, 97–99, 106, 136
monist, 200
practical, 117
research, 165–168, 173
science, xi, 168, 189
scientific methods, 186–187, 189
spirit, 72
theoretical, 73, 117, 162
thinking, 55, 72
thoughts, 165
view of world, xi, 78, 83, 96, 218

way, 6, 89
worldview, 70–72, 83–84, 161, 164, 170, 188, 194, 197–198
Mayer, Julius Robert, 76, 127, 217
morality, 73, 82–84, 117, 178, 181
Morgenstern, Christian, 60
Mystery Dramas, 44
Mystery of Golgotha, 43, 51–53, 144

N

natural science, x–xi, 76, 163, 165, 177, 188
facts of, 191
modern, 187
and sensory perception, 190
task of, 106
nature, xii, 11, 29, 31, 50, 62, 77, 99, 106, 129, 169, 176, 192
affairs of, 54
creative, 191
Greek, 34
human, 4, 19, 45–46, 53, 56–57, 63, 65, 196, 198
inanimate, 134–135
inorganic, 135
of intellect, 10
knowledge of, 75
law of, 54, 110, 124, 128
manifold, 200
material, 46
Moon, 39
of movement, 170
Nordic, 34
organic, 135
supersensory, 20
threefold, xi
true, 47
of velocity, 216
view of, 163
whole of, 6, 33, 54

O

objects, 19–20, 55, 103, 106, 131, 198, 206–207, 210–212, 215
  dead, 24, 62
  external sensory, 123
  living, 24
  material, 170
Occult Science, 45–46, 59, 149
occult senses, 146–148
Old Moon, 37–38, 45–46, 48
Old Testament, 51

P

philosophe inconnu, 43
philosophy, 4–5, 88, 103, 189, 196–197
  contemporary, 191
  natural science and, 190
  representatives of, 190–191
  schools of, 200–201
  and sense perception, 193
physical body, 48, 59–60, 137, 146, 164, 189–190, 193–194, 214
physical plane, 5, 8, 11, 15, 17, 19–21, 23–24, 26–27, 29–30, 36–37, 39–45, 51–52, 54, 59
physical world, 3–4, 16, 23, 63, 139
  images of, 11
  outer, 5, 8, 141
Plato, 5

R

reality, 7, 12, 15, 32, 80, 89, 106, 114, 144, 164, 169, 177, 211–212, 214
  astronomical understanding of, 75–76
  of criminal anthropology, 194
  external, 5, 9–10, 120
  genuine, 215
  image of, 5, 8
  of intellect, 10
  outer, 8
  realm of, 10
  spiritual, x, xii, 153, 216
  subjective, 10
  of thought, 9
  true, 148
realm
  of creative life, 49
  of fantasy, 215
  human, 64
  material, 165
  of reality, 10
  spiritual, xi, 61, 64
  supersensory, 20–21
religions, 142–145, 158–159, 165, 184
Riddles of Philosophy, The, 56, 81, 89, 154, 190

S

School of Spiritual Science, 167
science, 33, 72–73, 91, 131, 144–145, 159, 181, 186
  biological, 138, 163
  contemporary, 182
  conventional, xi
  current state of, 77
  earthly, 49
  European, 132, 134, 136
  external, 4, 70, 156, 183
  life of outer, 26
  of materialism, 98–99
  mechanical, 130
  modern, x, 119
  natural. *See* natural science
  objections of, 116
  occult, 156, 177
  ordinary, 141, 155
  physical, 45
  of senses, 185

sensory, 157
spiritual. *See* spiritual science
scientific conscience, 83
scientific research, 75, 116, 138, 165, 169
sensory physiology, 88–89
soul, 3, 11, 24, 57, 98, 114, 144, 164, 166, 184, 189
  ability, 4
  activity, 4
  animal, 137
  brilliant, 97
  conscious life of, 53
  deeper depths of, 49
  effort in, 60
  element, 167
  experience of, 54
  hidden depths of, 36, 41, 45, 53, 63
  human, 6, 17, 19–20, 44, 52–53, 56, 58, 158–159, 177
  inner tolerance of, 47–48
  life, 39, 146, 148, 197–198
  mood of, 59
  physical reflection of, 154
  unconscious life of, 12–14
  world, 139, 178, 198
Spirits of Form, 48
Spirits of Movement, 48
spiritual inwardness, 167
spiritual life, 57, 151, 168, 186
  of European cultural world, 143, 145
  forces, 17
  of human being, 81
  of humankind, 162
spiritual science, x, xii, 12, 15, 35, 41, 55–56, 63, 66, 72, 78, 90, 100, 114–117, 137–138, 140–142, 145, 147, 151, 159, 163, 165, 172, 175, 177, 182–185, 187, 194–197, 214–216, 218

actual, 150
facts of, 157
field of, 166
ground of, 186
instrument of, 143
research results of, 164
science and, 120
sense of, 162
spiritual facts and, 158
teachings of, 154
true, 170
truths of, 16
validity of, xi
whole content of, 42–43
spiritual world, 3–4, 8, 14–16, 23, 40, 42, 46, 48, 60–63, 65, 70, 99, 111, 120, 139–140, 142, 147, 149, 151, 155, 158, 162, 169, 176–177, 183
  content of, 153
  dependence on, 201
  existence of, 174
  fields of, 168
  knowledge of, x, 6
  nature of, 27
  physical and, 4
  purely, 148
  real, 154
  scraps of, 165
  secrets of, 5, 41
  threshold of, 21
  validity of, 136
supersensory world, 3–4, 20, 51–52

T
Theodora, 44
theosophists, 73, 157, 163
theosophy, 69–70, 73, 143, 145–146, 150, 157–159, 177, 182
  basic teachings of, 157, 181

thought, 4–5, 8, 10, 21, 40, 54, 70, 73, 78, 101, 113, 136–137, 149, 168–169, 186–187, 217
  abstract, 24, 26
  cosmic world of, 172
  dead, 26
  feelings and, 72, 81
  free activity of, 175
  genuine scientific, 116
  and ideas, 38
  life, 37
  living, 27–28, 37, 148
  machines, 29
  materialistic train of, 161
  mobile, 26–27, 30
  perception of, 148
  reality of, 9
  right, 107
  spiritual, 165
  subconscious, 53
  theoretical, 97
  tingles and prickles, 25
  train of, 85
  transition of, 62
  whole strand of, 160
  world of, 42
truth, 8, 16, 37, 53–54, 60, 99, 106, 110, 122, 155, 157, 200–201
  absolute, 121, 128
  Christian, 158
  epistemological, 87, 123
  of freedom, 86
  intuitive, 121
  logical, 123
  mathematical, 121, 124
  objective, 120
  possibility of, 44
  trail of, 187
  unconditional love of, 71
Tyndall, 76

W

worldview, xii, 6, 76–77, 80, 118, 134–135, 146, 154, 168–169, 182, 200, 213, 217
  atomistic, 170
  Copernican, 129–130
  Galilean, 163
  Greek, 5
  history of, 4
  'honest' representatives of, 162
  materialistic, 70–73, 83–85, 99, 161, 164, 170, 188, 194, 197–198
  materialistic mechanical, 74–75, 81–85, 97–99, 106, 117, 136
  modern, 116, 201
  mystical, 198
  naïve, 197
  principle of, 7
  psychological, 198
  Ptolemaic, 130
  religious, 159
  spiritual, 99, 136, 158
  spiritual-scientific, 4, 63, 139, 165, 184, 198
  theosophical, 143
Wrangell, F. von, 75, 78, 81–90, 92, 100–103, 105, 108, 112, 115, 120, 137, 142, 147, 150, 152, 157, 160–161, 163, 172–173, 175, 178–180, 182, 184
  Science and Theosophy, xi–xii, 69, 116, 118, 144, 186

Z

Zimmermann, Robert, 97

A note from Rudolf Steiner Press

We are an independent publisher and registered charity (non-profit organisation) dedicated to making available the work of Rudolf Steiner in English translation. We care a great deal about the content of our books and have hundreds of titles available – as printed books, ebooks and in audio formats.

As a publisher devoted to anthroposophy…

- We continually commission translations of previously unpublished works by Rudolf Steiner and invest in re-translating, editing and improving our editions.

- We are committed to making anthroposophy available to all by publishing introductory books as well as contemporary research.

- Our new print editions and ebooks are carefully checked and proofread for accuracy, and converted into all formats for all platforms.

- Our translations are officially authorised by Rudolf Steiner's estate in Dornach, Switzerland, to whom we pay royalties on sales, thus assisting their critical work.

So, look out for Rudolf Steiner Press as a mark of quality and support us today by buying our books, or contact us should you wish to sponsor specific titles or to support the charity with a gift or legacy.

office@rudolfsteinerpress.com
Join our e-mailing list at www.rudolfsteinerpress.com

RUDOLF STEINER PRESS